DALLAS
& FORT WORTH

EMILY TOMAN

Contents

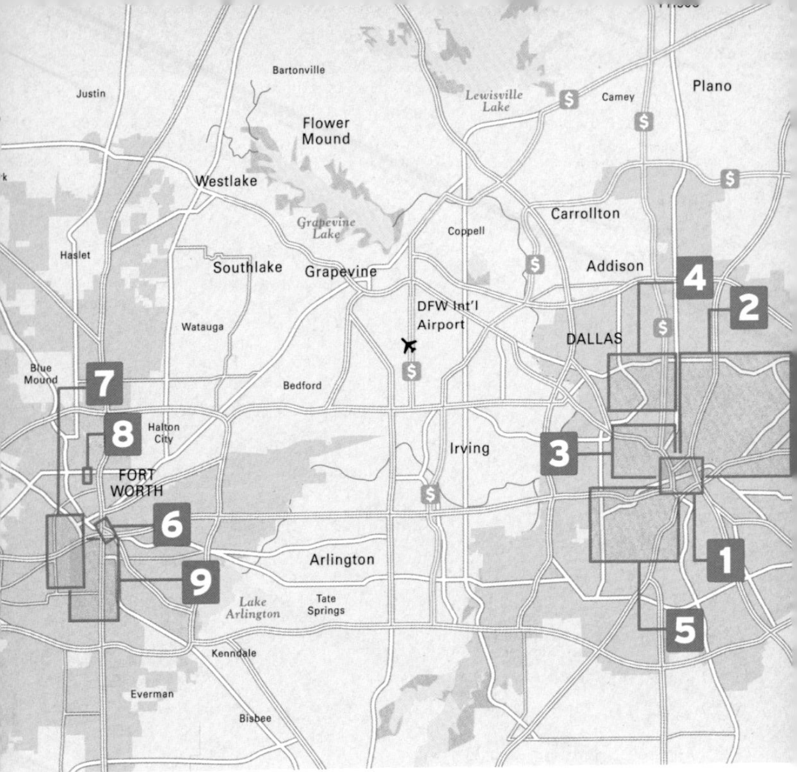
Bartonville
Justin
Lewisville Lake
Camey
Plano
Flower Mound
Westlake
Grapevine Lake
Coppell
Carrollton
Haslet
Southlake
Grapevine
Addison
4
2
DFW Int'l Airport
Watauga
DALLAS
Blue Mound
7
Bedford
8
Halton City
Irving
3
FORT WORTH
6
1
Arlington
9
Lake Arlington
Tate Springs
5
Kenndale
Everman
Bisbee

Maps

1
2
3
A
B
C
D
E
F

SEE MAP 3

Pike Park
Phelps Park
Harry Hines Blvd
Lyte St
Akard St
N Harwood St
Moody St
Payne St
Olive St
N Akard St
Cedar Springs Rd
McKinney Ave
Harwood St
Olive St
N Pearl St
Thomas St
366
Jack Evans St
Routh St
Boll St
N Hawkins St
1 2 American Airlines Center
3
4 5 6 Morton H. Meyerson Symphony Center
7
8
Ashland St
N Field St
Caroline St
Alamo St
Woodall Rodgers Service N Rd
Woodall Rodgers Service S Rd
12 Klyde Warren Park
Olive St
Flora St
Leonard St
Ross Ave
San Jacinto St
Crockett St
14
15
13
Olive St
Victory
N Houston St
Museum Wy
Park
11
10
9
N Saint Paul St
N Pearl St
Pearl M
N Harwood St
Broom St
Munger Ave
Freeman St
N Akard St
Victory Ave
Ln
N Lamar St
16
Magnolia St
N Field St
18
Wenchell
Federal St
Olive St
M St. Paul
Continental Ave
Woodall Rodgers Fwy
McKinney Ave
Laws St
Corbin St
DOWNTOWN
Federal St
Bryan St
Live Oak St
San Jacinto St
Bullington St
Dallas World Aquarium 17
Griffin St
Hord St
N Griffin Blvd
Patterson St
Federal St
20 Thanks-Giving Square
21
Pacific Ave
Akard M
19
N Record St
N Market St
Ross Ave
45 44
West End M
Griffin
N Field St
N Akard St
Elm St
51
Main St
52
50
Sixth Floor Museum 46
N Houston St
49
48
Commerce St
Browder St
Lane St
Jackson St
Old Red 47 Museum
S Austin St
HISTORIC DISTRICT
Commerce St

SEE MAP 4

Wood St
Pioneer Plaza
S Ervay St
S Market St
Jackson St
53
Young St
City Hall Plaza
S Record St
Wood St
Founders Square
Marilla Dr
Reunion Tower 54
Union Station M
Ferris Park
Union Station
Young St
W Reunion Blvd
S Lamar St
S Griffin Blvd
Ceremonial Dr
Canton St
Browder St
Reunion Blvd E
Reunion Arena Park
Dallas Convention Center
North Dr
Convention Center M
S Market St
Griffin Blvd
S Akard St
Reunion Arena
S Houston St
Hotel St
Griffin St W
Peters St
Griffin St
35E
77

SEE MAP 5

56
To 57 Bill's Records

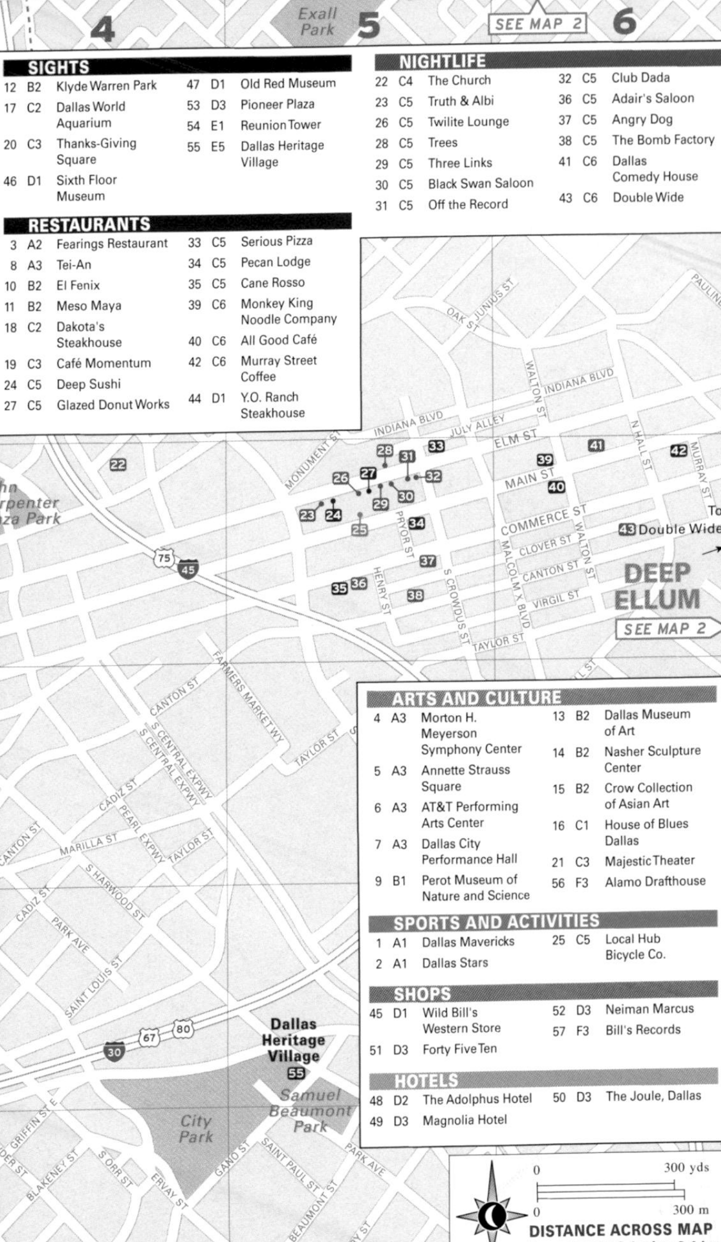
4
Exall Park
5
SEE MAP 2
6
SIGHTS
12 B2 Klyde Warren Park
17 C2 Dallas World Aquarium
20 C3 Thanks-Giving Square
46 D1 Sixth Floor Museum
47 D1 Old Red Museum
53 D3 Pioneer Plaza
54 E1 Reunion Tower
55 E5 Dallas Heritage Village
NIGHTLIFE
22 C4 The Church
23 C5 Truth & Albi
26 C5 Twilite Lounge
28 C5 Trees
29 C5 Three Links
30 C5 Black Swan Saloon
31 C5 Off the Record
32 C5 Club Dada
36 C5 Adair's Saloon
37 C5 Angry Dog
38 C5 The Bomb Factory
41 C6 Dallas Comedy House
43 C6 Double Wide
RESTAURANTS
3 A2 Fearings Restaurant
8 A3 Tei-An
10 B2 El Fenix
11 B2 Meso Maya
18 C2 Dakota's Steakhouse
19 C3 Café Momentum
24 C5 Deep Sushi
27 C5 Glazed Donut Works
33 C5 Serious Pizza
34 C5 Pecan Lodge
35 C5 Cane Rosso
39 C6 Monkey King Noodle Company
40 C6 All Good Café
42 C6 Murray Street Coffee
44 D1 Y.O. Ranch Steakhouse
PAULINE ST
OAK ST
JUNIUS ST
WALTON ST
INDIANA BLVD
JULY ALLEY
ELM ST
MAIN ST
COMMERCE ST
CLOVER ST
CANTON ST
VIRGIL ST
TAYLOR ST
N HALL ST
MURRAY ST
MONUMENT ST
PRYOR ST
HENRY ST
S CROWDUS ST
MALCOLM X BLVD
John Carpenter Plaza Park
To 43 Double Wide
DEEP ELLUM
SEE MAP 2
75
45
FARMERS MARKET WY
S CENTRAL EXPWY
CADIZ ST
PEARL EXPWY
MARILLA ST
S HARWOOD ST
PARK AVE
SAINT LOUIS ST
67
80
30
Dallas Heritage Village
City Park
Samuel Beaumont Park
GRIFFIN ST E
BROWDER ST
BLAKENEY ST
S ORR ST
ERVAY ST
GANO ST
SAINT PAUL ST
BEAUMONT ST
HICKORY ST
ARTS AND CULTURE
4 A3 Morton H. Meyerson Symphony Center
5 A3 Annette Strauss Square
6 A3 AT&T Performing Arts Center
7 A3 Dallas City Performance Hall
9 B1 Perot Museum of Nature and Science
13 B2 Dallas Museum of Art
14 B2 Nasher Sculpture Center
15 B2 Crow Collection of Asian Art
16 C1 House of Blues Dallas
21 C3 Majestic Theater
56 F3 Alamo Drafthouse
SPORTS AND ACTIVITIES
1 A1 Dallas Mavericks
2 A1 Dallas Stars
25 C5 Local Hub Bicycle Co.
SHOPS
45 D1 Wild Bill's Western Store
51 D3 Forty Five Ten
52 D3 Neiman Marcus
57 F3 Bill's Records
HOTELS
48 D2 The Adolphus Hotel
49 D3 Magnolia Hotel
50 D3 The Joule, Dallas
0
300 yds
0
300 m
DISTANCE ACROSS MAP
Approximate: 2.1 mi or 3.4 km

MAP 2

1 2 3
A B C D E F

To
1 Half-Price Books

SKILLMAN ST
E NORTHWEST HWY
EAST LOVERS LN
SEE MAP 4
NORTH CENTRAL EXPRESSWY
E MOCKINGBIRD LN
MOCKINGBIRD LN
MARTEL AVE
MCCOMMAS BLVD
GREENVILLE AVE
ABRAMS RD
VICKERY BLVD
MILLER AVE
MC MILLAN AVE
N HENDERSON AVE
RICHMOND AVE
SEARS ST
GASTON AVE
BENNETT AVE
LA VISTA DR
LEWIS ST
Lakewood Country Club
LIVE OAK ST
ROSS AVE
N MUNGER BLVD
JUNIUS ST
BRYAN ST
N PEAK ST
N HASKELL AVE
LINDSLEY AVE
E GRAND AVE
Tenison Park Golf Course
SEE MAP 3
GRAHAM AVE
GURLEY AVE
N CARROLL AVE
COLUMBIA AVE
Samuell Grand Park
E R L THORNTON FREEWY
WASHINGTON ST
ELM ST
MAIN ST
DOLPHIN RD
SEE MAP 1
EXPOSITION AVE
GREENVILLE AVE
S HASKELL AVE
1ST AVE
Fair Park
75
30

2 3 6 7 8 9 11 12 13 14 15 16 18 19 20 21 22 23 24 25 26 27 28 29 30 31 32 33 34 35 36 39 40 41 42 43 44 45 46 47

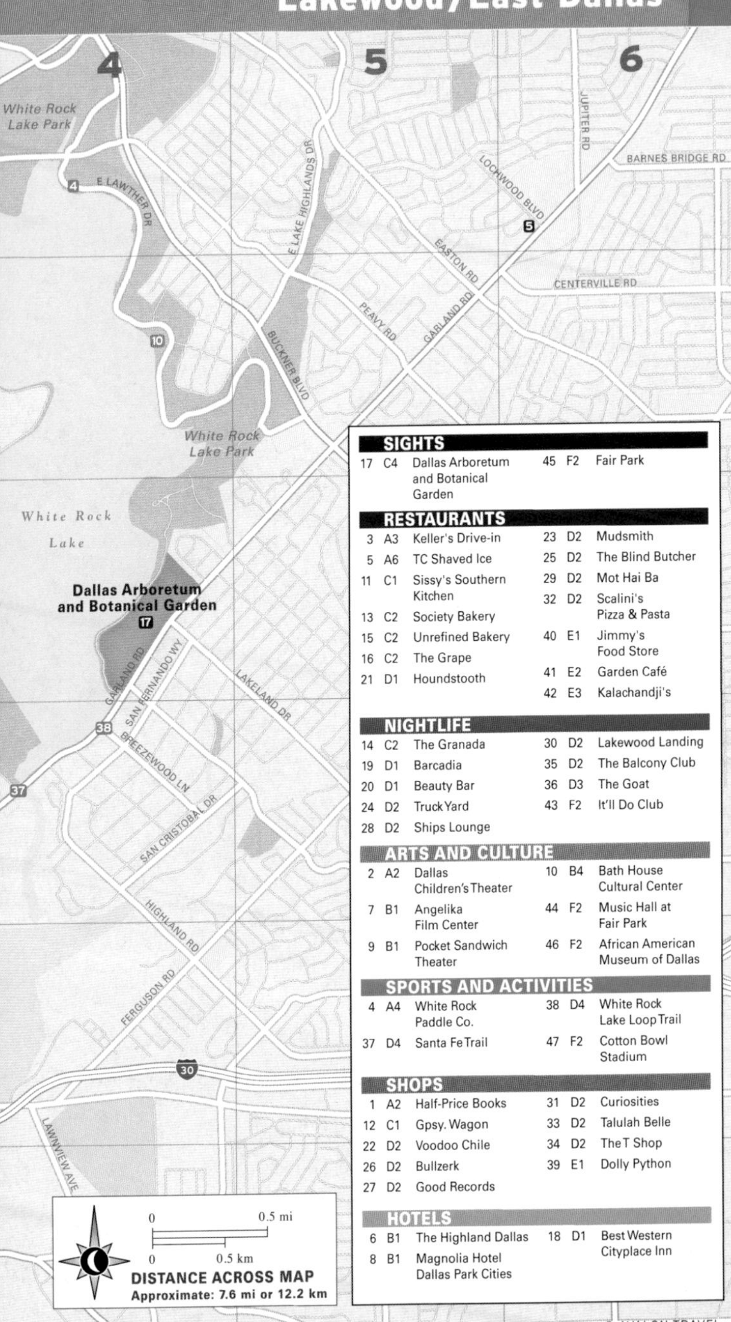
4
5
6
White Rock Lake Park
E LAWTHER DR
E LAKE HIGHLANDS DR
JUPITER RD
BARNES BRIDGE RD
LOCHWOOD BLVD
EASTON RD
CENTERVILLE RD
PEAVY RD
GARLAND RD
BUCKNER BLVD
White Rock Lake Park
White Rock Lake
Dallas Arboretum and Botanical Garden
SAN FERNANDO WY
LAKELAND DR
BREEZEWOOD LN
SAN CRISTOBAL DR
HIGHLAND RD
FERGUSON RD
LAWNVIEW AVE
SIGHTS
17 C4 Dallas Arboretum and Botanical Garden
45 F2 Fair Park
RESTAURANTS
3 A3 Keller's Drive-in
5 A6 TC Shaved Ice
11 C1 Sissy's Southern Kitchen
13 C2 Society Bakery
15 C2 Unrefined Bakery
16 C2 The Grape
21 D1 Houndstooth
23 D2 Mudsmith
25 D2 The Blind Butcher
29 D2 Mot Hai Ba
32 D2 Scalini's Pizza & Pasta
40 E1 Jimmy's Food Store
41 E2 Garden Café
42 E3 Kalachandji's
NIGHTLIFE
14 C2 The Granada
19 D1 Barcadia
20 D1 Beauty Bar
24 D2 Truck Yard
28 D2 Ships Lounge
30 D2 Lakewood Landing
35 D2 The Balcony Club
36 D3 The Goat
43 F2 It'll Do Club
ARTS AND CULTURE
2 A2 Dallas Children's Theater
7 B1 Angelika Film Center
9 B1 Pocket Sandwich Theater
10 B4 Bath House Cultural Center
44 F2 Music Hall at Fair Park
46 F2 African American Museum of Dallas
SPORTS AND ACTIVITIES
4 A4 White Rock Paddle Co.
37 D4 Santa Fe Trail
38 D4 White Rock Lake Loop Trail
47 F2 Cotton Bowl Stadium
SHOPS
1 A2 Half-Price Books
12 C1 Gpsy. Wagon
22 D2 Voodoo Chile
26 D2 Bullzerk
27 D2 Good Records
31 D2 Curiosities
33 D2 Talulah Belle
34 D2 The T Shop
39 E1 Dolly Python
HOTELS
6 B1 The Highland Dallas
8 B1 Magnolia Hotel Dallas Park Cities
18 D1 Best Western Cityplace Inn
0 0.5 mi
0 0.5 km
DISTANCE ACROSS MAP
Approximate: 7.6 mi or 12.2 km
© AVALON TRAVEL

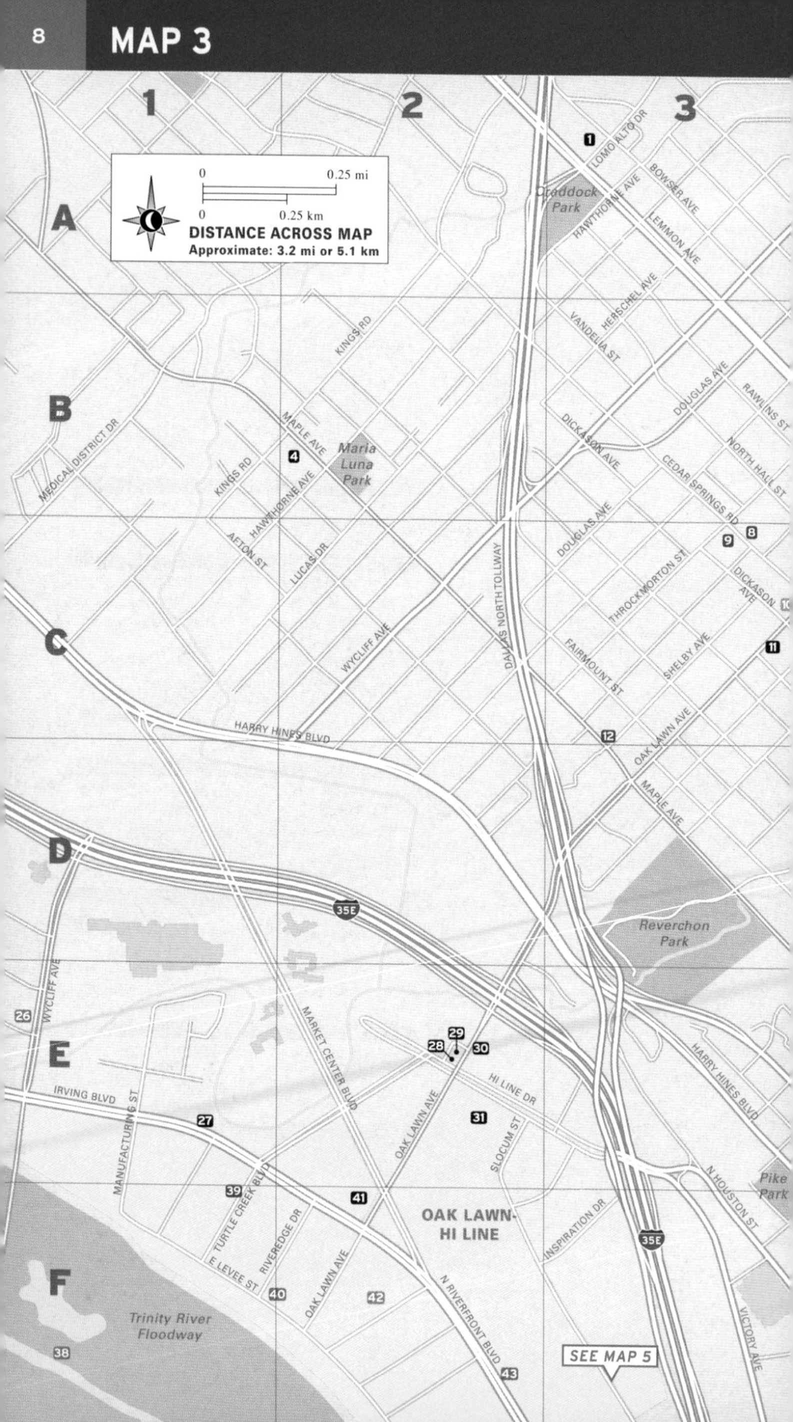

0 0.25 mi
0 0.25 km
DISTANCE ACROSS MAP
Approximate: 3.2 mi or 5.1 km
1
2
3
A
B
C
D
E
F
LOMO ALTO DR
Craddock Park
HAWTHORNE AVE
BOWSER AVE
LEMMON AVE
HERSCHEL AVE
VANDELIA ST
KINGS RD
DOUGLAS AVE
RAWLINS ST
DICKASON AVE
CEDAR SPRINGS RD
NORTH HALL ST
MEDICAL DISTRICT DR
MAPLE AVE
Maria Luna Park
KINGS RD
HAWTHORNE AVE
AFTON ST
LUCAS DR
DOUGLAS AVE
DALLAS NORTH TOLLWAY
THROCKMORTON ST
DICKASON AVE
WYCLIFF AVE
FAIRMOUNT ST
SHELBY AVE
HARRY HINES BLVD
OAK LAWN AVE
MAPLE AVE
35E
Reverchon Park
WYCLIFF AVE
MARKET CENTER BLVD
HI LINE DR
HARRY HINES BLVD
IRVING BLVD
MANUFACTURING ST
OAK LAWN AVE
SLOCUM ST
N HOUSTON ST
Pike Park
TURTLE CREEK BLVD
RIVEREDGE DR
OAK LAWN-HI LINE
INSPIRATION DR
35E
E LEVEE ST
OAK LAWN AVE
N RIVERFRONT BLVD
Trinity River Floodway
VICTORY AVE
SEE MAP 5
1
4
8
9
10
11
12
26
27
28
29
30
31
38
39
40
41
42
43

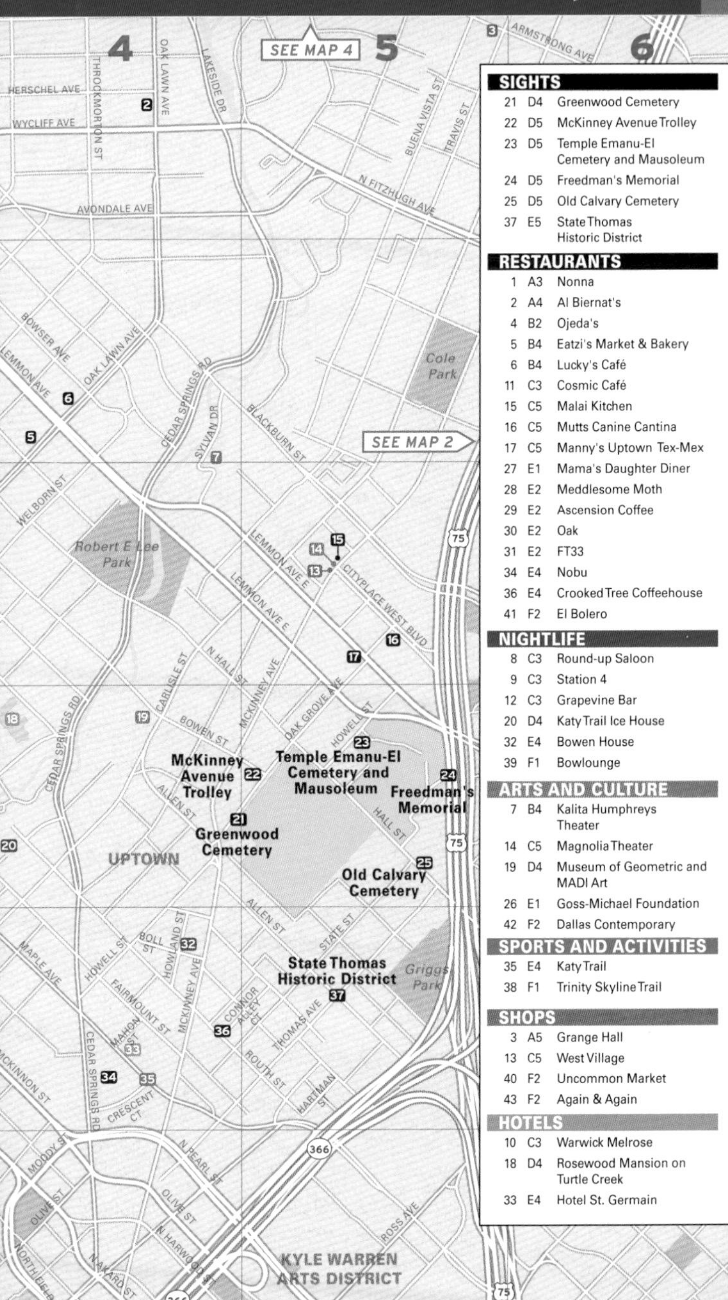
SIGHTS
21 D4 Greenwood Cemetery
22 D5 McKinney Avenue Trolley
23 D5 Temple Emanu-El Cemetery and Mausoleum
24 D5 Freedman's Memorial
25 D5 Old Calvary Cemetery
37 E5 State Thomas Historic District
RESTAURANTS
1 A3 Nonna
2 A4 Al Biernat's
4 B2 Ojeda's
5 B4 Eatzi's Market & Bakery
6 B4 Lucky's Café
11 C3 Cosmic Café
15 C5 Malai Kitchen
16 C5 Mutts Canine Cantina
17 C5 Manny's Uptown Tex-Mex
27 E1 Mama's Daughter Diner
28 E2 Meddlesome Moth
29 E2 Ascension Coffee
30 E2 Oak
31 E2 FT33
34 E4 Nobu
36 E4 Crooked Tree Coffeehouse
41 F2 El Bolero
NIGHTLIFE
8 C3 Round-up Saloon
9 C3 Station 4
12 C3 Grapevine Bar
20 D4 Katy Trail Ice House
32 E4 Bowen House
39 F1 Bowlounge
ARTS AND CULTURE
7 B4 Kalita Humphreys Theater
14 C5 Magnolia Theater
19 D4 Museum of Geometric and MADI Art
26 E1 Goss-Michael Foundation
42 F2 Dallas Contemporary
SPORTS AND ACTIVITIES
35 E4 Katy Trail
38 F1 Trinity Skyline Trail
SHOPS
3 A5 Grange Hall
13 C5 West Village
40 F2 Uncommon Market
43 F2 Again & Again
HOTELS
10 C3 Warwick Melrose
18 D4 Rosewood Mansion on Turtle Creek
33 E4 Hotel St. Germain
SEE MAP 4
SEE MAP 2
4
5
6
HERSCHEL AVE
WYCLIFF AVE
THROCKMORTON ST
OAK LAWN AVE
LAKESIDE DR
ARMSTRONG AVE
BUENA VISTA ST
TRAVIS ST
N FITZHUGH AVE
AVONDALE AVE
BOWSER AVE
LEMMON AVE
CEDAR SPRINGS RD
SYLVAN DR
BLACKBURN ST
Cole Park
WELBORN ST
Robert E Lee Park
LEMMON AVE E
CITYPLACE WEST BLVD
N HALL ST
CARLISLE ST
MCKINNEY AVE
OAK GROVE AVE
HOWELL ST
BOWEN ST
McKinney Avenue Trolley
Temple Emanu-El Cemetery and Mausoleum
Freedman's Memorial
ALLEN ST
HALL ST
Greenwood Cemetery
UPTOWN
Old Calvary Cemetery
NORTH PEAK
STATE ST
BOLL ST
HOWLAND ST
MAPLE AVE
State Thomas Historic District
Griggs Park
FAIRMOUNT ST
CONNOR ALLEY CT
THOMAS AVE
MAHON ST
ROUTH ST
HARTMAN ST
MCKINNON ST
CRESCENT CT
MOODY ST
N PEARL ST
OLIVE ST
N HARWOOD ST
ROSS AVE
NORTHFIELD ST
N AKARD ST
KYLE WARREN ARTS DISTRICT
75
366
© AVALON TRAVEL

1
2
3
A
B
C
D
E
F
NORTHWEST HWY
BERKSHIRE LN
BERKSHIRE
LN
VILLANOVA ST
Preston Center Plaza
LUTHER LN
MCCRAW DR
SHERRY LN
SHERRY LN
SHADYWOOD LN
FARQUHAR LN
STONEGATE RD
COLGATE AVE
DALLAS NORTH TOLLWAY
CARUTH BLVD
CARUTH BLVD
Smith Park
LILAC LN
GREENBRIER DR
GREENBRIER DR
SOUTHWESTERN BLVD
BRYN MAWR DR
CHADBOURNE RD
PRESTON PARK DR
DEVONSHIRE DR
EASTERN AVE
DOUGLAS AVE
BRIARWOOD LN
HANOVER AVE
HANOVER ST
WESTCHESTER DR
PURDUE AVE
PURDUE AVE
MENIER ST
STANFORD AVE
STANFORD AVE
STANFORD AVE
W AMHERST AVE
W AMHERST AVE
AMHERST AVE
W LOVERS LN
PARK CITIES
To
Canary
HYER ST
HYER ST
ARMSTRONG PKWY
GRASSMERE LN
NEWMORE AVE
BOAZ ST
DRUID LN
DRUID LN
LOMO ALTO DR
GLENWICK LN
GLENWICK LN
KAYWOOD DR
W GREENWAY BLVD
INWOOD RD
EMERSON AVE
EMERSON AVE
CAILLET ST
MORTON ST
ROBIN RD
EASTERN AVE
UNIVERSITY BLVD
PRESTON PKWY
WESTWICK RD
MCFARLIN BLVD
WATEKA DR
WATEKA DR
LARCHMONT ST
LINNET LN
NEOLA DR
WINDSOR LN
ORIOLE DR
DRANE DR
WINDSOR PKY
THRUSH ST
SHANNON LN
WENONAH DR
To
Frontiers of Flight Museum
WENONAH DR
STANHOPE ST
SHENANDOAH ST
NAKOMA DR
NORMANDY AVE
LOMO ALTO DR
WANETA
ROBIN RD
WANETA DR
SAN CARLOS ST
LARK LN
Greenway Park
POTOMAC AVE
Country Club
MOCKINGBIRD LN
WESTSIDE DR
SOUTHERN AVE
LIVINGSTON AVE
LIVINGSTON AVE
EDMONDSON AVE

4
5
6
NorthPark Center
0 0.25 mi
0 0.25 km
DISTANCE ACROSS MAP
Approximate: 3.5 mi or 5.6 km
NORTHWEST HWY
Northcrest Park
WENTWOOD DR
SIGHTS
27 E1 Frontiers of Flight Museum
28 E5 Southern Methodist University
30 E6 George W. Bush Presidential Library and Museum
RESTAURANTS
2 A6 La Duni Latin Kitchen and Coffee Studio
5 B3 Flying Fish
6 B3 Carlo's Bakery
9 B3 Sprinkles Cupcakes
13 D1 Neighborhood Services
14 D1 Shinsei
15 D1 Rise No. 1
17 D2 Rafa's Café Mexicano
20 D5 East Hampton Sandwich Co.
23 D5 Bubba's Cooks Country
24 D5 Kuby's Sausage House
25 D5 Peggy Sue BBQ
26 D5 Mustang Donuts
34 F3 Café Pacific
ARTS AND CULTURE
1 A6 Museum of Biblical Art
16 D1 Inwood Theatre
33 F3 Highland Park Village Theater
35 F5 Meadows Museum at SMU
SHOPS
3 A6 NorthPark Center
7 B3 Ylang 23
8 B3 Castle Gap Jewelry
10 B3 Swoozie's
11 B3 Anteks Curated
12 D1 Canary
18 D2 Elements
19 D5 Snider Plaza
22 D5 The Urban Manor
22 D5 Jackson Armory
31 F3 Draper James
32 F3 Highland Park Village
HOTELS
4 B2 Hilton Dallas/ Park Cities
29 E5 Hotel Lumen
AMHERST AVE
E LOVERS LN
Curtis Park
WESTMINSTER AVE
RANKIN ST
DURHAM ST
Daniel Cemetery
MILTON AVE
CLEBURNE ST
WILLARD DR
VASSAR AVE
HURSEY ST
SNIDER PLZ
ROSEDALE AVE
SEE MAP 2
Porter Park
Goar Park
DANIEL AVE
Burleson Park
HAYNIE AVE
DICKENS AVE
UNIVERSITY BLVD
Williams Park
Southern Methodist University
BOAZ
AIRLINE EXT
DUBLIN ST
FONDREN DR
MCFARLIN BLVD
DYER ST
George W. Bush Presidential Library and Museum
SMU BLVD
ASBURY ST
GOLF DR
GRANADA AVE
BINKLEY AVE
75
Owenby Stadium
NORMANDY AVE
CHALET CT
Potomac Park
Mockingbird
POTOMAC AVE
KEY ST
AUBURNDALE AVE
HILLCREST AVE
BISHOP BLVD
E MOCKINGBIRD LN
DREXEL DR
SEWANEE ST
AIRLINE RD
FAIRFIELD AVE
ETON AVE
OXFORD AVE
SAINT JOHNS DR
SEE MAP 3
CORNELL AVE

SEE MAP 3
Ronald Kirk Pedestrian Bridge
Margaret Hunt Hill Bridge
Moore Park
Trinity Greenbelt
WEST DALLAS
Trinity Overlook Park
Kessler Parkway Park
To Comfort Suites West Dallas-Cockrell Hill
Stevens Park Golf Course
Kidd Springs Park
Lake Cliff Park
OAK CLIFF
SEE INSET (INS)
Texas Theatre
Page Park
Ruth Meade Park
To Oak Cliff Nature Preserve
© AVALON TRAVEL

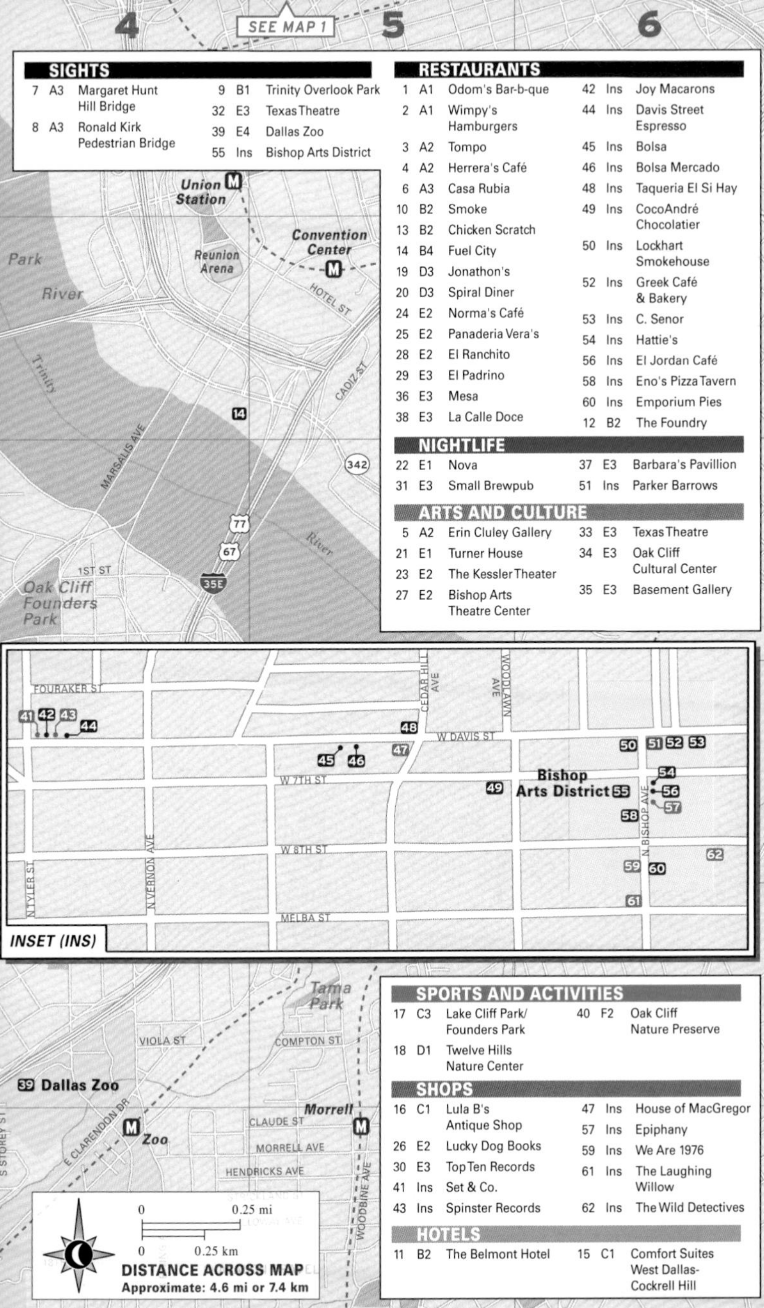
4
SEE MAP 1
5
6
SIGHTS
7 A3 Margaret Hunt Hill Bridge
8 A3 Ronald Kirk Pedestrian Bridge
9 B1 Trinity Overlook Park
32 E3 Texas Theatre
39 E4 Dallas Zoo
55 Ins Bishop Arts District
RESTAURANTS
1 A1 Odom's Bar-b-que
2 A1 Wimpy's Hamburgers
3 A2 Tompo
4 A2 Herrera's Café
6 A3 Casa Rubia
10 B2 Smoke
13 B2 Chicken Scratch
14 B4 Fuel City
19 D3 Jonathon's
20 D3 Spiral Diner
24 E2 Norma's Café
25 E2 Panaderia Vera's
28 E2 El Ranchito
29 E3 El Padrino
36 E3 Mesa
38 E3 La Calle Doce
42 Ins Joy Macarons
44 Ins Davis Street Espresso
45 Ins Bolsa
46 Ins Bolsa Mercado
48 Ins Taqueria El Si Hay
49 Ins CocoAndré Chocolatier
50 Ins Lockhart Smokehouse
52 Ins Greek Café & Bakery
53 Ins C. Senor
54 Ins Hattie's
56 Ins El Jordan Café
58 Ins Eno's Pizza Tavern
60 Ins Emporium Pies
12 B2 The Foundry
NIGHTLIFE
22 E1 Nova
31 E3 Small Brewpub
37 E3 Barbara's Pavillion
51 Ins Parker Barrows
ARTS AND CULTURE
5 A2 Erin Cluley Gallery
21 E1 Turner House
23 E2 The Kessler Theater
27 E2 Bishop Arts Theatre Center
33 E3 Texas Theatre
34 E3 Oak Cliff Cultural Center
35 E3 Basement Gallery
Union Station
Convention Center
Reunion Arena
Park
River
Trinity
HOTEL ST
CADIZ ST
MARSALIS AVE
River
1ST ST
Oak Cliff Founders Park
FOURAKER ST
CEDAR HILL AVE
WOODLAWN AVE
W DAVIS ST
W 7TH ST
Bishop Arts District
N BISHOP AVE
W 8TH ST
N VERNON AVE
N TYLER ST
MELBA ST
INSET (INS)
Tama Park
VIOLA ST
COMPTON ST
Dallas Zoo
E CLARENDON DR
Zoo
Morrell
CLAUDE ST
MORRELL AVE
HENDRICKS AVE
WOODBINE AVE
S STOREY ST
0 0.25 mi
0 0.25 km
DISTANCE ACROSS MAP
Approximate: 4.6 mi or 7.4 km
SPORTS AND ACTIVITIES
17 C3 Lake Cliff Park/ Founders Park
18 D1 Twelve Hills Nature Center
40 F2 Oak Cliff Nature Preserve
SHOPS
16 C1 Lula B's Antique Shop
26 E2 Lucky Dog Books
30 E3 Top Ten Records
41 Ins Set & Co.
43 Ins Spinster Records
47 Ins House of MacGregor
57 Ins Epiphany
59 Ins We Are 1976
61 Ins The Laughing Willow
62 Ins The Wild Detectives
HOTELS
11 B2 The Belmont Hotel
15 C1 Comfort Suites West Dallas-Cockrell Hill

SIGHTS
15 C3 Sundance Square
22 F3 Fort Worth Water Gardens
RESTAURANTS
4 B3 Riscky's Bar-B-Q
5 B3 Yolk
7 B3 Reata
16 C3 Bird Café
20 D1 Buon Giorno
21 D2 Bailey's Bar-B-Que
NIGHTLIFE
9 C3 Four Day Weekend
10 C3 Flying Saucer
13 C3 Scat Jazz Lounge
17 C3 Silver Leaf Cigar Lounge
18 C3 Hyena's Comedy Club
ARTS AND CULTURE
2 A3 Coyote Drive-in
6 B3 Sid Richardson Museum
11 C3 Circle Theatre
12 C3 Milan Gallery
14 C3 Jubilee Theatre
19 C3 Bass Performance Hall
SPORTS AND ACTIVITIES
1 A1 Panther Island Pavilion
HOTELS
3 B3 Worthington Renaissance
8 C2 Etta's Place ed & Breakfast
23 F3 Sheraton Fort Worth Downtown
To 1 Panther Island Pavilion
To 2 Coyote Drive-in
Heritage Park
Sundance Square
Burk Burnett Park
Fort Worth Water Gardens
PEACH ST
MILLS ST
CHERRY ST
N MAIN ST
BLUFF ST
E 2ND ST
E 3RD ST
THROCKMORTON ST
HOUSTON ST
MAIN ST
COMMERCE ST
CALHOUN ST
W 6TH ST
W 7TH ST
W 8TH ST
9TH ST
W 10TH ST
FLORENCE ST
MACON ST
TEXAS ST
W 13TH ST
TAYLOR ST
MONROE ST
JENNINGS AVE
W 11TH ST
13TH ST
14TH ST
15TH ST
W LANCASTER AVE
347
287
180
SEE MAP 7
SEE MAP 9
0 200 yds
0 200 m
DISTANCE ACROSS MAP
Approximate: 0.7 mi or 1.1 km
© AVALON TRAVEL

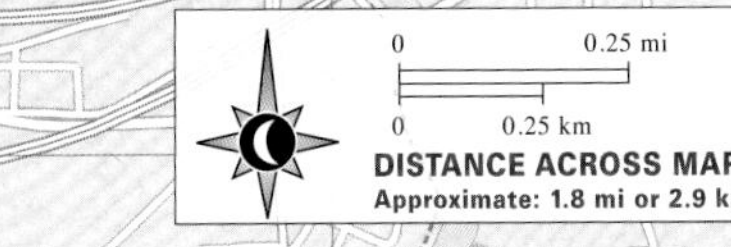

SIGHTS

18	C2	Will Rogers Memorial Center	23	C2	Fort Worth Botanic Garden

RESTAURANTS

1	A3	Angelo's	16	C1	Edelweiss
2	B2	Righteous Foods	17	C1	Curly's Frozen Custard
11	B3	Terra Mediterranean Grill	22	C2	Montgomery Street Cafe
13	B3	Fred's Texas Cafe			

NIGHTLIFE

5	B2	Fort Worth Swing Dance Syndicate	9	B3	Lola's Saloon
8	B2	Capital Bar	10	B3	The Abbey Pub
			14	B3	Magnolia Motor Lounge

ARTS AND CULTURE

3	B2	Amon Carter Museum of American Art	12	B3	Movie Tavern
4	B2	Fort Worth Community Arts Center	19	C2	Casa Mañana
6	B2	Kimbell Art Museum	20	C2	Fort Worth Museum of Science and History
7	B2	Modern Art Museum of Fort Worth	21	C2	National Cowgirl Museum and Hall of Fame

SPORTS AND ACTIVITIES

25	D2	Trinity Park

SHOPS

15	B3	Revint Boutique	24	D2	Montgomery Street Antique Mall

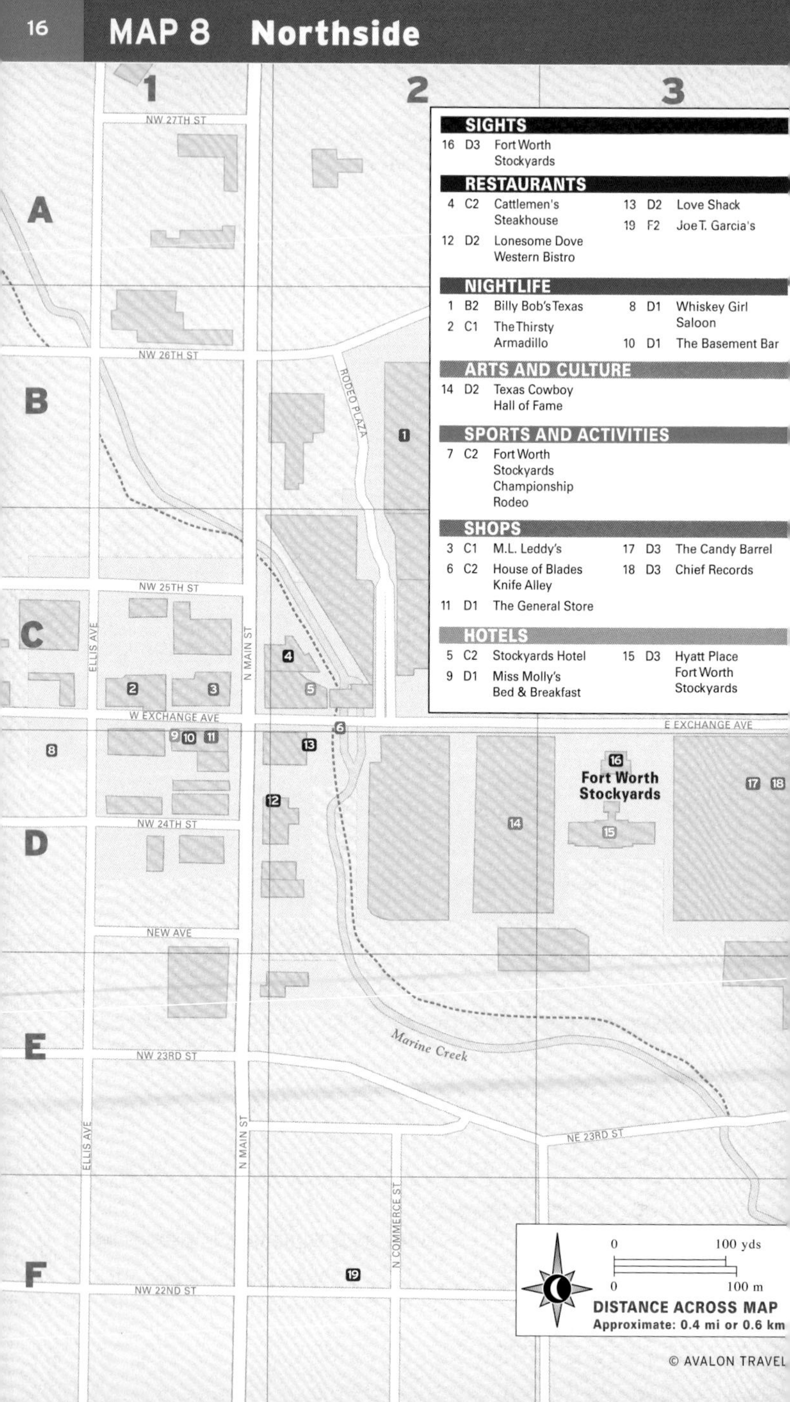
16
MAP 8 Northside
1
2
3
A
B
C
D
E
F
SIGHTS
16 D3 Fort Worth Stockyards
RESTAURANTS
4 C2 Cattlemen's Steakhouse
12 D2 Lonesome Dove Western Bistro
13 D2 Love Shack
19 F2 Joe T. Garcia's
NIGHTLIFE
1 B2 Billy Bob's Texas
2 C1 The Thirsty Armadillo
8 D1 Whiskey Girl Saloon
10 D1 The Basement Bar
ARTS AND CULTURE
14 D2 Texas Cowboy Hall of Fame
SPORTS AND ACTIVITIES
7 C2 Fort Worth Stockyards Championship Rodeo
SHOPS
3 C1 M.L. Leddy's
6 C2 House of Blades Knife Alley
11 D1 The General Store
17 D3 The Candy Barrel
18 D3 Chief Records
HOTELS
5 C2 Stockyards Hotel
9 D1 Miss Molly's Bed & Breakfast
15 D3 Hyatt Place Fort Worth Stockyards
NW 27TH ST
NW 26TH ST
RODEO PLAZA
NW 25TH ST
ELLIS AVE
N MAIN ST
W EXCHANGE AVE
E EXCHANGE AVE
Fort Worth Stockyards
NW 24TH ST
NEW AVE
Marine Creek
NW 23RD ST
NE 23RD ST
N COMMERCE ST
NW 22ND ST
0
100 yds
0
100 m
DISTANCE ACROSS MAP
Approximate: 0.4 mi or 0.6 km
© AVALON TRAVEL

1
2
3
A
B
C
D
E
F
SEE MAP 6
SEE MAP 7
Trinity Park
Newby Park
Forest Park
Fort Worth Zoo
Log Cabin Village
Daggett Park
Texas Christian University
Harris Hospital
All Saints Hospital
Saint Josephs Hospital
Smith Hospital
Elizabeth Boulevard Historic District
Clear Fork Trinity River
30
80
377
303
DAGGETT AVE
BROADWAY AVE
PETER SMITH ST
TUCKER ST
PENNSYLVANIA AVE
CANNON ST
ANNIE ST
HATTIE ST
LEUDA ST
W TERRELL AVE
COOPER ST
WEST FWY
GRANBURY
PARKVIEW DR
15TH AVE
12TH AVE
9TH AVE
SUMMIT AVE
ADAMS ST
S JENNINGS AVE
MAY ST
CALHOUN ST
CRAWFORD ST
BRYAN AVE
MAIN ST
OAK GROVE ST
GALVESTON AVE
W ROSEDALE ST
IRWIN ST
MISTLETOE BLVD
W MAGNOLIA AVE
HARRISON AVE
CLARA ST
BUCK AVE
HURLEY AVE
7TH AVE
6TH AVE
LAKE ST
S ADAMS ST
HEMPHILL ST
GRAINGER ST
ST. LOUIS AVE
EDWIN ST
JEROME ST
ALLEN AVE
PARK PLACE AVE
COLONIAL PKWY
S HENDERSON ST
WASHINGTON AVE
ALSTON AVE
JEFFERSON AVE
RICHMOND AVE
ROCKRIDGE TER
FOREST PARK BLVD
WINDSOR PL
WARNER RD
8TH AVE
FAIRMOUNT AVE
W ARLINGTON AVE
W HAWTHORNE AVE
LILAC ST
MITCHELL AVE
CARLOCK ST
TRAVIS AVE
JENNINGS AVE
GLENCO TER
STANLEY AVE
JESSAMINE ST
RAMSEY AVE
PAGE AVE
ELIZABETH BLVD
MULKEY ST
PARK HILL DR
PARK HILL WAY
ROBERT ST
S UNIVERSITY DR
GREENE AVE
WAITS AVE
LUBBOCK AVE
MCPHERSON AVE
FRAZIER AVE
TOWNSEND DR
GORDON AVE
LOWDEN ST
W BOWIE ST
W BERRY ST
COCKRELL AVE
MERIDA AVE
SANDAGE AVE
MCCART AVE
CLEBURNE RD
LIVINGSTON AVE
ORANGE AVE
MISSION ST
BEWICK ST
BIDDISON ST
MONDA ST

SIGHTS
17 C1 Log Cabin Village
18 C1 Fort Worth Zoo
21 D2 Elizabeth Boulevard Historic District

RESTAURANTS
3 B1 Ol' South Pancake House
4 B2 FunkyTown Donuts
6 B2 Ellerbe Fine Foods
8 B2 Avoca Coffee
9 B2 Lili's Bistro on Magnolia
10 B2 Melt
12 B3 Yucatan Taco Stand
13 B3 Hot Damn, Tamales!
14 B3 Paris Coffee Shop
15 B3 Jesus BBQ
19 C2 Chadra Mezza & Grill

NIGHTLIFE
2 A3 Shipping and Receiving Bar
7 B2 The Bearded Lady
11 B3 Chimera Brewing Company
22 E1 The Aardvark

ARTS AND CULTURE
1 A3 Stage West

SHOPS
20 C2 Butler's Antiques

HOTELS
5 B2 Texas White House Bed & Breakfast
16 C1 Courtyard Fort Worth University Drive

0 0.5 mi
0 0.5 km
DISTANCE ACROSS MAP
Approximate: 2.5 mi or 4.0 km
AVALON TRAVEL

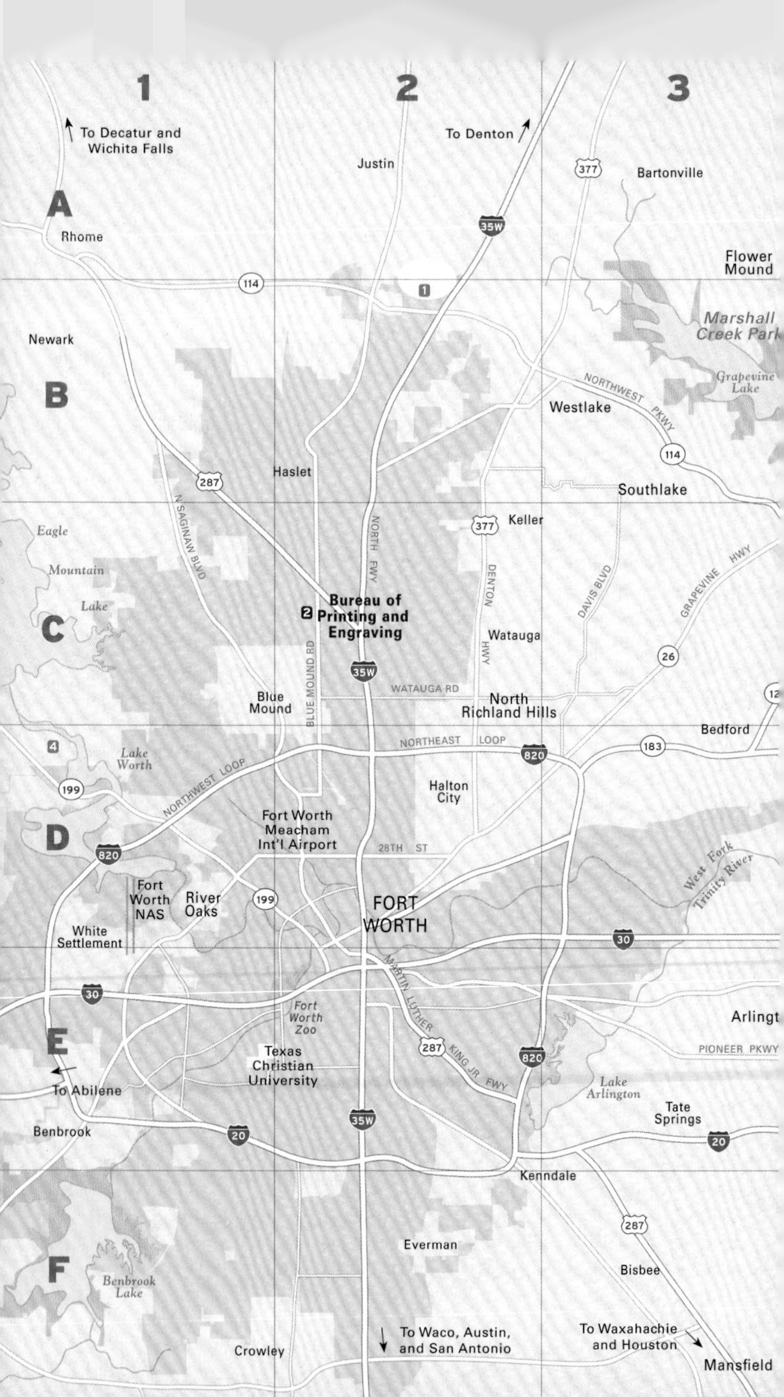

1
2
3
A
B
C
D
E
F
To Decatur and Wichita Falls
To Denton
Justin
377
Bartonville
35W
Rhome
Flower Mound
114
1
Marshall Creek Park
Newark
NORTHWEST PKWY
Grapevine Lake
Westlake
114
Haslet
287
Southlake
Eagle Mountain Lake
377
Keller
N SAGINAW BLVD
NORTH FWY
DENTON HWY
DAVIS BLVD
GRAPEVINE HWY
2 Bureau of Printing and Engraving
Watauga
26
35W
WATAUGA RD
Blue Mound
BLUE MOUND RD
North Richland Hills
Bedford
183
4
Lake Worth
NORTHEAST LOOP
820
199
NORTHWEST LOOP
Halton City
Fort Worth Meacham Int'l Airport
820
28TH ST
West Fork Trinity River
Fort Worth NAS
River Oaks
199
FORT WORTH
White Settlement
30
MARTIN LUTHER KING JR FWY
30
Fort Worth Zoo
Arlingt
Texas Christian University
287
820
PIONEER PKWY
To Abilene
Lake Arlington
Tate Springs
35W
Benbrook
20
20
Kenndale
287
Everman
Bisbee
Benbrook Lake
To Waco, Austin, and San Antonio
To Waxahachie and Houston
Crowley
Mansfield

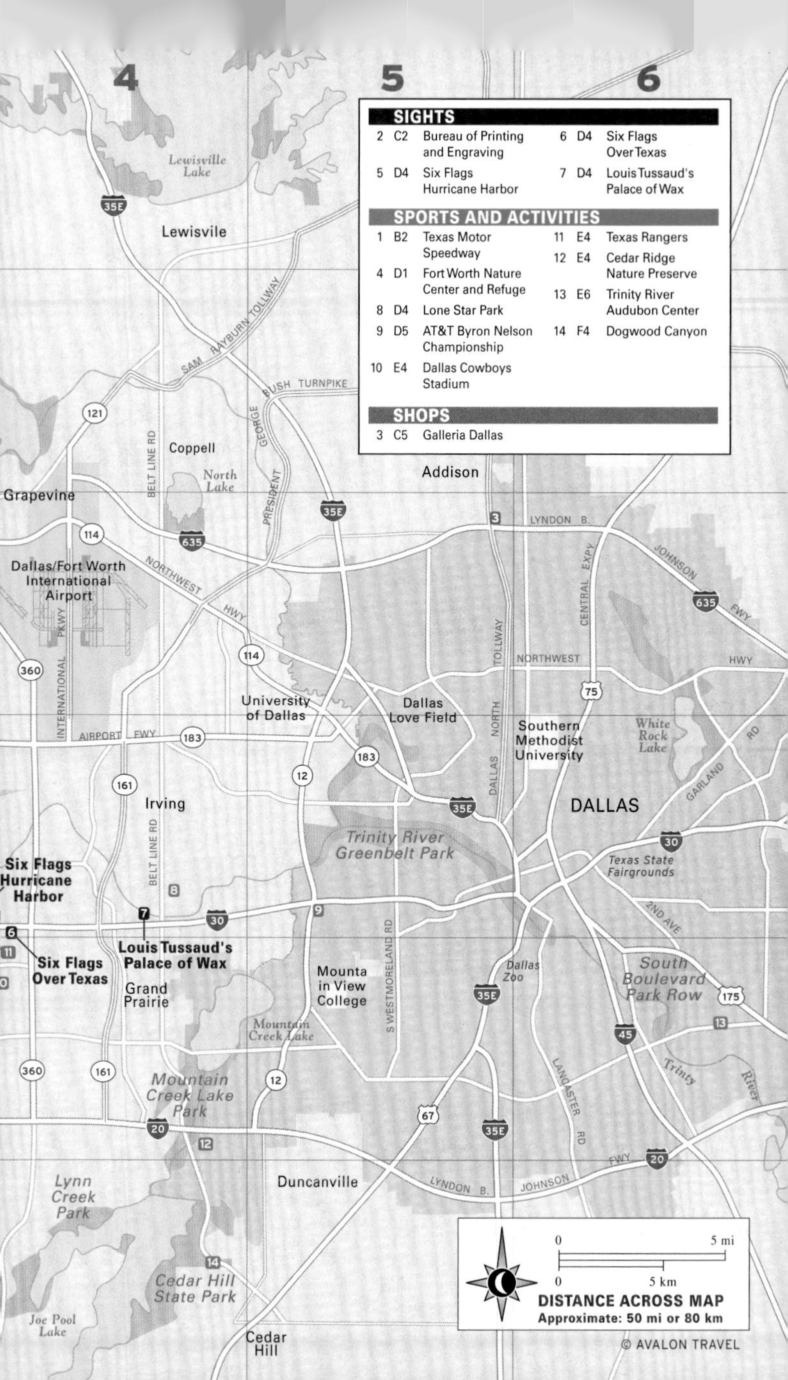

4
5
6
SIGHTS
2 C2 Bureau of Printing and Engraving
5 D4 Six Flags Hurricane Harbor
6 D4 Six Flags Over Texas
7 D4 Louis Tussaud's Palace of Wax
SPORTS AND ACTIVITIES
1 B2 Texas Motor Speedway
4 D1 Fort Worth Nature Center and Refuge
8 D4 Lone Star Park
9 D5 AT&T Byron Nelson Championship
10 E4 Dallas Cowboys Stadium
11 E4 Texas Rangers
12 E4 Cedar Ridge Nature Preserve
13 E6 Trinity River Audubon Center
14 F4 Dogwood Canyon
SHOPS
3 C5 Galleria Dallas
Lewisville Lake
Lewisvile
SAM RAYBURN TOLLWAY
BUSH TURNPIKE
GEORGE PRESIDENT
Coppell
North Lake
BELT LINE RD
Grapevine
Addison
LYNDON B. JOHNSON FWY
Dallas/Fort Worth International Airport
INTERNATIONAL PKWY
NORTHWEST HWY
CENTRAL EXPY
DALLAS NORTH TOLLWAY
University of Dallas
Dallas Love Field
AIRPORT FWY
Southern Methodist University
White Rock Lake
GARLAND RD
Irving
DALLAS
Trinity River Greenbelt Park
Texas State Fairgrounds
Six Flags Hurricane Harbor
2ND AVE
Louis Tussaud's Palace of Wax
Six Flags Over Texas
Grand Prairie
Mounta in View College
S WESTMORELAND RD
Dallas Zoo
South Boulevard Park Row
Mountain Creek Lake
Mountain Creek Lake Park
LANCASTER RD
Trinity River
Lynn Creek Park
Duncanville
LYNDON B. JOHNSON FWY
Cedar Hill State Park
Joe Pool Lake
Cedar Hill
0 5 mi
0 5 km
DISTANCE ACROSS MAP
Approximate: 50 mi or 80 km
© AVALON TRAVEL

DISCOVER

Discover Dallas & Fort Worth

Big oil and big hair, cowboys and cattle fields—these are the images of Dallas and Fort Worth that prevail.

Established as a profitable trading post on the banks of the Trinity River, Dallas grew into a vibrant community of merchants, and then a cosmopolitan city as the center of the Texas oil boom. With all that money and status came wealthy socialites with sky-high hair, designer clothing, and flashy BMW convertibles. Thirty miles away, cowboys herded millions of cattle down the Chisholm Trail, founding Fort Worth as the "place where the West begins." That city's western culture continues to thrive.

Over the years, however, all kinds of people moved here and the cities have changed. Transplants from both coasts have set down roots in DFW, influencing the region's dining and shopping scenes with a homegrown, handmade philosophy. Today, diversity is everywhere, from the colorful *quinceañera* celebrations in Oak Cliff to the massive Korean spa center in Northwest Dallas. The Fort Worth Cultural District boasts world-renowned art museums full of Picassos and Andy Warhols. Punk rock bars and craft breweries are peppered in with the more classic jazz clubs and dance halls in Deep Ellum. Historic cemeteries preserve the region's heritage in West Dallas while restaurant rows in Trinity Groves and on Fort Worth's Magnolia Avenue showcase modern redevelopment.

Look beyond the rodeos and honky-tonks and Dallas and Fort Worth will defy your expectations.

Clockwise from top left: the Modern Art Museum of Fort Worth's stunning architecture; great egret at the Trinity River Audubon Center; view from the Ronald Kirk Pedestrian Bridge; The Wild Detectives bookstore and cafe.

Neighborhoods

Downtown Dallas/Deep Ellum

The city center houses important history and art museums that top the list of Dallas attractions. Dealey Plaza, the site of President John F. Kennedy's assassination in 1963, still fascinates visitors. Spanning 19 blocks, the Dallas Arts District bursts with activity most of the year. Besides the major sights, event venues, and all-star restaurants, downtown has a mostly commercial feel compared to the more community-oriented neighborhoods around it. Although the city has invested in more public spaces, locals don't spend much time here when they leave the office—that's what Deep Ellum is for. A few blocks east of downtown, it's the heart of Dallas nightlife.

Lakewood/East Dallas

The diverse landscape of Lakewood and East Dallas ranges from the peaceful nature of White Rock Lake and iconic turn-of-the-20th-century mansions to the walkable Greenville Avenue restaurant and shopping strip. The sense of pride is palpable here because these thriving destinations resulted from grassroots neighborhood planning rather than big Dallas money.

Uptown/Oak Lawn/Design District

Situated side by side just north of downtown, these neighborhoods smoothly transition from one to the next, but each is distinct. Uptown has historical charm hidden within its new mixed-use real estate, drawing young professionals who enjoy the proximity to trendy restaurants. Oak Lawn is home to an LGBT community where no one feels like an outsider, whether chilling at a dive bar or dancing under neon lights. The more upscale Design District is a haven for contemporary fashion and interior design galleries along with well-established antiques shops.

Dealey Plaza

White Rock Lake

Park Cities

These separate municipalities, Highland Park and University Park, include some of Dallas's wealthiest enclaves as well as Southern Methodist University's college-town environment. The area embodies the perception of Dallas as rich, white, and conservative, though it is not lacking in culture. The Meadows Museum at SMU boasts some of the most significant Spanish art in the world, for example, and NorthPark Center brings diverse communities together with festivals throughout the year.

West Dallas/Oak Cliff

The neighborhoods south of the Trinity River have a communal spirit unlike anywhere else in the city, and their recent gentrification has drawn comparisons to Austin and Brooklyn. In the Bishop Arts District, and along Davis Street and Jefferson Boulevard, you'll find artisan shops and small-scale event spaces. A closer look at this neighborhood reveals a community of young artists and entrepreneurs, devoted baby boomers who grew up here and never left, and a majority Hispanic population looking to retain its place in a rapidly changing landscape.

Downtown Fort Worth

It features top attractions like Bass Performance Hall and Sundance Square, but downtown Fort Worth is more than an entertainment district. You'll find plenty of service businesses and great transportation options—like the trolley and the bike-share program—that give the neighborhood a more livable, down-home feel compared to Dallas's city center.

West Fort Worth

This neighborhood is home to the Fort Worth Cultural District, which boasts world-renowned art museums and performing arts centers along with long-standing restaurants and shops. In recent years, West 7th Street has been redeveloped into a vibrant live-work-play area, akin to Dallas's

Uptown, attracting young professionals. The west side of town is also where you'll find the best outdoor recreation along the Trinity River.

Northside

The Fort Worth Stockyards are the center of the action north of downtown, featuring rodeos every weekend, daily cattle drives, old-fashioned honky-tonks and saloons, steak houses, and souvenir shopping. Elsewhere, the Coyote Drive-In is a popular destination for families and nightlife seekers alike.

Southside/TCU

The area has charming, historic neighborhoods full of early-20th-century architecture. Magnolia Avenue has exploded into a "restaurant row," featuring a variety of locally owned cafes, bars, and live music venues. Near Texas Christian University, you'll find a college-town vibe along with more upscale shopping centers.

When to Go

You can get the most out of your visit to Dallas and Fort Worth in the spring (March-May) or fall (September-November) when the milder temperatures help accommodate some of the best events—from the Deep Ellum Arts Festival in April to the State Fair of Texas in October. During these months, you can fully explore the city on foot or by bike without risking heat stroke.

The summer routinely sees triple-digit temperatures that make it hard to justify leaving the house. If you're stuck in Dallas around this time, splurge on a nice hotel with an indoor pool and a breezy bar. From flash floods to ice storms, the winter brings unpredictable weather that could ruin your best-laid plans (e.g., Dallas's attempt to host Super Bowl XLV).

Ferris wheel at the State Fair of Texas

The Best of Dallas and Fort Worth

It takes at least a week to soak up all that Dallas and Fort Worth have to offer. That's due in part to the tricky transportation; getting from one region to another can be cumbersome without a car. Curate a two-day trip carefully to hit as many highlights as possible without wasting any time navigating the auto-centric metropolis. This sample itinerary will help you make the best of a typical weekend.

Day 1

Get an early start in downtown Dallas with coffee at at **Murray Street Coffee.** From there, head to the West End's Dealey Plaza, where President John F. Kennedy was assassinated on November 22, 1963. If you arrive before the **Sixth Floor Museum** opens at 10am, explore the **Grassy Knoll** and the **JFK Memorial Plaza** first to maximize your time.

From Dealey Plaza, hop on the **D Link,** that flashy pink and yellow shuttle you see around downtown, and ride to the **Dallas Arts District.** You could easily spend the rest of the day here touring the art museums: the **Dallas Museum of Art,** the **Nasher Sculpture Center,** and the **Crow Collection of Asian Art.** Stroll through **Klyde Warren Park,** a stunning green space situated on a freeway deck with skyline views. You can also experience the park at night; it stays open until 11pm. Grab a food truck snack, catch a yoga session, or take in a concert on the lawn.

For a late night, go barhopping in Deep Ellum, the city's liveliest neighborhood between 10pm and 2am. Hit **Twilite Lounge** for an old Hollywood vibe, **Adair's Saloon** if you're in a honky-tonk mood, or the **It'll Do Club** where some of the best DJs in town bring crowds to the dance floor. For

Klyde Warren Park

Fun and Cheap

It's easy to run up a tab exploring Dallas and Fort Worth's vast landscape of museums, restaurants, and shops. Still, there are plenty of ways to enjoy the cities on a budget.

Sightseeing

The free **Dallas Streetcar** runs every 20 minutes 5:30am-midnight. Ride from **Union Station** downtown across the Trinity River to the **Bishop Arts District** in Oak Cliff. Browse the mom-and-pop boutiques up and down the redbrick paths of Bishop Avenue. Stop to snap some pictures in front of the neighborhood murals, including the provocative portrait of Lee Harvey Oswald. Don't leave Bishop Arts without a visit to **Emporium Pies;** the $5 splurge is definitely worth it.

Take a ride on the free **McKinney Avenue Trolley** from Uptown to all the **Dallas Arts District** hot spots. Other than some special exhibitions, the **Dallas Museum of Art** is always free, including a docent tour at 2pm Saturdays. Channel your inner child at the museum's Art Stop where you can sketch, draw, or sculpt your own artwork from available objects. Peek inside the **Cathedral Shrine of Guadalupe,** and admire its 19th-century Gothic Revival architecture.

Spend an afternoon at the **Fort Worth Stockyards** where you can watch a twice-daily cattle drive at 11:30am or 4pm, and go souvenir shopping at **Stockyards Station.**

Find your Zen at the **Fort Worth Water Gardens,** a modern architectural marvel that you may recognize from the 1976 sci-fi flick *Logan's Run*. It's especially beautiful at night against the city skyline.

Food & Drink

If you can resist the temptation to buy every vendor's homemade salsa or hand-poured candle, a stroll through the **Dallas Farmers Market** won't cost you a dime (plus, free samples).

Fort Worth Stockyards cattle drive

Along the perimeter of the Shed, you'll find purveyors of seasonal produce, free-range meats, and fresh cheeses. Inside are more offbeat artisanal items like banana pudding and habanero jam. Swing by the indoor market for more shops and vendors. If it's happy hour pull up a barstool at **Taqueria La Ventana** for $2 margaritas.

A couple of blocks off the McKinney Avenue Trolley line in Uptown, spend happy hour at **Parliament,** a swanky 1900s-era lounge that serves up some of the fanciest-yet-affordable house cocktails for around $5.

Recreation

Spend the day outdoors without spending any money. Take a stroll on the 9.3-mile **White Rock Lake Loop Trail** and absorb the scene of rowers, bird-watchers, nature photographers, and hard-core athletes. Linger at Winfrey Point and TP Hill, the park's highest points.

For just $10 a day (10am-3pm), you can rent a bike from **Dallas City Tour** and go sightseeing around downtown or hit the neighborhood trails. Hop on the **Katy Trail** from its southern terminus and ride through Uptown, or head east on the **Santa Fe Trail** all the way to White Rock Lake.

those midnight calorie cravings, join the line at **Serious Pizza** for a massive slice of New York-style pie; the place stays open until 3am on weekends.

Day 2

Spend your second 24 hours in Fort Worth, beginning with breakfast at **Paris Coffee Shop,** a local institution and the most authentic glimpse into the city's cowboy character.

Next, make your way to the **Fort Worth Cultural District** for a day of world-class art, beginning at the **Kimbell Art Museum.** While the collection is small, you'll want to spend a few hours lingering inside the Louis Khan-designed building. Then, head to the **Modern Art Museum of Fort Worth,** the Kimbell's counterpart for post-World War II talent.

Weather permitting, spend the rest of the daylight hours walking or biking along the **Trinity River.** The surrounding park features a duck pond, a picturesque bridge, shady lounge areas, and a tiny fishing pier. Before embarking on the quintessential country-and-western evening, make a detour to **Angelo's** for local barbecue that far outshines the touristy restaurants.

Arrive at the **Fort Worth Stockyards** in time for the 8pm championship rodeo every Friday and Saturday. Watch competitive bull riders, cattle roping, and barrel racing along with rodeo clowns offering comic relief. After the show, go two-stepping at **Billy Bob's Texas,** the massive nightclub frequented by country music legends. Ride the mechanical bull, play pool, sing karaoke, or grab a late-night bite from the Honky Tonk Kitchen.

With More Time

If you have more time to spend in Dallas, dedicate a few daytime hours to Deep Ellum. Although known for its nightlife, the walkable neighborhood east of downtown offers plenty of afternoon diversions. Start at **Pecan Lodge** for the best barbecue brisket in Texas. Get in line before the restaurant opens at 11am, and be prepared to wait. After lunch, take a self-guided tour of **Deep Ellum street art.** Check out the *Dallas Morning News*'s mobile-friendly walking guide to 42 murals: www.interactives.dallasnews.com/2016/deep-ellum/42-murals.

In Fort Worth, head to the **Fort Worth Stockyards** earlier in the day to see one of the twice-daily cattle drives at 11:30am or 4pm. You can also catch a historical reenactment of the original Pawnee Bill's Wild West Show on Saturdays at 2:30pm and 4:30pm in the Cowtown Coliseum. Dating to 1909, the show features cowboy trick roping, shooting, and riding. Tickets are $11.50-18.50.

Best Eats

- **Barbecue at Pecan Lodge:** There's a reason the line extends down the block every single weekend—it's that good. This Deep Ellum outpost opens at 11am, but people start lining up at least a half hour sooner for the mouthwatering brisket smoked to perfection.
- **Cheeseburger and tots at Keller's Drive-in:** Forget the fancy $15 burgers touted at trendy Dallas hotspots. The 50-year-old Keller's Drive-in harks back to a simpler time. For less than $3, chow down on a juicy double-meat patty in a poppy seed bun and take in the old-school carhop ambience.
- **Chicken-fried steak at Fred's Texas Café:** Often overlooked amid the popular burgers, Fred's chicken-fried steak is some of the best you'll find in Dallas and Fort Worth. The first indication? Its sheer size, covering the plate edge to edge.
- **Fuel City Tacos:** Set inside a truck stop, this roadside taco stand is a local legend for its super-simple street tacos made with corn tortillas, meat, onions, and cilantro. Plus, you can't beat the atmosphere: the Dallas skyline in one direction, and a pasture of longhorns in the other.
- **Fletcher's Corny Dog at the Texas State Fair:** What could be so great about "America's original corn dog"? If you're lucky enough to visit Dallas during fair season, you'll find out. There's just something special about this hand-battered, deep-fried hot dog that cannot be replicated.
- **Margarita at Joe T. Garcia's:** Dallas is the birthplace of the frozen margarita, so there's a lot of competition. However, you might do better to try this Tex-Mex institution in Fort Worth. Pair it with an enchilada dinner in the restaurant's garden villa.

Mile-High Cream Pie at Norma's Café

- **Mile-High Cream Pie at Norma's Café:** Perhaps the most famous dessert in town, this pie is a slice of heaven with creamy filling topped with a thick and fluffy meringue. The Oak Cliff-based diner created the confection in 1959, and it has stood the test of time.
- **Tortilla soup at The Mansion at Turtle Creek:** Throughout the Mansion's long history as one of the finest restaurants in Dallas, one recipe has received more acclaim than any artfully plated cuisine: the tortilla soup. Legendary Dallas chef Dean Fearing created the dish decades ago, and it's a mainstay of the Mansion's menu.

Sights

Highlights

Klyde Warren Park

★ **Best History Museum:** Nothing shaped Dallas more than the assassination of President John F. Kennedy. The **Sixth Floor Museum** features a comprehensive exhibit that puts the national tragedy into greater perspective (page 32).

★ **Best Community Gathering Space:** Transformed from freeway to green space, **Klyde Warren Park** is a shining example of creative city planning. The bustling park is also a prime spot for people watching (page 33).

★ **Best Way to Get Around:** Linking Downtown Dallas and Uptown, the **McKinney Avenue Trolley** adds some vintage charm to your modern-day sightseeing. Plus, it's free (page 36).

★ **Best Look at Recent History:** Regardless of your political leanings, the **George W. Bush Presidential Library and Museum** features a fascinating display of the Bush years (page 39).

★ **Best Neighborhood Gateway:** The newest addition to the Dallas skyline, the **Margaret Hunt Hill Bridge** helped create a vibrant dining and entertainment scene in West Dallas (page 41).

★ **Best Downtown Charm:** In stark contrast to Dallas, the historic **Sundance Square** gives downtown Fort Worth a refreshing, small-town vibe. The free parking and 24-hour security helps, too (page 44).

★ **Best Glimpse of Cowboy Culture:** At the **Fort Worth Stockyards,** the city's western heritage is on display daily in the form of rodeos, bull riding and cattle drives (page 46).

Dallas and Fort Worth feature the old and the new. Travelers can spend half a day buried in archives that document the assassination of President John F. Kennedy, then spend the other half soaking up the contemporary architecture of the nearby Dallas Arts District. From historic preservation to urban creativity, the region has more than a few surprises.

Every weekend, weather permitting, locals gather atop a Downtown Dallas freeway deck to toss Frisbees, play croquet, watch their kids run and romp through fountains, or just take a shady afternoon nap. The strip of concrete once carried thousands of cars commuting through the city. Now, replaced with lush grass and various amenities, Klyde Warren Park brings people together at the human scale. In fact, you can ditch the car altogether in this part of town. Fully restored vintage trolley cars transport visitors between Downtown and Uptown, rolling beneath soaring skyscrapers and past newly constructed shopping centers.

The stunning white arch of the Margaret Hunt Hill Bridge—and the rest of the skyline—is best viewed from the West Dallas Gateway where you can walk along the adjacent pedestrian bridge.

If you're seeking Old West archetypes, you'll find the best of them in Fort Worth, "where the West begins." North of town, cowboys herd cattle through the cobblestone streets of the Fort Worth Stockyards. Cowboy culture also serves as the backdrop of Sundance Square in downtown, where a massive mural of longhorns pays tribute to the 19th century livestock industry.

From dusty cattle trails to fancy bridges, sightseeing around Dallas and Fort Worth blends the past with the present.

Previous: Sixth Floor Museum at Dealey Plaza; Dallas Arboretum and Botanical Garden

Downtown Dallas

Map 1

DALLAS HERITAGE VILLAGE

In the shadow of the city's glossy skyscrapers lies 20 acres frozen in time. Dallas Heritage Village contains the largest collection of 19th-century pioneer structures in Texas. About 24,000 artifacts compose the permanent installation, illustrating what it was like to live and work during the frontier days of Dallas. The collection includes Victorian furnishings and accessories, medical tools, and fascinating archival photographs. On a walk down "Main Street," you can watch a blacksmith at work, and peek into the library or the saloon. Guided tours are available, providing a more curated experience; they last no more than two hours. Arrive after 1pm to avoid school field trips, and pack a picnic to enjoy in the park.

MAP 1: 1515 S. Harwood St., 214/421-5141, www.dallasheritagevillage.org; Tues.-Sat. 10am-4pm, Sun. noon-4pm; adults $9, seniors $7, children $5

DALLAS WORLD AQUARIUM

Located in downtown's historic West End, the Dallas World Aquarium features five exhibits not limited to underwater creatures. The first thing you'll see is a multilevel, spiraling rain forest full of free-flying exotic birds, lazy two-toed sloths, and other critters. Throughout the aquarium and zoo, you'll find giant river otters, crocodiles, and many species of monkeys. A 20,000-gallon tunnel surrounds visitors with curious creatures from the tropical waters of the Indian and Pacific Oceans, such as the pot-bellied seahorse and harlequin shrimp. Ticket prices are a bit steep—two adults will pay over $40—but there's a lot to see here. Expect to spend all day, and arrive early to beat the afternoon crowds.

MAP 1: 1801 N. Griffin St., 214/720-2224, www.dwazoo.com; daily 10am-5pm; adults $20.95, seniors $16.95, children $14.95, under 2 free

★ SIXTH FLOOR MUSEUM

The former Texas School Book Depository became known as something else on November 22, 1963, when President John F. Kennedy's assassin, Lee Harvey Oswald, perched from the building's 6th-floor window and fired the fatal shots that changed Dallas forever. Its image tarnished, the city was not eager to preserve the building; it was even in danger of being demolished. After Dallas finally reckoned with the horrific yet historic event, the structure overlooking Dealey Plaza was opened as the Sixth Floor Museum on Presidents Day in 1989. The crime scene itself has been re-created to its condition just 45 minutes after the assassination, with boxes of books stacked haphazardly and a replica of the rifle used. The historical exhibit chronicles the events with images, video footage, artifacts, and crime scene evidence so engaging you can't look away—especially when using the audio guide, included with admission.

As you leave the museum and walk toward the infamous Grassy Knoll, a ragtag group of conspiracy theorists offer their side of the story, usually involving a second shooter. After you roam the grounds of Dealey Plaza, look for the white "X" on the road, marking the exact spot where Kennedy was shot.

Buy tickets online in advance to reserve a spot; the museum only lets a certain amount of people in at 30-minute intervals. Peak vacation times—summer, spring break, the holidays—draw huge crowds, so plan ahead and be prepared to wait. At other times of the year, crowds are unpredictable, but there's rarely a day without JFK tourists.

MAP 1: 411 Elm St., 214/747-6660, www.jfk.org; Mon. noon-6pm, Tues.-Sun. 10am-6pm; adults $16, seniors $14, youth $13, children under 5 free

★ KLYDE WARREN PARK

One of the most ambitious (and wildly successful) projects Dallas has undertaken in recent years is the 5-acre freeway deck green space known as Klyde Warren Park. In 2012, eight lanes of concrete once clogged with cars were transformed into a privately managed public green space. The linear park connects the Dallas Arts District with the rest of downtown and Uptown, and features a range of free activities on any given day. Several playground areas will occupy the kids for a couple of hours. There are also bistro tables, free board games, a small dog park, a walking path, and plenty of open space for picnics and lounging. Local food trucks line up during lunchtime most days, while a brick-and-mortar restaurant, Savor Gastropub, serves brunch, dinner, and cocktails. Check the online calendar for recurring events like yoga sessions, story time, live music, and movie screenings.

MAP 1: 2012 Woodall Rodgers Freeway, 214/716-4500, www.klydewarrenpark.org

OLD RED MUSEUM

Built in 1892 as the Dallas County Courthouse, the Old Red Museum offers a thorough history lesson on local culture and a peek at stunning Romanesque Revival-style architecture. Play close attention to the details like the four mythical serpent sculptures that adorn the top and the stately clock tower that illuminates at night. Inside, the grand staircase has been restored to its original glory along with the 100 or so stained glass windows. You can receive a free guided tour of all four floors of the building at 2pm Monday-Friday, but call ahead first. Four permanent exhibits chronicle the history of Dallas, beginning with the first settlement in 1841 and continuing through the turn of 21st century.

MAP 1: 100 S. Houston St., 214/757-1914, www.oldred.org; daily 9am-5pm; general admission $10, seniors, students, and military $8, children under 3 free

PIONEER PLAZA

This park's bronze herd of 49 longhorn steers commemorates the 19th-century cattle drives that brought the early settlers to what we now know as Dallas. Located just outside the Kay Bailey Hutchison Convention Center, Pioneer Plaza is a neat display, especially for kids, set among trees, native plants, and water features. Although good for the classic tourist photo if you're already in the area, it's not worth going out of your way. Wander over to the adjacent Pioneer Park Cemetery, which includes graves dating back more than 150 years.

MAP 1: 1428 Young St., 214/953-1184

REUNION TOWER

It's the most recognizable feature of the Dallas skyline, stretching 561 feet into the sky, but Reunion Tower (aka "the Ball") is only the 15th-tallest building in the city. What it lacks in height it makes up for in 360-degree immersive views of downtown. It's hard to imagine what Dallas looked like before the tower was built in 1978. The circular architecture was designed to accommodate the revolving restaurant at the top of the ball, which is home to chef Wolfgang Puck's Five Sixty restaurant. In 2008, the tower underwent a $23 million renovation to its interior. A few years later, the high-tech GeO-Deck opened, making the Ball more accessible. In addition to the view, you can explore touch screens and interactive games. For the best view, visit just before sunset to see the myriad colors reflecting off the skyscrapers. For just a few dollars more, you can do both with the Day and Night ticket, which gets you onto the deck twice in one day.

MAP 1: 300 Reunion Blvd., 214/712-7040, www.reuniontower.com; Geo-Deck Sun.-Thurs. 10:30am-8:30pm, Fri.-Sat. 10:30am-9:30pm; Wolfgang Five Sixty Sun.-Thurs. 5-10pm, Fri.-Sat. 5-11pm; general admission $8-17, Day and Night $13-22

THANKS-GIVING SQUARE

During a hectic day of sightseeing, Thanks-Giving Square is a quiet, calming retreat amid towering skyscrapers and downtown traffic. Established in 1976 by public-private partnership, the park and chapel are meant to foster gratitude among visitors regardless of their spiritual affiliation. The most striking feature is the spiraling stained glass ceiling inside the chapel. To capture the city's most photographed landmark, just lie flat on the chapel floor with your camera pointed straight up. Thanks-Giving Square also features a cascading waterfall and three granite pillars that frame the public space.

MAP 1: 1627 Pacific Ave., 214/969-1977, www.thanksgiving.org; free

Lakewood/East Dallas — Map 2

DALLAS ARBORETUM AND BOTANICAL GARDEN

Flanking the wild prairies of White Rock Lake is a very different kind of park: a perfectly manicured display that has become one of the top arboretums in the world. The Dallas Arboretum boasts 66 acres of gardens, each with its own character. There are endless beds of roses and tulips, lush lawns perfect for picnicking, and gorgeous walkways. You could spend all day taking photographs; it's a prime place for special event pictures. A few highlights include Crape Myrtle Alley, where the trees form a long tunnel; Pecan Grove, where you can see cherry blossoms in spring and about 50,000 pumpkin varieties in the fall; and the Rory Meyers Children's Adventure

Garden, which has racked up national awards for its 150 educational activities and breathtaking views of the lake. Arrive after 2pm on weekdays to avoid the crowds. The arboretum's two biggest events are Dallas Blooms in the spring, and Autumn at the Arboretum in the fall. Visit during those seasons to get the most out of the park. Check the website for discounts year-round.

MAP 2: 8525 Garland Rd., 214/515-6500, www.dallasarboretum.org; daily 9am-5pm; adults $15, seniors $12, children $10, 2 and under free

FAIR PARK

Most visitors find their way to Fair Park to attend a big annual event—from the iconic State Fair of Texas to the fantastic Fourth of July fireworks show. But this 277-acre historic site is best appreciated on its own, un-obscured by throngs of festivalgoers. Debuting in 1936 with the Texas Centennial Exposition, Fair Park is a relic of an era when officials constructed mini-cities within their cities to display new ideas to the public in the form of art, architecture, nature shows, and technological exhibits. Today, Fair Park is the last surviving pre-1950s world's fair site in the United States, featuring the country's largest collection of art deco designs. Visitors can tour the fairgrounds on foot using a map marked with about 60 stops where you can access information via cellphone. Fair Park also houses several museums worth visiting such as the Hall of State, which was built for the Texas Centennial; the Texas Discovery Gardens, home to a butterfly house and insectarium; and the Children's Aquarium.

MAP 2: 1121 First Ave., 214/426-3400, www.fairpark.org; Fairground hours: daily 10am-5pm; admission to the fairgrounds is free, special event fees vary; Hall of State: free admission, unless otherwise noted during special events; Texas Discovery Gardens: $8 adults, $6 seniors, $4 children; Children's Aquarium at Fair Park: $8 adult, $6 seniors and children, free ages 2 and under

Uptown

Map 3

FREEDMAN'S MEMORIAL

A towering granite archway marks the entrance to this important piece of Dallas history. The remains of thousands of freed slaves rest in Freedman's Memorial, commemorating the post-Civil War town, established in 1869, by the same name. The memorial features several heart-wrenching bronze sculptures depicting slaves, but you won't find many tombstones here. That's because most residents couldn't afford them, and the graves went unmarked. In fact, part of the burial ground wasn't even discovered until the widening of Central Expressway in 1990 unearthed the remains. After that, about 1,500 more graves were found and moved to what became Freedman's Memorial.

MAP 3: N. Central Expy. and Calvary Dr.

GREENWOOD CEMETERY

Hidden behind an ivy-covered brick wall just a block or so from Uptown's barhopping nightlife, Greenwood Cemetery feels completely undiscovered. Established as Trinity Cemetery in 1875, the historic burial ground has a spookier vibe than its neighboring cemeteries. Perhaps it emanates from the graves of Dallas's earliest and most prominent residents, whose stories ended tragically. One former mayor, Benjamin Long, was shot and killed in a saloon while trying to stop a theft. Attorney J. M. Thurmond was shot dead in a courtroom during an argument with a rival attorney. Greenwood Cemetery also includes the graves of both Union and Confederate soldiers, their tombstones stained black with age.

MAP 3: 3020 Oak Grove Ave.

OLD CALVARY CEMETERY

This slice of Dallas history lies in the shadow of the CityPlace residential tower, just off the Central Expressway. But once you start down the tree-shaded stone path in Old Calvary Cemetery, you'll forget all about the frenzied modern life occurring outside. Established in 1878, this historic burial ground served Dallas's early settlers from France, Ireland, Italy, Germany, Poland, and Czechoslovakia. The most notable grave is that of Maxime Guillot, marked by a large stone pillar. The bilingual carriage maker opened Dallas's first manufacturing plant in the early 1850s and served as an interpreter for the French colonists of La Reunion in present-day Oak Cliff. Burials ceased at Old Calvary around 1945 after the larger Calvary Hill Cemetery was established farther north.

MAP 3: 2500 N. Hall St.

TEMPLE EMANU-EL CEMETERY AND MAUSOLEUM

The final resting place for Dallas's early Jewish settlers, the Temple Emanu-El Cemetery and Mausoleum dates back to 1884. The German-born immigrants buried here were among the first to arrive in Dallas via the Texas and Pacific Railroad, which marked the beginning of the city's enormous commercial growth. The Jewish community played a prominent role in Dallas's legendary retail industry. The tombstones bear some big names: Sanger, of what became the Sanger-Harris department store chain; Linz, of Linz Jewelers, operating through the 1980s; and the most famous, Neiman, of Neiman-Marcus. The small but beautifully maintained cemetery still serves Temple Emanu-El, one of the largest reform congregations in the Southwest.

MAP 3: 3430 Howell St.

★ MCKINNEY AVENUE TROLLEY

The adorable antique trolley cars running through Uptown are hard to miss amid the neighborhood's modern architecture and luxury SUVs. The McKinney Avenue Transit Authority (MATA) operates five early-20th-century cars that have been completely restored—and they're not just for show. These vintage streetcars provide practical transportation around Uptown and Downtown Dallas for tourists exploring the city and locals headed to

Historic Cemeteries

Perhaps no other place in Dallas contains such a stark juxtaposition of the past and the present as the trendy Uptown neighborhood, which is home to a cluster of centuries-old cemeteries. All four burial grounds are within walking distance of each other, providing a fascinating and convenient history lesson. Start at **Greenwood Cemetery** (3020 Oak Grove Ave.) to learn about some of Dallas's founders, then head north to **Temple Emanu-El Cemetery and Mausoleum** (3430 Howell St.) for a look at the city's rich Jewish heritage. Next is **Freedman's Memorial** (N. Central Expy. and Calvary Dr.), which honors a once forgotten community of freed slaves. End your self-guided tour at **Old Calvary Cemetery** (2500 N. Hall St.) where the city's early European settlers rest.

The Dallas Historical Society hosts a guided tour of the four cemeteries around Halloween every year for $20. Visit www.dallashistory.org for more information.

work. They're always free to ride and they connect with other public transportation, including the DART train and the Katy Trail. Each trolley has a name and a story. For example, "Betty" was built in 1926. When she went out of service 30 years later, she became a playhouse for the grandchildren of the Dallas railway company president. Like all of the trolley cars, Betty was restored to her original state inside and out, with the addition of air-conditioning, of course.

The McKinney Avenue Trolley runs Monday-Thursday 7am-10pm, Friday 7am-midnight, Saturday 10am-midnight, and Sunday 10am-10pm. Times vary, so check the schedule on the MATA website.

MAP 3: 3153 Oak Grove Ave., 214/855-0006, www.mata.org; free

STATE THOMAS HISTORIC DISTRICT

Flanked by the eight-acre Griggs Park and stellar skyline views, the State Thomas Historic District contains the largest remaining collection of Victorian-era homes in Dallas. The neighborhood features one- and two-story frame houses representing Italianate, Queen Anne, Classic Revival, and farmhouse architecture of the day. The homes were built between the 1870s and 1920s for the wealthy elite of what was once "North Dallas." The walkable, tree-canopied streets provide a hidden escape from the more crowded areas of Uptown. On foot, you can admire the Victorian architecture and duck into cozy neighborhood bars like **State and Allen** (2400 Allen St., 214/239-1990, www.stateandallen.com) or **City Council** (2901 Thomas Ave., 214/965-9595, www.citycouncilbar.com).

MAP 3: Allen St. and Thomas Ave.

Top: George W. Bush Presidential Library and Museum; **Bottom:** McKinney Avenue Trolley

Park Cities

Map 4

FRONTIERS OF FLIGHT MUSEUM

The lesser-known story of Dallas features a rich aviation history centered on Love Field Airport. The former World War I training base welcomed the first round-the-world flight crew in 1924 and became one of the busiest terminals in the country. The nearby Frontiers of Flight Museum embodies that history, showcasing an astonishing array of rare aircraft, aviation artifacts, and NASA relics in a 100,000-square-foot space. The chronological exhibits captivate children, who can view astronaut suits, an actual moon rock, and the command module from Apollo 7, which orbited Earth for 10 days in October 1968. Air Force pilots and museum guides offer tours of warplanes, including the world's only SR-71 Blackbird simulator, the fastest air-breathing manned aircraft. While the museum is a must-see for those with kids in tow, adults enjoy the nostalgia induced by the vintage scenes of Braniff Airlines—particularly the flight attendant fashions. Expect to spend about two hours strolling through the exhibits, and check the museum calendar for events like air shows, astronaut visits, and film screenings.

MAP 4: 6911 Lemmon Ave., 214/350-3600, www.flightmuseum.com; Mon.-Sat. 10am-5pm, Sun. 1pm-5pm; adults $10, seniors $8, students and children $7, free under 3

★ GEORGE W. BUSH PRESIDENTIAL LIBRARY AND MUSEUM

Walking through the museum of such a recent past feels surreal, but necessary. Whatever your politics, the George W. Bush Presidential Library and Museum captures the events of eight tumultuous years in well-organized, interactive exhibits. Visitors receive portable audio guides, but you can also download the mobile app before the tour. The 9/11 terrorist attacks play a prominent role, of course. The difficult-to-watch display includes actual pieces of the twin towers, the bullhorn Bush used at ground zero, scores of photographs, and oral histories. The museum's biggest draw is the Decision Points Theater, where visitors put themselves in the president's position. The theater presents the group a tough situation, such as Hurricane Katrina or the invasion of Iraq, and gives them four minutes to gather information from advisers via a video and make a decision—after which President Bush himself appears on screen to deliver his decision and rationale. Admission is pricey, plus parking costs $7, but the museum is worth a one-time visit.

MAP 4: 2943 SMU Blvd., 214/346-1650, www.georgewbushlibrary.smu.edu; Mon.-Sat. 9am-5pm, Sun. noon-5pm; adults $16, seniors $13, youth $10-14, active military free

SOUTHERN METHODIST UNIVERSITY

Established in 1911 by the United Methodist Church, SMU is lauded for its humanities, science, business, and law schools, claiming several notable alumni. Among them are former First Lady and neighborhood resident Laura Bush, Nobel Prize-winning physicist James Cronin, and

Oscar-winning actress Kathy Bates. The pristine Park Cities campus covers 234 acres north of downtown Dallas, creating a vibrant small-town vibe that mixes lifelong residents with students from all over the world.

Besides housing the George W. Bush Presidential Library, the university also hosts campus-wide events like art lectures, concerts, exhibitions, and independently organized TED talks. The red-and-blue SMU pride is most evident during Mustang football season at Gerald J. Ford Stadium. In its 100-year history, the team has claimed three national titles and 10 conference titles, and birthed NFL legends like Don Meredith, Doak Walker, and Raymond Berry.

Another major point of interest is the Meadows Museum at SMU, which features one of the finest collections of Spanish art outside of Spain. You'll see significant 18th-century works by Francisco de Goya as well as more modern pieces by Pablo Picasso.

MAP 4: 6425 Boaz Ln., 214/768-2000, www.smu.org

West Dallas/Oak Cliff **Map 5**

BISHOP ARTS DISTRICT

Visitors liken this neighborhood to the famously hip enclaves of Austin and Brooklyn—anything but Dallas. Established in the 1920s and '30s as the city's busiest trolley stop, the Bishop Arts District has retained its historical charm, and is home to locally owned boutiques and restaurants housed in old brick buildings along tree-lined sidewalks.

Just twenty years ago, the district comprised vacant storefronts, occupied by a few Oak Cliff artists. The area had experienced decades of decline since the mid-1960s, and city leaders invested more in economic development to the north. Luckily, forward-thinking developers stepped in and began revitalizing the neighborhood into what exists today. In 2016, plans came full circle as the city launched its new **Dallas Streetcar** (www.dart.org), a free Bishop Arts transit service running from downtown's **Union Station** (400 S. Houston St.).

If you're driving to Bishop Arts, expect to park a few blocks from the action. Once you're here, you can browse stores featuring quirky gifts and home décor, tour art studios, and snap photos in front of striking murals. The street art depicts famous Oak Cliff natives, such as Yvonne Craig as Batgirl in the 1960s TV hit *Batman*. You'll also find a more controversial image of a menacing Lee Harvey Oswald. Breakfast, lunch, and dinner options abound in Bishop Arts, but only a few restaurants stay open past midnight.

MAP 5: N. Bishop and W. Davis Sts., www.bishopartsdistrict.com

DALLAS ZOO

A towering bronze giraffe—Texas's tallest statue—watches over Interstate 35 and Marsalis Avenue as commuters are herded to and from the asphalt jungle of downtown. Just beyond the sculpture, some arguably gentler animals reside.

Founded in 1888, the Dallas Zoo spans 106 acres and includes about 430 species. The zoo features two main sections: ZooNorth where visitors can find koalas, otters, endangered tigers, and the largest living tortoise species; and the Wilds of Africa, showcasing every habitat found on that continent. The latter section expanded with Giants of the Savanna, an 11-acre exhibit where visitors can observe a matriarchal family of elephants along with the region's other species including zebras, ostriches, cheetahs, and lions. The most popular activity involves coming face to face with giraffes from atop a feeding ridge where the affable animals eat lettuce from visitors' hands.

In 2009, the city privatized management of the zoo while retaining ownership of the land. Since then, attendance and donations have surged, and acclaimed new exhibits have opened every year. In the spring of 2017, the Simmons Hippo Outpost opened, bringing the animals back to Dallas for the first time in 15 years. Visitors can easily spend all day exploring the zoo. But if you only have a few hours, head straight through the tunnel to the Wilds of Africa, then double back to ZooNorth if you have time. Spring is peak season for school field trips, but the swarm of kiddos usually thins out by the afternoon. Also, the zoo becomes unbearably crowded during Dollar Day ($1 admission), which falls on a Thursday toward the end of the summer.

MAP 5: 650 S. R. L. Thornton Freeway, 469/554-7500, www.dallaszoo.com; daily 9am-5pm; adults $15, children and seniors $12, free 2 and under, $8 parking

★ MARGARET HUNT HILL BRIDGE

Designed by internationally renowned Spanish architect Santiago Calatrava, the Margaret Hunt Hill Bridge was a dramatic addition to the Dallas skyline in 2012. The elegant white arch reaches 400 feet high as 58 cables envelop the six-lane roadway. The bridge stretches across the Trinity River, connecting **Woodall Rodgers Freeway** in downtown to **Singleton Boulevard** in West Dallas, a once forgotten industrial area that has since transformed into a vibrant entertainment district with panoramic views of the city. The bridge is best viewed at nightfall from the Felix Lozada Gateway Plaza, which hosts outdoor festivals, food trucks, live music, and wellness events. The bridge closes to vehicular traffic every spring for the Trinity Levee Run and a massive yoga practice.

In true Dallas fashion, this world-class piece of architecture was named after the philanthropist and daughter of oil tycoon H. L. Hunt Jr., whose petroleum company helped fund the bridge's construction. Its official moniker, Margaret Hunt Hill, doesn't exactly roll off the tongue, so many locals have dubbed it "Large Marge" or simply "the Calatrava bridge." The latter nickname won't last long: The architect's second Trinity River Corridor project, the Margaret McDermott Bridge, is scheduled to open along Interstate 30 in 2017, carrying pedestrians and cyclists only.

MAP 5: Singleton Blvd. and N. Beckley Ave., www.trinityrivercorridor.com

Top: Margaret Hunt Hill Bridge; **Bottom:** Sundance Square

RONALD KIRK PEDESTRIAN BRIDGE

For an even grander view of the Margaret Hunt Hill Bridge, walk or bike down the adjacent Ronald Kirk Pedestrian Bridge, another defining feature of the West Dallas Gateway. Built in 1933, the roadway originally served as one of the main connectors that transported motorists across the Trinity River into downtown. As new traffic relief projects took shape nearby, the city redesigned the bridge exclusively for pedestrians and cyclists, and debuted it in 2014. Formerly known as the Continental Avenue Bridge, city officials renamed the sight after Dallas's first African American mayor. The linear gathering space features a playground, climbing blocks, splash pads, a life-sized chessboard, and seating. Fitness groups meet for boot camp, Zumba, and yoga, and food trucks assemble on the gateway plaza. Shade is scarce, so lather on the sunscreen, and bring an umbrella if visiting on a sunny afternoon. Better yet, watch the sunset from the bridge while walking off the dinner you had at the **Trinity Groves** restaurant park (3011 Gulden Ln., www.trinitygroves.com).

MAP 5: 109 Continental Ave., www.dallascontinentalbridge.com

TEXAS THEATRE

At about 1:45pm on November 22, 1963, a suspicious man slipped into the Texas Theatre without paying, and took a seat near the back during a screening of *War Is Hell*. He left in handcuffs, accused of assassinating the president of the United States, John F. Kennedy, a little more than an hour earlier before killing local police officer J. D. Tippit. The Oak Cliff theater went down in history as the site where Lee Harvey Oswald was captured. Today, it's a beautifully restored art-house cinema and events space managed by Dallas-based Aviation Cinemas, featuring a carefully curated weekly lineup of indie flicks, avant-garde shows, and the occasional blockbuster release. The theater features a historical marker out front and offers tours by appointment. Tours show visitors where Oswald sat, and cover the venue's origins involving 1920s film and aviation tycoon Howard Hughes. The iconic neon lettering on the building's façade and the large, illuminated star overlooking the box office make for popular photo opportunities.

MAP 5: 231 W. Jefferson Blvd., 214/948-1546, www.thetexastheatre.com; Thurs. 5:30pm-midnight, Fri. 4pm-2am, Sat. 5:30pm-2am, Sun. 4pm-11pm; general $10, student, senior, child, or bicycle rider $8.50

TRINITY OVERLOOK PARK

Partly obstructed by the state jail's dull, brown façade, the skyline view at Trinity Overlook Park pales in comparison to that of the West Dallas Gateway bridges. Still, it offers a different, more intimate perspective with direct access down to the floodway via the Trinity Skyline Trail. Hiking beneath the bridges, past peculiar graffiti and rocky riverbanks, feels a little more adventurous than the typical roadside photo op. Also, the sheer size of this vast green space comes into view, and it's no wonder that city officials have been fighting over how to use the 10,000-acre corridor. Politicians have been pushing an unpopular plan to build a high-speed toll road in the floodway to relieve traffic congestion elsewhere. Urban planners and

neighborhood activists have urged leaders to preserve the parkland as a recreational amenity. The civic saga, which has spanned nearly two decades, is the defining issue for the people of Dallas. Despite its popularity among tourists and locals alike, visitors should avoid trekking through the corridor alone after dark; the floodway still attracts the occasional drifter.
MAP 5: 110 W. Commerce St., www.trinityrivercorridor.com

Downtown Fort Worth Map 6

FORT WORTH WATER GARDENS

Designed in 1974 by modern architect Philip Johnson, the Fort Worth Water Gardens offer an unexpected, almost hidden retreat right across from the bustling Fort Worth Convention Center on the south side of downtown. Water cascades down a 360-degree concrete terrace into a pool at the bottom. Visitors can venture into the modernist landscape via exposed stone steps, surrounded by falling water. You'll also find a calm turquoise-blue pool enclosed by native trees, and an aerating pond dotted with spray fountains. Despite the austere design and hard concrete edges, the water gardens are surprisingly serene. A few downtown buildings peek over the trees just enough to remind you that you're in the city. In the evening, lights illuminate the fountains, offering a whole new architectural perspective on a park that locals too often overlook. Weekends attract more crowds. Visit on a weekday morning or afternoon to experience more solitude.
MAP 6: 1502 Commerce St., 817/392-7111; daily 7:30am-10pm; free

★ SUNDANCE SQUARE

The heart of downtown Fort Worth is 35 blocks of cobblestone streets lined with local eats, indie shops, and world-class performing arts. Developed in the mid-1980s out of restored turn-of-the-20th-century buildings, Sundance Square evokes a European-style walkability mixed with a small-town vibe rooted in cowboy culture. The massive Chisholm Trail Mural at the square's center commemorates the cattle drives that passed through the area in the 1860s. That's where the city's big annual events happen—the Main Street Arts Festival, the Main Table community dinner, the pre-Thanksgiving Parade of Lights, the Christmas tree lighting, and the New Year's Eve party. You'll also spot the plaza's weekly yoga practice, live music jam sessions, and outdoor movie screenings.

Garage parking is free after 5pm on weekdays and all day weekends. For free valet, look for the red umbrellas.
MAP 6: 420 Main St., 817/255-5700, www.sundancesquare.com

Fort Worth Bcycle

Sometimes, the best way to explore a city is on two wheels. Fort Worth's bike share program **BCycle** makes it incredibly easy to do so. Just walk up to any of the 45 stations across the city, and use a touch screen kiosk to buy a 24-hour pass for $8. When the bike unlocks, hop on and ride. After 30 minutes, dock it at the nearest station, and grab another. Repeat. The bikes are comfortable and easy to ride, plus they come with a handy basket on the front.

There are several bike sharing stations around Sundance Square, or you can start your ride at Panther Island along the bank of the Trinity River. You'll also find plenty of bikes along Magnolia Avenue's restaurant row in Southside. Fort Worth, with its slower pace and walkable urban strips, is friendlier to cyclists than Dallas. In fact, Cowtown was ahead of the curve, rolling out its program in 2013, expanding it to include 350 bikes.

For more information, including a map of bike sharing stations, visit www.fortworth.bcycle.com.

West Fort Worth

Map 7

FORT WORTH BOTANIC GARDEN

Spanning 110 acres, the Fort Worth Botanic Garden's charm lies in its simplicity. It's a popular place for photography and special events, but it's not cluttered with amenities that detract from its natural beauty. A few of the 22 gardens are particularly stunning. The historic Rose Garden, built in 1933, features sprawling rose beds, a reflection pond, and romantic sandstone paths perfect for a sunset stroll. The garden was recently renovated after a plant disease wiped out most of the roses. Don't miss the 7.5-acre Japanese Garden, which only blooms during the fall and spring. You'll see hundreds of cherry trees, maples, magnolias, and bamboo, all framing a picturesque wooden bridge. The garden also hosts a monthly Japanese tea ceremony and an annual spring festival. Admission to the Japanese Garden is $4-7 while the rest of the gardens are free.

MAP 7: 3220 Botanic Garden Blvd., 817/392-5510, www.fwbg.org; daily 8am-8pm; free

WILL ROGERS MEMORIAL CENTER

Built in 1936 for the Texas Centennial, and featuring a 200-foot art deco tower, the 85-acre Will Rogers Memorial Center is analogous to Dallas's Fair Park, but with a lot more cowboys. Honoring the building's namesake, the bronze statue out front, *Riding into the Sunset,* depicts the Western icon and his horse, Soapsuds. Inside, the mosaic ceiling gives visitors a colorful Texas history lesson. Since 1944, the center has hosted the annual Fort Worth Stock Show and Rodeo, which today draws over a million people during its 24-day run. A collection of vintage photos documents the tradition, including performances of Gene Autry and Roy Rogers, who were

Stock Show regulars. You can also find other events here year-round, from holiday ballet performances to local handmade gift markets.

MAP 7: 3401 W. Lancaster Ave., 817/392-7469, www.fortworth.com

Northside

Map 8

★ FORT WORTH STOCKYARDS

Along these cobblestone streets, and in the wood frame saloons that lined them, early-20th-century cattle traders built what became known as the "Wall Street of the West." The Fort Worth Stockyards, a National Historic District, cover 98 acres devoted to preserving the city's livestock legacy and western heritage in the form of museums, rodeos, restaurants, gift shops, and bars. It's the only place to experience the quintessential cowboy culture for which Fort Worth is famous.

Twice-daily cattle drives occur at 11:30am and 4pm. Ranchers herd enormous steers down East Exchange Avenue past the **Stockyards Visitor Center** (130 E. Exchange Ave., 817/624-4741)—a good starting point for your visit. For a thorough lesson on the significance of this place, spring for a guided historical walking tour, which costs $5-9 per person. The tours depart from **Stockyards Station** (140 E. Exchange Ave., 817/625-9715, tourmanager@stockyardsstation.com), a hub for souvenir and gift shops. The year-round weekend rodeo takes place in the **Cowtown Coliseum** (121 E. Exchange Ave., 817/625-1025).

MAP 8: 130 E. Exchange Ave., 817/624-4741, www.fortworthstockyards.org

Southside/TCU

Map 9

ELIZABETH BOULEVARD HISTORIC DISTRICT

Towering stone pillars mark the entrance to historic Elizabeth Boulevard, which is lined with early-20th-century mansions protected by Fort Worth's first residential historic district. Characterized by stunning Mediterranean stucco, Spanish Colonial villas, and Prairie Style rooflines, Elizabeth Boulevard is a shining example of neighborhood activism. It started when developer John C. Ryan began construction in 1911 on what would become home to Fort Worth's most prominent residents. Then came the Great Depression, which left the estates vacant and forgotten. After World War II, the wealthy began moving to the suburbs, except for a dedicated group of residents who by the 1970s had helped restore the boulevard to its former glory—and protect it from urban sprawl.

Look for the grand gates at Elizabeth Boulevard and 8th Avenue, and take a leisurely drive or walk down the seven-block street. Keep in mind that these are private residences. Some of the homes open to the public

Top: Bureau of Engraving and Printing; **Bottom:** Fort Worth Stockyards

just once a year for the Candlelight Christmas Tour, held the first weekend in December.

MAP 9: Elizabeth Blvd. between 8th and College Aves.

FORT WORTH ZOO

The Fort Worth Zoo has 12 exhibits, all of which are captivating—from Raptor Canyon to Meerkat Mounds. But elephants and gorillas still win the popularity contest here. If you have limited time, head to Asian Falls on the southwest end of the zoo to see three generations of elephants (the family welcomed two babies in 2013). There's also an almost mythical-looking Malaysian tiger and white tiger. The World of Primates exhibit, near the zoo entrance, is home to six western lowland gorillas along with smaller primates like the gibbon and colobus monkeys that can be seen swinging through their jungle habitat. The 30,000-square-foot Museum of Living Art showcases the surprising beauty of scaly reptiles and amphibians, and offers a nice air-conditioned break during the heat of the day.

You can see most of the zoo in about three to four hours, or you can easily extend your visit through the entire day. School field trips tend to wind down by the afternoon, making weekdays a better bet if you want to beat the crowds.

MAP 9: 1989 Colonial Pkwy., 817/759-7555, www.fortworthzoo.org; March 4-July 7 Mon.-Fri. 10am-5pm, Sat.-Sun. 10am-6pm; July 8-Oct. 29 daily 10am-5pm; adults $14, children and seniors $10, 2 and under free

LOG CABIN VILLAGE

A working gristmill, a spinning wheel, a candle-making caldron, and a blacksmith shop are just a few of the authentic examples of early pioneer life you'll see in the Log Cabin Village. The city-owned living-history museum features six 19th-century cabins relocated from various areas of Fort Worth and restored for educational purposes. Each was owned by a real pioneer family whose story unfolds through details preserved or replicated inside the cabin, including hand-carved furniture, ceramic dishes, and eerie daguerreotypes. The Texas history lesson doesn't overlook the role of slaves, who raised the children who became the founders of Fort Worth. Depending on your interest level, you could spend just 30 minutes strolling the entire village or a few hours reading plaques and visiting with historical interpreters. Once a month, the village features live demonstrations and hands-on activities for kids and families.

MAP 9: 2100 Log Cabin Village Ln., 817/392-5881, www.logcabinvillage.org; Tues.-Fri. 9am-4pm, Sat.-Sun. 1pm-5pm; adults $5.50, ages 4-17 and seniors $5, groups of 10 or more $4.50, 3 and under free

Greater Dallas and Fort Worth

Map 10

BUREAU OF ENGRAVING AND PRINTING

Fun fact: More than half of the nation's currency is printed in Fort Worth, of all places. The rest of it comes from Washington DC. The Bureau of Engraving and Printing operates a "money factory" in north Fort Worth, offering public tours during which visitors can watch from an overhead walkway as machines manufacture billions of dollars. You can stroll through two floors of interactive exhibits to learn the history of U.S. currency and how it's made. It's a fun (and free) way to spend a rainy afternoon. Self-guided tours are available Tuesday-Friday 8:30am-5:30pm. Be prepared to leave behind cell phones, cameras, and backpacks, and go through a security screening upon entering the federal facility.

MAP 10: 9000 Blue Mound Rd., 817/231-4000, www.moneyfactory.gov; Tues.-Fri. 8:30am-5:30pm; free

LOUIS TUSSAUD'S PALACE OF WAX

If you have money to burn and kids to entertain, Louis Tussaud's Palace of Wax can easily occupy an entire afternoon with lifelike (but sometimes laughable) wax figures. Designed after an Arabian-style palace, the flashy museum features more than 200 renditions of notable people organized in different exhibits including famous monsters, the hall of presidents, the life of Jesus, and scenes from popular movies like *Harry Potter* and *The Wizard of Oz*. It's fun to take goofy pictures with Oprah, Michael Jackson, or the cast of *Star Trek*. In the same building, the Ripley's Believe It Or Not! museum features "weird" stories and artifacts. The museums have separate (and pretty steep) admission prices, so skip Ripley's and opt for the Palace of Wax.

MAP 10: 601 E. Palace Pkwy., Grand Prairie, 972/263-2391, www.ripleys.com/grandprairie/wax; Mon.-Thurs. 10am-6pm, Fri.-Sun. 10am-8pm; adults $19.99, children $12.99

SIX FLAGS HURRICANE HARBOR

Every day, I-30 commuters drive past this park's iconic waterslide—two towering spirals of dark tubes that descend 80 feet to a pool below. The Black Hole is a fixture of Hurricane Harbor, part of the Six Flags chain of water parks. Other thrill rides have debuted over the years, including the Tornado, a blue-and-yellow-checkered funnel; and Der Stuka, perhaps the scariest slide, which plummets riders into a seven-story free fall. The park also offers plenty of attractions for those who just want to chill out in the water; you can float the Lazy River, lie out in the Suntan Lagoon, or wade around at Boogie Beach. The park is open May through September. Go on weekdays during the summer to beat the crowds, and hit up your favorite rides near opening or closing time when the lines are shortest. Bring sunblock for warm days and a jacket for chilly nights.

MAP 10: 1800 E. Lamar Blvd., Arlington, 817/640-8900, www.sixflags.com/hurricaneharbortexas; hours vary; adults $34.99, children under 48 inches $29.99, under 2 free

SIX FLAGS OVER TEXAS

From classic wooden roller coasters like Judge Roy Scream, built in 1980, to the soon-to-open Joker "free-fly coaster" with spinning seats, Six Flags continues to update its attractions almost every season. Located on the other side of the interstate from Hurricane Harbor, Six Flags Over Texas is open March through December and hosts popular seasonal festivities like Fright Fest and Holiday in the Park.

Must-see attractions include Gotham City on the east side, featuring some of the most popular roller coasters in the park. Bring the little ones to Bugs Bunny Boomtown's kid-friendly rides and Looney Toons entertainment. Don't miss the park's most famous thrill ride, the 153-foot-high Texas Giant, the tallest steel-wood hybrid roller coaster in the world. No visit is complete without a nighttime ride on the huge, historic Silver Star Carousel at the park gates, and an indulgence in a sugary funnel cake from one of the nearby food stands. For fewer crowds, go during April, May, September, or October.

MAP 10: 2201 Road to Six Flags, 817/640-8900, www.sixflags.com/overtexas; hours vary; $59.99 online, $74.99 at the gate

Restaurants

Look for ★ to find recommended Restaurants

Highlights

★ **Best Tex-Mex:** The rise of Tex-Mex began with **El Fenix** a century ago, making it your best bet for the iconic cuisine (page 54).

★ **Best Meal with a Conscience:** At **Café Momentum,** you can dine on charcuterie, beef filet and fingerling potatoes while helping at-risk teens turn their lives around (page 55).

★ **Best Vegetarian:** Set inside a beautiful Hare Krishna temple, **Kalachandji's** inviting atmosphere is just as impressive as its meat-free Indian cuisine (page 61).

★ **Best Steakhouse:** For quality steak and a glimpse at Dallas' 1 percent, duck inside **Al Biernat's** where you can rub elbows with local celebrities (page 63).

★ **Best Farm-to-Table Eatery:** The menu at **FT33** changes daily, but you can always expect fresh, local ingredients prepared for the adventurous palate (page 64).

★ **Best for Dog-Lovers:** The dog-friendly patio reaches a whole new level at **Mutts Canine Cantina,** which features a members-only off-leash dog park with day passes available (page 64).

★ **Best Tapas:** Because of its creative take on traditional Spanish tapas, **Casa Rubia** has become the hottest restaurant in the Trinity Groves dining mecca, racking up numerous awards (page 74).

★ **Best Barbecue:** As new trendy barbecue joints open left and right, locals know that **Angelo's** remains the best spot for hickory-smoked meats with a truly Texan ambiance (page 78).

★ **Best Breakfast:** Open 24 hours, **Ol' South Pancake House** has the best selection of pancakes, including the popular German pancake and plenty of build-your-own options (page 81).

★ **Best Sweet Treat:** The basic breakfast staple becomes a decadent dessert at **FunkyTown Donuts,** which features flavors like key lime pie, raspberry dark chocolate, and double-stuffed Oreo (page 82).

PRICE KEY

$ Entrées less than $10
$$ Entrées $10–20
$$$ Entrées more than $20

Dallas has become a food destination—and not just for steak, barbecue, and Tex-Mex. The local culinary scene has come to life over the past several years, embracing the farm-to-table philosophy by sourcing quality ingredients from local purveyors. Chefs are akin to rock stars; some have even achieved national reality TV fame.

At the same time, tried-and-true greasy spoons and taco shacks hold their own against contemporary cuisine. Even when Norma's Café is packed with customers pining for chicken-fried steak and mile-high pies, you can still get seated almost immediately. At Fuel City, you can gas up your car and gorge on the city's best street, tacos sold 24 hours a day. Not much has changed at El Fenix, the 100-year-old birthplace of Dallas' Tex-Mex cuisine.

Time-tested establishments and experimental restaurants coexist to create a diverse culinary landscape. While Angelo's has solidified its barbecue reputation over six decades, Pecan Lodge became an instant hit in 2010, its lunch line wrapping around the block. Wealthy Dallasites have long enjoyed steak dinners at the upscale Al Biernat's while in recent years, The Blind Butcher has attracted the more laid-back, Lower Greenville crowd.

Street food remains a staple in Dallas—from the Tigers Blood at Aunt Stelle's Sno Cone shack, now almost 60 years old, to the Chinese dumplings at the ultra-hip Monkey King Noodle Company. Plus, a variety of creative food trucks can be found almost anywhere people gather.

Make no mistake: Steak, barbecue and Tex-Mex are essentials. But the Dallas-Fort Worth food scene is so much more than that.

Previous: Joe T. Garcia's garden patio; Café Momentum chefs, Adolph Martin and Malik Runnels

Downtown Dallas

Map 1

BARBECUE

PECAN LODGE $$

Beginning as a vendor in the Dallas Farmers Market shed, Pecan Lodge quickly outgrew its space after word got around about its mesquite-smoked barbecue and burnt ends. Even at its Deep Ellum smokehouse, people wait in line for an hour or more. The trick is to go with a group and place a large order of five pounds or more to gain access to the express line. For sides, go for the fried okra and mac and cheese.

MAP 1: 2702 Main St., 214/748-8900, www.pecanlodge.com; Tues.-Thurs. 11am-3pm, Fri.-Sat. 11am-10pm, Sun. 11am-3pm

STEAK HOUSES

DAKOTA'S STEAKHOUSE $$$

To skirt the deed restrictions that prohibited the sale of alcohol on the grounds of the former First Baptist Church, Dakota's Steakhouse set up shop underground—and not just as some basement bistro. A glass elevator takes diners down to the lavish garden-style courtyard complete with a granite waterfall and lava rock fire pit. Serving USDA Prime steaks aged for at least 28 days, Dakota's food is on par with other great steak houses in town. The ambience, however, puts it at the top.

MAP 1: 600 N. Akard St., 214/740-4001, www.dakotasrestaurant.com; Mon.-Thurs. 11am-2:30pm and 5:30pm-10pm, Fri. 11am-2:30pm and 5:30pm-10:30pm, Sat. 5pm-10pm

Y.O. RANCH STEAKHOUSE $$$

For more adventurous meat eaters, Y.O. Ranch Steakhouse specializes in wild game along with traditional steak dinners. The menu features unexpected dishes like rattlesnake chili pie, bacon-wrapped venison, and buffalo filet mignon. You can also feel good about the lives these animals led before ending up on your plate, roaming free on the restaurant's 48,000-acre Hill Country ranch.

MAP 1: 702 Ross Ave., 214/744-3287, www.yoranchsteakhouse.com; Mon.-Thurs. 11am-10pm, Fri.-Sat. 11am-11pm, Sun. 11am-9pm

MEXICAN

★ EL FENIX $$

When Dallasites think Tex-Mex, the first restaurant that comes to mind is likely El Fenix, the pioneer of the iconic local cuisine. The downtown restaurant opened in 1925 in an old grocery store, marking the start of a mini Tex-Mex empire throughout Dallas. Loyal diners still show up weekly for Wednesday's $5.99 enchilada special that lasts all day, and the tortilla soup is among the best in the city.

MAP 1: 1601 McKinney Ave., 214/747-1121, www.elfenix.com; Sun.-Mon. 11am-9pm, Tues.-Sat. 11am-10pm

FUEL CITY $

This truck stop taco stand has become legendary for its simple $1.62 street tacos, served with diced onions, cilantro, and your choice of meat. Fuel City draws a huge lunch crowd, but the line moves fast. You can enjoy your tacos on the patio, complete with a view of the skyline and longhorns roaming the pasture next door. It doesn't get more "Dallas" than that.

MAP 1: 801 S. Riverfront Blvd., 214/426-0011, www.fuelcity.com; daily 24 hours

MESO MAYA $$

If you grow tired of Tex-Mex, Meso Maya offers a different take on cuisine from south of the border. The restaurant specializes in authentic dishes from Oaxaca, Veracruz, Yucatan and other states. Built in 1938, this historic downtown building was a pillar of the Little Mexico community that started Dallas down the path to producing "Tex-Mex." Only in recent years has the "Tex" begun to fade as foodies crave something fresher—like Meso Maya's mole enchiladas, made with freshly ground cocoa beans, or the sweet corn tamal.

MAP 1: 1611 McKinney Ave., 214/484-6555, www.mesomaya.com; Sun.-Thurs. 11am-10pm, Fri.-Sat. 11am-11pm

AMERICAN

ALL GOOD CAFÉ $$

One of the Deep Ellum hangouts that attract a huge daytime crowd, All Good Café is known for its hearty breakfast sourced from local purveyors. Try the breakfast tacos, the *migas*, or the chicken-fried steak with farm-fresh eggs. Get there when it opens to avoid the long wait for a table. The diner also serves lunch and dinner.

MAP 1: 2934 Main St., 214/742-5362, www.allgoodcafe.com; Mon. 8am-2pm, Tues.-Sat. 8am-9pm, Sun. 8am-7pm

★ CAFÉ MOMENTUM $$

Here is some excellent local cuisine that also makes a difference in the community. Café Momentum employs juvenile offenders who might otherwise become tragic statistics. The interns are trained in different areas of the restaurant industry from cooking to managing. After a year, they can receive job placement with one of the restaurant's community partners. Café Momentum's food is just as impressive as its conscience. The simple menu features a charcuterie board, shrimp and grits, beignets, and beautifully presented main courses like beef fillet with fingerling potatoes.

MAP 1: 1510 Pacific Ave., 214/303-1234, www.cafemomentum.org; Thurs.-Sat. 5:30pm-11pm

FEARINGS RESTAURANT $$$

Local celebrity chef Dean Fearing has built one of the most famous fine-dining establishments in Dallas, focusing on upscale southwestern cuisine. Fearing got his start at the Mansion on Turtle Creek before opening his own restaurant inside the Ritz-Carlton Hotel in 2007. It's still where you'll find the best steak in town, along with wagyu beef, Maine lobster,

Top: brisket at Pecan Lodge; **Bottom:** Café Momentum's fried pie

and pork tenderloin. Although the price point is high, the atmosphere and dress code is relaxed. Feel free to arrive in your jeans and cowboy boots.

MAP 1: 2121 McKinney Ave., 214/922-4848, www.fearingsrestaurant.com; Mon.-Thurs. 6:30am-2:30pm and 6pm-10:30pm, Fri. 6:30am-2:30pm and 6pm-11pm, Sat. 6:30am-3pm and 6pm-11pm, Sun. 6:30am-2:30pm and 6pm-10pm

ASIAN

DEEP SUSHI $$

Open since 1996, this veteran Deep Ellum establishment is a go-to spot for a good sushi fix. You can't go wrong with most of the rolls and sashimi, but be sure to ask about off-menu specials. The restaurant's narrow space can get a little cramped inside during peak hours, so try to score a patio table. You can make a reservation online.

MAP 1: 2624 Elm St., 214/651-1177, www.deepsushi.com; Mon.-Wed. 10am-10pm, Thurs. 10am-11pm, Fri. 10am-midnight, Sat. 5pm-midnight, Sun. 5pm-10pm

MONKEY KING NOODLE COMPANY $$

Although it operates from an outdoor food stand, Monkey King Noodle Company serves up some of the finest Chinese street food in town at a reasonable price. Choose from handcrafted noodles, wontons, and soups, but be prepared to dine outside.

MAP 1: 2933 Main St., 469/713-2648, www.monkeykingnoodlecompany.com; Mon.-Sat. 11am-10pm, Sun. 11am-3pm

TEI-AN $$$

Located on One Arts Plaza with one of the best rooftop views in the city, Tei-An specializes in fresh soba, a Japanese pasta made by hand. The acclaimed chef Teiichi Sakurai is also known for his ramen, fresh sushi, and seaweed salad. Make a reservation to ensure at spot at this popular Arts District restaurant.

MAP 1: 1722 Routh St., Suite 110, 214/220-2828, www.tei-an.com; Tues.-Thurs. 11:30am-2pm and 6pm-10:30pm, Fri. 11:30am-2pm and 5:30pm-10:30pm, Sat. 5:30pm-10:30pm, Sun. 11:30am-2pm and 6pm-10:30pm

ITALIAN

CANE ROSSO $$

For discerning pizza snobs, Cane Rosso is regarded as one of the best pizzerias in Dallas. In fact, it has topped all the "best of" lists in town. Not to be confused with New York style, the restaurant specializes in Neapolitan-style pizzas baked in a 900-degree oven, cooking in just 90 seconds. The dough is made fresh daily, and many of the ingredients are imported straight from Italy.

MAP 1: 2612 Commerce St., 214/741-1188, www.canerosso.com; Mon. 5pm-10pm, Tues.-Sun. 11am-3pm and 5pm-11pm

SERIOUS PIZZA $

Don't be too intimidated by the long lines inside Serious Pizza. The New York-style, counter-service restaurant gets hungry concertgoers through quickly. One slice for $3.25 is a steal when you see how massive it is. On weekends, the pizza joint is one of the last Deep Ellum hot spots to shut down for the night, staying open until 3am.

MAP 1: 2807 Elm St., 214/761-9999, www.seriouspizza.com; Sun.-Thurs. 11:30am-11pm, Fri.-Sat. 11:30am-3am

DESSERT

GLAZED DONUT WORKS $

If it's not a concert, the only other time people form a line down the block in Deep Ellum is to get their hands on some sugary goodness from Glazed Donut Works. The small-batch bakery uses brioche dough fermented for 18-24 hours, and house-made toppings. You can get the classic vanilla bean or more creative flavors like Samoa or chocolate berry bomb. There are also several vegan options. For something savory, splurge on the grilled cheese donut with bacon.

MAP 1: 2644 Elm St., 214/741-2275, www.glazeddonutworks.com; Thurs.-Fri. 7am-11am and 9pm-2am, Sat. 9am-4pm and 9pm-2am, Sun. 9am-4pm

COFFEE

MURRAY STREET COFFEE $

This spacious, two-story coffee shop offers plenty of quiet and comfy nooks in which to relax, read, or work. It's also a convenient stop during an afternoon stroll through Deep Ellum, located within walking distance of shops, bars, and restaurants. Murray Street serves locally roasted coffees as well as the South American staple, mate.

MAP 1: 103 Murray St., 214/655-2808, www.murraystreetcoffee.com; Mon.-Fri. 7am-4pm, Sat. 8am-4pm

Lakewood/East Dallas — Map 2

AMERICAN

THE BLIND BUTCHER $$

Devout carnivores should find their way to the Blind Butcher, a hip, meat-centric restaurant with a laid-back bar atmosphere. It's great for small bites and shareables while barhopping around the Lower Greenville scene. The best options include duck pastrami with chips and warm beer goat cheese, a cured meat and cheese board, and pork belly poutine. Ask your server to recommend the best craft beer to pair with your house-cured meat.

MAP 2: 1919 Greenville Ave., 214/887-0000, www.theblindbutcher.com; daily 11am-2am

GARDEN CAFE $$

This restaurant's name doesn't only refer to its vegetarian-friendly menu. The Garden Café actually grows some of its vegetables on-site and provides an oasis for outdoor dining. Lush, green arches open up to the half-acre garden, which is just one example of the restaurant's sustainable practices.

Dallas Farmers Market

Dallas Farmers Market

Since it was privatized a few years back, the Dallas Farmers Market has grown into a vibrant foodie destination. Local purveyors set up shop in the Shed every weekend, peddling their farm-fresh eggs, free-range meats, and locally grown produce. Across the street, the Market features more permanent establishments, including restaurants, bars, bakeries, and gift shops, open during the week. Here's how to make the most of your visit to the Dallas Farmers Market:

- The Shed is open weekends only. Get there first thing in the morning for the best selection of fruits and vegetables, usually located on the perimeter.

- In the center aisles of the Shed, and scattered among the produce vendors, you'll find more offbeat artisan fare like T-Rex Pickles made with craft beer, the colorful array of Pappardelle's Pasta, and personal-sized banana pudding cups from Pudding on Smiles.

- ATMs are available on-site, and most vendors accept debit and credit cards now. Bring your own bag to transport your goods, since you will likely make some impulse buys.

- The Market, an indoor food hall filled with more vendors, is open daily. It's one of the best spots in town for truly local souvenir shopping. You'll find Texas-themed home décor gifts at Lone Chimney Mercantile, clever Dallas T-shirts at Bullzerk, and specialty ingredients for the home kitchen at Stock and Body.

The popular brunch dishes, such as the build-your-own omelets, are made with pasture-raised meat and eggs.

MAP 2: 5310 Junius St., 214/887-8330, www.gardencafe.net; daily 7am-3pm

KELLER'S DRIVE-IN $

For more than five decades, Keller's has harnessed the old-school drive-in culture of the 1950s. The carhops—many who have worked full-time since the early days—take your order in person once you flash your headlights to show that you're ready. The burgers are nothing gourmet, but they're cheap, fresh, and consistent. You can enjoy a beer inside your car, as long as it's parked. On a Saturday night, you'll see tailgaters post up for hours on end, showing off their classic hot rods.

MAP 2: 6537 Northwest Hwy., 214/368-1209; daily 11am-10pm

SISSY'S SOUTHERN KITCHEN $$

This tiny A-frame's canary-yellow doors open to reveal a huge, shotgun-style house where Sissy's Southern Kitchen makes brined and pressure-fried chicken. The Mississippi Delta culture radiates in the Southern Colonial design, featuring tuft banquettes, Spode Delamere china, and art nouveau light fixtures, salvaged from the original Neiman Marcus building after its 1913 fire. If you're dining with three or more people, order a bucket of chicken and family-style sides, including mac and cheese, collard greens, "sloppy slaw," and biscuits.

MAP 2: 2929 N. Henderson Ave., 214/827-9900, www.sissyssouthernkitchen.com; Tues.-Fri. 11am-2pm and 5pm-10:30pm, Sat. 11am-3pm and 5pm-10:30pm, Sun. 11am-3pm

THE GRAPE $$$

Having endured for 45 years in Dallas's ever-evolving restaurant scene, the Grape maintains its reputation for Sunday brunch. Its wildly popular cheeseburger (available on the brunch menu) piles on peppered bacon, Vermont white cheddar, and horseradish. Besides brunch, the happy hour menu, available 4:30pm-7pm Monday-Friday, features half-priced wine, $3 well drinks, $2 beers, and a short list of small plates—a good deal, considering the Grape's pricey dinner menu.

MAP 2: 2808 Greenville Ave., 214/828-1981, www.thegraperestaurant.com; Mon. 5:30pm-9pm, Tues.-Thurs. 5:30pm-10pm, Fri.-Sat. 5:30pm-11pm, Sun. 10:30am-2pm and 5:30pm-10pm

ASIAN

MOT HAI BA $$$

This chic little spot has garnered rave reviews from local critics, but still manages to fly under the radar in terms of the hype. Mot Hai Ba, taking its name from the Vietnamese words for appetizer, main course, and dessert, specializes in North Vietnamese food with complex flavor profiles. Take, for example, the grilled duck hearts served in a green papaya salad with citrus and garlic, or the fried oysters with lemongrass caramel, papaya, and Thai chili.

MAP 2: 6047 Lewis St., 214/826-0968, www.mothaibadallas.com; Tues.-Thurs. 5pm-10pm, Fri.-Sat. 5pm-11pm

INDIAN

★ KALACHANDJI'S $$

Well known as Dallas's oldest vegetarian restaurant, Kalachandji's is much more than that. The chefs practice India's ancient Ayurveda, a holistic approach to cooking that promotes good health for not just the body but also the mind and soul. The buffet changes daily but usually includes some type of soup, rice, curry, and a veggie entrée like enchiladas or lasagna. The restaurant is inside a Hare Krishna temple, so you might catch a service in session. The temple also offers tours by appointment.

MAP 2: 5430 Gurley Ave., 214/821-1048, www.kalachandjis.com; Tues.-Fri. 11:30am-2pm and 5:30pm-9pm, Sat.-Sun. noon-3pm and 5:30pm-9pm

ITALIAN

JIMMY'S FOOD STORE $

Some of the city's best restaurants source their meats from this little Italian grocery store tucked away in Old East Dallas. The DiCarlo family, originally from Sicily, opened Jimmy's 50 years ago and became locally famous for their meatballs and sausages, made fresh daily. The aisles are full of specialty sauces, cheeses, breads, pastas, spices, desserts, and other staples along with a wide selection of Italian wines. The deli counter at the back of the shop is a popular lunch spot, serving Italian subs, prosciutto panini, Philly roast pork, and Cuban sandwiches. Continue past the back counter into the "secret" dining room—a quiet reprieve from the often cramped, bustling market. Stop by on a Saturday afternoon for free wine tastings.

MAP 2: 4901 Bryan St., 214/823-6180, www.jimmysfoodstore.com; Mon.-Sat. 9am-7:30pm

SCALINI'S PIZZA & PASTA $$

There's nothing too fancy about Scalini's—and that's a good thing. At this quaint Italian eatery, you can blend in with the locals and soak up Lakewood's authentic neighborhood vibe, in between browsing the adjacent gift shops. Scalini's crispy thin-crust pesto pizza is by far the best offering. You can also build your own pies.

MAP 2: 2021 Abrams Rd., 214/821-8088, www.scalinisdallas.com; Mon.-Thurs. 11am-10pm, Fri.-Sat. 11am-11pm, Sun. noon-10pm

DESSERT

SOCIETY BAKERY $

This local empire has racked up national accolades for its sugary treats ever since it debuted in 2003. Society Bakery is known for its seasonal cupcake flavors like key lime pie, s'mores, pink champagne, and banana pudding in the summer. These pastry chefs can create just about any custom cake or cookie for special events.

MAP 2: 3610 Greenville Ave., 214/827-1411, www.societybakery.com; Mon.-Fri. 8am-6pm, Sat. 8am-5pm

TC SHAVED ICE $

Dallas loves its sno-cone shacks. It's one of the only ways we know how to cope with our triple-digit summer heat. TC Shaved Ice is one of the city's two legendary stands (the other being Aunt Stelle's in Oak Cliff). You'll find traditional snowballs in every familiar flavor like Tiger's Blood, Pink Lady, and Dreamsicle. Spring for the large Knockout—shaved ice topped with a scoop of ice cream.

MAP 2: 10999 Garland Rd., 214/649-2212; daily 11am-10pm

UNREFINED BAKERY $

Specializing in organic, gluten-free, and soy-free baked goods, Unrefined Bakery is worth the indulgence no matter your dietary restrictions. Plus, you can feel a little less guilty knowing that the muffins, cinnamon rolls, cupcakes, and sweet breads are made with, as the name suggests, unrefined flour and sugar.

MAP 2: 3426 Greenville Ave., Suite 150, 214/826-2414, www.unrefinedbakery.com; Mon.-Sat. 10am-6pm, Sun.10:30am-5:30pm

COFFEE

HOUNDSTOOTH $

With its open, light-filled ambience and clean, modern design, Houndstooth lacks the cozy feel of traditional coffee shops. But the baristas are serious about their craft, serving the locally roasted Tweed Coffee. The coffee is top-notch, but expect to pay about $5 for a basic pour-over brew.

MAP 2: 1900 N. Henderson Ave., 972/863-9080, www.houndstoothcoffee.com; Mon.-Fri. 6:30am-7pm, Sat.-Sun. 7am-7pm

MUDSMITH $

The coffee is consistently good at Mudsmith, if you can bear to mess up the beautiful latte art. The menu includes nondairy milk options like almond and coconut, and a wide selection of uncommon syrups including lavender, rose, mint, and blackberry. Venture to the back room for a more rustic, man-cave atmosphere, complete with mounted moose heads, red leather armchairs, and a wall-to-wall bookshelf.

MAP 2: 2114 Greenville Ave., 214/370-9535, www.mudsmithcoffee.com; Mon.-Fri. 6:30am-11pm, Sat. 7am-11pm, Sun. 7am-10pm

Uptown

Map 3

MEXICAN

EL BOLERO $$

El Bolero offers a refreshing reprise with its multiregional Mexican cuisine served in a bright and modern atmosphere. The extensive menu includes several seafood options worth considering such as lobster fajitas, which are offered as a lunch special every Friday. For dessert, try the churros with caramel, dark chocolate sauce, and berries.

MAP 3: 1201 Oak Lawn Ave., Suite 160, 214/741-1986, www.elboleromexican.com; Mon.-Thurs. 11am-10pm, Fri. 11am-11pm, Sat. 10am-11pm, Sun. 10am-10pm

MANNY'S UPTOWN TEX-MEX $

The yellow frame house with green trim makes this West Village eatery easy to spot. Manny's offers pretty standard Tex-Mex fare, but with special attention paid to the brisket tacos and brisket enchiladas. For its location—within walking to distance to Uptown shops and bars—the menu prices are surprisingly inexpensive.

MAP 3: 3521 Oak Grove Ave., 214/252-1616, www.mannysuptowntexmex.com; Mon.-Thurs. 11am-10pm, Fri. 11am-11pm, Sat. 8am-11pm, Sun. 8am-10pm

OJEDA'S $

Open since 1969, Ojeda's is one of Dallas's classic Tex-Mex institutions. The family-owned restaurant serves just about every staple from fajita nachos to sour cream enchiladas. You'll also find the puffed taco, a Texas specialty not seen on every Tex-Mex menu. Bonus: Breakfast is served all day.

MAP 3: 4617 Maple Ave., 214/528-8383, www.ojedasrestaurant.com; Mon.-Thurs. 10:30am-9:30pm, Fri. 10:30am-10:30pm, Sat. 10am-10:30pm, Sun. 10am-9:30pm

AMERICAN

★ AL BIERNAT'S $$$

It's one of the best places in Dallas for a serious steak, but out-of-towners often overlook Al Biernat's. Probably because it's not in downtown with the other well-known steak houses. It's a neighborhood restaurant, drawing wealthy and prominent Dallasites. Of the menu's 15 steak options, you can't go wrong with the prime rib or bone-in filet. Seafood is the other big star at Al's, including Chilean sea bass, grilled scallops on coconut rice, and horseradish-crusted halibut. It's a classy place, so dress appropriately.

MAP 3: 4217 Oak Lawn Ave., 214/219-2201, www.albiernats.com; Mon.-Fri. 11:30am-2:30pm and 5:30pm-10pm, Sat. 5:30pm-11pm, Sun. 11am-2:30pm and 5:30pm-9pm

EATZI'S MARKET & BAKERY $$

Cheerful French music reverberates around this European-style market, which seems to have every post covered: the bakery bursting with baguettes, mountains of cheese selections, a sizzling grill, and a mouthwatering dessert case. Eatzi's is just like any other high-end restaurant, but in take-out form. While the patio is a nice and breezy spot to dine, it's best to hit up Eatzi's for gourmet food to go—great for a picnic or a cozy dinner back in the hotel room.

MAP 3: 3403 Oak Lawn Ave., www.eatzis.com; 214/526-1515; daily 7am-10pm

★ FT33 $$$

Backed by Dallas's rock-star chef Matt McCallister, FT33 turns food into an art form. With local ingredients sourced from North Texas farmers and ranchers, the modern menu changes with the seasons. If you can't decide among the dizzying array of dishes, ask about the restaurant's tasting menus or prix fixe dinner.

MAP 3: 1617 Hi Line Dr., 214/741-2629, www.ft33dallas.com; Tues.-Thurs. 6pm-10pm, Fri.-Sat. 5:30pm-11pm

LUCKY'S CAFÉ $

You can't miss this joint's bright red neon sign reaching skyward from Oak Lawn Avenue. Lucky's Café is always a reliable choice for breakfast, served all day. The old-school diner serves some of the best pancakes in town. Enjoy a little booze with your breakfast? Try the banana cognac pancakes with pure maple syrup. Plus, unlike most greasy spoons, Lucky's also serves craft beer, wine, and cocktails.

MAP 3: 3531 Oak Lawn Ave., 214/522-3500, www.luckysdallas.com; daily 7am-10pm

MAMA'S DAUGHTER'S DINER $$

This family-owned diner has thrived for three generations of women—"Mama," daughter, and granddaughter—by serving up some of the best Southern comfort food in the city. You can order breakfast all day, and the $10 lunch specials offer huge portions for the money.

MAP 3: 2014 Irving Blvd., 214/742-8646, www.mamasdaughersdiner.com; daily 6am-3pm

MEDDLESOME MOTH $$

The most striking feature of Meddlesome Moth is its three stained glass windows, salvaged from Dallas's original Hard Rock Café. Titled "the Trinity," the windows depict playful paintings of Chuck Berry, Elvis Presley, and Jerry Lee Lewis. Located in the Design District, this gastropub attracts beer nerds with its 40 taps of hard-to-find brews. The food menu, which includes lots of shareable plates, even shows which beer pairs best with each item.

MAP 3: 1621 Oak Lawn Ave., 214/628-7900, www.mothinthe.net; Mon.-Thurs. 11am-midnight, Fri.-Sat. 11am-1am, Sun. 10am-10pm

★ MUTTS CANINE CANTINA $$

This Uptown hangout takes "dog friendly" to a whole new level. Part restaurant, part dog park, Mutts Canine Cantina features a huge outdoor patio and communal beer garden with $6 craft beer selections that rotate regularly. The concession-style menu is big on burgers, hot dogs, and shakes.

While leashed pups are allowed on the patio, the adjacent one-acre park gives them room to run wild.

MAP 3: 2889 Cityplace West Blvd., 214/377-8723, www.muttscantina.com; Mon.-Thurs. 4pm-8pm, Fri. noon-8pm, Sat.-Sun. 11am-8pm

OAK $$$

For those who appreciate an artful presentation, the food at Oak is almost too pretty to eat. The eclectic and swanky Design District restaurant serves a variety of cuisine fused to create something all its own. The dinner menu is decidedly more upscale, with seared scallops and braised veal, while the lunch menu is a little more casual, featuring items like a prime beef burger and steak frites.

MAP 3: 1628 Oak Lawn Ave., Suite 110, 214/712-9700, www.oakdallas.com; Mon.-Thurs. 11am-2pm and 5pm-10pm, Fri. 11am-2pm and 5pm-11pm, Sat. 5pm-11pm

ASIAN

MALAI KITCHEN $$

Located in the West Village shopping center, Malai Kitchen is a great spot to grab lunch or dinner before a movie at the Magnolia. The Thai-Vietnamese bistro offers refined cuisine in a sleek but laid-back atmosphere. The standout dish is the iron pot green curry chicken. There are also Asian beers brewed in-house; you can sample a flight of three for $8.

MAP 3: 3699 McKinney Ave., Suite 319, 214/599-7857, www.malaikitchen.com; Mon.-Thurs. 11am-10pm, Fri.-Sat. 11am-11pm, Sun. 10am-10pm

NOBU $$$

One of the hottest restaurant empires in the country, chef Nobu Matsuhisa's Dallas location is no less impressive than its brethren. Located inside the Rosewood Crescent Hotel, Nobu serves upscale Japanese cuisine that features seven types of wagyu beef, including one flamed in cognac at the table. And yes, the number 136 next to the menu item is the price, so be prepared to splurge. The excellent sushi and sashimi is a little easier on the wallet. Don't skip the decadent miso cappuccino for dessert.

MAP 3: 400 Crescent Ct., 214/252-7000, www.noburestaurants.com; Sun.-Thurs. 6pm-10pm, Fri.-Sat. 6pm-11pm

INDIAN

COSMIC CAFÉ $

The exterior of Cosmic Café is enough to spark the curiosity of any adventurous diner. The intricate Indian designs flow throughout the restaurant. The vegetarian menu includes staples like hummus, naan, samosas, and curried vegetables (all of which are included in the restaurant's popular Buddha's Delight). You'll also find other veggie options in the form of tacos, enchiladas, pizza, and a black bean burger. Be sure to venture out to the back patio for to see more Indian murals.

MAP 3: 2912 Oak Lawn Ave., 214/521-6157, www.cosmiccafedallas.com; Mon.-Thurs. 11am-10:30pm, Fri.-Sat. 11am-11pm, Sun. noon-10pm

ITALIAN

NONNA $$$

It's easy for locals to forget that one of the city's finest Italian restaurants is hidden in a dull strip shopping center at the edge of Oak Lawn and Highland Park. Still, even a *New York Times* food critic managed to find Nonna and rank it among the best in the country. Famous for its white clam pizza, the small, upscale restaurant fills up fast, so make reservations.

MAP 3: 4115 Lomo Alto Dr., 214/521-1800, www.nonnadallas.com; Mon.-Thurs. 5:30pm-9pm, Fri.-Sat. 5:30pm-9:30pm

COFFEE

ASCENSION COFFEE $

This chic café serves coffee roasted in-house, some of the best in the city. But if you're hungry for something more substantial than a blueberry scone, Ascension Coffee also has a stellar brunch menu with dishes like smoked salmon hash and ricotta and berry hotcakes. It's also a classy, laid-back place for a glass of wine or a craft beer.

MAP 3: 1621 Oak Lawn Ave., 214/741-3211, www.ascensiondallas.com; Mon.-Wed. 7am-9pm, Thurs.-Fri. 7am-10pm, Sat. 8am-10pm, Sun. 8am-6pm

CROOKED TREE COFFEEHOUSE $

Located in a small bungalow with minimal signage, Crooked Tree Coffeehouse feels like, well, someone's home. It has several cozy nooks in which hide away with a laptop or a good book. The shop serves locally roasted coffee and espresso along with loose-leaf tea, hot chocolate, and Italian sodas. Stop in on a weekend evening for live music sessions.

MAP 3: 2414 Routh St., 214/953-1142; Mon.-Thurs. 6am-11pm, Fri. 6am-midnight, Sat. 7am-midnight, Sun. 8am-9pm

Park Cities

Map 4

TEX-MEX

RAFA'S CAFÉ MEXICANO $$

Dallas is teeming with Tex-Mex restaurants, but one way to tell a good one from a bad one is longevity. Rafa's Café has operated in the same Lovers Lane space for more than 20 years, serving straightforward staples like enchiladas, fajitas, and chiles rellenos. The house queso and the seven-layer dip are local favorites. Beware: parking is a pain during lunchtime.

MAP 4: 5617 W. Lovers Ln., 214/357-2080, www.rafascafe.com; Sun. 11am-9:30pm, Tues.-Thurs. 11am-9:30pm, Fri.-Sat. 11am-10pm

BARBECUE

PEGGY SUE BBQ $$

Located in the quaint and walkable Snider Plaza shopping center, Peggy Sue BBQ has a comfortable, checkered-tablecloth vibe. While the meats may not impress barbecue snobs, they do hit the spot. The best thing about Peggy Sue's? Fried pie a la mode, and moderately priced wine by the glass.

MAP 4: 6600 Snider Plaza, 214/987-9188, www.peggysuebbq.com; Sun.-Thurs. 11am-9pm, Fri.-Sat. 11am-10pm

AMERICAN

BUBBA'S COOKS COUNTRY $

Hungry college kids with high metabolisms chow down on gravy-smothered chicken-fried steak at Bubba's Cooks Country, but don't be fooled. The 35-year-old retro diner serves up mountainous portions of Southern food that could knock you out for the rest of the afternoon. Will it be worth it? Probably.

MAP 4: 6617 Hillcrest Ave., 214/373-6527, www.bubbasdallas.com; daily 6:30am-10pm

EAST HAMPTON SANDWICH CO. $$

Five years ago, a twentysomething Dallas native opened a sandwich shop. Now, it's something of a local empire. East Hampton Sandwich Co. takes an upscale approach to the fast-casual deli with items like the lobster grilled cheese, Meyer lemon chicken sandwich, and the asparagus and gruyere with red chili vinaigrette. If you're looking for Dallas's perfect sandwich, this place comes pretty close.

MAP 4: 6912 Snider Plaza, 214/363-2888, www.ehsandwich.com; daily 10:30am-9pm

NEIGHBORHOOD SERVICES $$$

One of several restaurants from famed local chef Nick Badovinus, Neighborhood Services remains a quiet success among Park Cities foodies. The upscale, seasonal comfort-food menu features nightly specials like lobster nachos and chicken fricassee pot pie along with regular dishes, including caramelized scallops, Gulf shrimp enchiladas, and several steak plates. The dark, intimate atmosphere makes for a nice date night, but the bar area can get noisy.

MAP 4: 5027 W. Lovers Ln., 214/350-5027, www.nhstheoriginal.com; Mon.-Thurs. 5pm-10pm, Fri.-Sat. 5pm-11pm

MUSTANG DONUTS $

This morning doughnut counter attracts more than just the neighborhood's SMU crowd. Locals bustle in for pastry staples like doughnut holes, éclairs, glazed twists, and cinnamon buns. For something even more indulgent (can we even call it breakfast at this point?), go for the blueberry cake doughnut. The lines are long but move quickly. Mustang Donuts is cash only.

MAP 4: 6601 Hillcrest Ave., 214/363-4878; daily 5am-noon

ASIAN

SHINSEI $$$

The product of two local celebrity chef families—the Fearings and the Rathbuns—Shinsei is known for its creative pan-Asian sushi and seafood. The offerings are constantly changing, but a few mainstays include the shrimp dumplings, Thai beef cheek, and the citrusy kampachi and fig.

Venture upstairs for a more laid-back cocktail lounge with plush furniture and large windows overlooking Inwood Road.

MAP 4: 7713 Inwood Rd., 214/352-0005, www.shinseirestaurant.com; Mon.-Thurs. 5pm-10:30pm, Fri. 11am-2pm and 5pm-11:15pm, Sat. 5pm-11:15pm

FRENCH

RISE NO. 1 $$$

An entire concept devoted to perfecting the soufflé, Rise No. 1 has carved out a special place in the Dallas dining scene. George W. and Laura Bush have listed it among their favorite restaurants. Whether sweet or savory, the essential French dish takes center stage, served in a cozy, bookish, softly lit atmosphere. Don't skip the famous "marshmallow" soup, a tomato-and-carrot bisque with goat cheese chunks and drizzled pesto.

MAP 4: 5360 W. Lovers Ln., Suite 220, 214/366-9900, www.risesouffle.com; Mon.-Thurs. 11am-10pm, Fri.-Sat. 11am-11pm, Sun. 11am-9pm

GERMAN

KUBY'S SAUSAGE HOUSE $

This old-fashioned German meat market carries 16 kinds of bratwurst along with gourmet cheeses, specialty mustard, sauerkraut, and other staples. If dining in, the "wurst teller" plate offers the best value: your choice of sausage served with potato salad, red cabbage, and sauerkraut. Kuby's is a delightfully unexpected pocket of German culture tucked away in SMU country.

MAP 4: 6601 Snider Plaza, 214/363-2231, www.kubys.com; Mon.-Thurs. 6am-6pm, Fri.-Sat. 6am-9pm, Sun. 9am-2pm

MEXICAN

LA DUNI LATIN KITCHEN AND COFFEE STUDIO $$

A trip to NorthPark Center without visiting La Duni would be a mistake. This long-standing Latin-American eatery is known for its weekend brunch, espresso bar, and desserts. The extensive menu includes a long list of entrees, but the coffee drinks and the sweet and savory snacks impress on their own. From flaky empanadas and rich queso verde to the guava rolls and butter conchas, La Duni is the perfect midday pit stop.

MAP 4: NorthPark Center, 8687 N. Central Expy., Suite 1516, 214/987-2260, www.laduni.com; Mon.-Thurs. 9am-8:30pm, Fri. 9am-9:30pm, Sat. 10am-10pm, Sun. 10am-8:30pm

SEAFOOD

CAFÉ PACIFIC $$$

This decades-old institution doesn't receive much media hype anymore; it doesn't need it. Café Pacific embraces its classic, old-Dallas vibe: black-and-white checkered tile, white tablecloths, soft chandeliers, and a dress code that prohibits T-shirts, shorts, and flip-flops. Among the patrons, you'll find politicians, business moguls, and other moneyed elite dining on caviar and escargot, red snapper and rainbow trout, lobster rolls and steak fillets.

MAP 4: 24 Highland Park Village, 214/526-1170, www.cafepacificdallas.com; Mon.-Sat. 11:30am-2:30pm and 5:30pm-10pm, Sun. 5pm-9pm

FLYING FISH $

Inspired by the small-town seafood joints of East Texas, the casual and kitschy Flying Fish serves up gumbo, fried catfish baskets, crab legs, shrimp po'boys, jambalaya, hushpuppies, and other Southern-style favorites. Traffic in this neighborhood is heavy, and parking is difficult during weekday lunchtime as the area's 9-to-5 office workers flock to Preston Center's restaurants. Weekends are much calmer.

MAP 4: 6126 Luther Ln., 214/696-3474, www.flyingfishinthe.net; daily 7am-10pm

DESSERT

CARLO'S BAKERY $

When Carlo's Bakery opened its Dallas location a few years ago, the line around the block didn't let up for weeks. An outpost of reality television's *Cake Boss*, where chef Buddy Valastro and his team create stunning custom cakes, the bakery features grab-and-go cannoli, lobster tails, cream puffs, and other pastries made famous by the show.

MAP 4: 8319 Preston Rd., 469/726-2669, www.carlosbakery.com; Sun.-Thurs. 7am-9pm, Fri.-Sat. 7am-10pm

SPRINKLES CUPCAKES $

Part of a California-based cupcake kingdom, the adorable Sprinkles offers different flavors every week, from Cuban coffee to salty caramel to lemon coconut. Beware: The cupcakes are very large and sweet, too much so for some people. Got a midnight craving? Next door to the Preston Center storefront, the pink cupcake ATM dispenses treats 24/7.

MAP 4: 4020 Villanova St., 214/369-0004, www.sprinkles.com; Mon.-Sat. 9am-9pm, Sun. 10am-8pm

West Dallas/Oak Cliff — Map 5

TEX-MEX

HERRERA'S CAFÉ $$

Locals swear by the sour cream chicken enchiladas at Herrera's Café, a long-standing Dallas restaurant that has bounced around town the past couple of decades. Its latest West Dallas location features a covered patio with sprawling shade trees, making it one of the best spots to sip a frozen margarita and snack on bottomless chips and salsa.

MAP 5: 3311 Sylvan Ave., 214/954-7180, www.herrerascafe.com; Mon. 11am-9pm, Wed.-Thurs. 11am-9pm, Fri. 11am-10pm, Sat. 9am-10pm, Sun. 9am-9pm

EL JORDAN CAFÉ $

For a straightforward Tex-Mex breakfast, this bustling Bishop Arts dive makes a heaping plate of *migas* served with roasted potatoes and refried beans. The breakfast burritos, while a bit greasy, are a steal at only $1.50

Top: Emporium Pies; **Bottom:** Mutts Canine Cantina

each. El Jordan also offers American fare, including French toast, biscuits and gravy, and omelets.

MAP 5: 416 N. Bishop Ave., 214/941-4451; Sun-Mon. 7am-2:30pm, Wed.-Sat. 7am-2:30pm

EL PADRINO $

The restaurant is so tiny you might drive past it multiple times before finally spotting the blue and orange storefront, sandwiched between two taller buildings on Jefferson Boulevard. El Padrino, which is Spanish for "the godfather," serves up good, cheap street tacos as well as breakfast burritos, fajita plates, soups, and tortas.

MAP 5: 408 W. Jefferson Blvd., 214/943-3993; Mon.-Sat. 8am-10pm, Sun. 8am-9pm

EL RANCHITO $$

Full of colorful Mexican décor and large oil-painted murals, El Ranchito feels like a party waiting to happen. And when the mariachi band begins making the rounds the party actually does get started. The decades-old Tex-Mex establishment is also known for hosting Elvis impersonator contests every January and August, attracting some pretty serious competitors. You'll find all the major menu staples along with some surprises like grilled baby goat sourced from a local farm.

MAP 5: 610 W. Jefferson Blvd., 214/946-4238, www.elranchito-dallas.com; Mon.-Thurs. 11am-10pm, Fri. 11am-11:30pm, Sat. 10am-11:30pm, Sun. 10am-10pm

BARBECUE

LOCKHART SMOKEHOUSE $$

Named for the famous Central Texas barbecue town from which the owners' family hails, Lockhart Smokehouse brings those revered recipes to the Bishop Arts District. Upon entering, head all the way to the back counter where you can see the pit master in action before ordering your meats and sides. Originally, the restaurant did not provide forks or sauce, requiring diners to eat barbecue the "right" way, but that gimmick didn't last long.

MAP 5: 400 W. Davis. St., 214/944-5521, www.lockhartsmokehouse.com; daily 11am-9pm

ODOM'S BAR-B-QUE $$

The service is slow, the staff isn't always attentive, and the food won't look pretty in Instagram photos. So, if you're looking to add some #travelporn to your social media feed, Odom's is not the place for you. The old-school, family-owned barbecue joint makes a deliciously messy baked potato loaded with butter, cheese, sour cream, and shredded beef.

MAP 5: 1971 Singleton Blvd., 214/631-3538, www.odomsbbq.com; daily 10:30am-11pm

AMERICAN

BOLSA $$

Known for their seasonal, locally sourced, and ever-changing menu, the folks at Bolsa are used to attracting suburbanites and out-of-towners. The cheese boards, bruschetta, and flatbreads bring together ingredients like

manchego and apple slaw, and pimento cheese and pickles. The bartenders whip up fancy, inventive cocktails, which are only $5 during happy hour.
MAP 5: 634 W. Davis St., 214/942-0451, www.bolsadallas.com; Mon.-Fri. 4:30pm-10pm, Sat. 10am-11pm, Sun. 10am-10pm

CHICKEN SCRATCH $$

Ideal for travelers with kids in tow, Chicken Scratch resembles a giant family picnic where you can let the little ones roam. The menu features fried chicken, biscuit sandwiches, nontraditional sides, and homemade sodas. The Popsicles, made with real, fresh fruit, are hard to pass up on a hot day.
MAP 5: 2303 Pittman St., 214/749-1112, www.cs-tf.com; Sun.-Thurs. 11am-10pm, Fri.-Sat. 11am-midnight

ENO'S PIZZA TAVERN $$

Located in an old, two-story brick building, Eno's serves crispy, thin-crust pizza in a casual, rustic environment. The truffle cheese bread is a delicious precursor to, well, more cheese and more bread. Pair with a craft beer for some serious carbo-loading that you won't regret. Try to score a table upstairs, which is quieter and offers a nice view of the Bishop Arts District.
MAP 5: 407 N. Bishop Ave., 214/943-9200, www.enospizza.com; Tues.-Thurs. 11:30am-10pm, Fri.-Sat. 11:30am-midnight, Sun.11:30am-10pm

HATTIE'S $$$

This upscale, Southern-style bistro is the quintessential spot for celebratory comfort food. Hattie's occupies a prominent corner in the Bishop Arts District, serving bacon-wrapped meatloaf, pecan-crusted catfish, and pork chops with tomato-ginger jam. The four-cheddar mac and cheese is among the best in the city. Make reservations, or expect to wait awhile for a table.
MAP 5: 418 N. Bishop Ave., 214/942-7400, www.hatties.com; Mon.-Sat. 11:30am-2:30pm, Tues.-Sun. 5:30pm-10pm, Sun. 11am-2:30pm

JONATHON'S $$

Located inside a tiny bungalow, Jonathon's is packed during weekend brunch with diners spilling out onto the sidewalk along Beckley Avenue, so expect a long wait time. They come for the fried chicken and waffles, but other indulgent dishes include the all-in-one Belgian waffle baked with bacon and topped with cheesy scrambled eggs, pork sausage, onions, chilies, and gravy. The Bloody Mary bar is also a hit.
MAP 5: 1111 N. Beckley Ave., 214/946-2221, www.jonathonsoakcliff.com; Tues.-Fri. 7am-10pm, Sat. 8am-9pm, Sun. 8am-2pm

NORMA'S CAFÉ $

Another Oak Cliff institution, Norma's Café has spent 60 years perfecting the home-cooked meal in its old-fashioned diner atmosphere. After gorging on chicken-fried steak, mashed potatoes, and cornbread, you might have to roll yourself out of there. Still, save room for one of the giant meringue cream desserts known as "mile-high pies."

MAP 5: 1123 W. Davis. St., 214/946-4711, www.normascafe.com; Mon.-Sat. 6am-8pm, Sun. 7am-8pm

SMOKE $$$

Chef Tim Byres wrote the book on smoking meats, and it won a James Beard Award. Located next to the Belmont, a remodeled boutique hotel, Smoke stands alone in the Dallas restaurant scene. The modern, upscale approach to barbecue is just one highlight. The brunch menu includes Smoke's famous ricotta cheese pancakes with vanilla poached apricots.

MAP 5: 901 Fort Worth Ave., 214/393-4141, www.smokerestaurant.com; Mon.-Thurs. 8am-10pm, Fri.-Sat 8am-11pm

SPIRAL DINER $$

Despite its completely vegan menu, Spiral Diner appeals to a variety of palates. In addition to hummus wraps and tofu sandwiches, you'll find pretty good vegan versions of Philly cheesesteak, spaghetti and meatballs, and quesadillas. Check the bakery case for rotating dessert specials like Neapolitan cake and peanut butter cups. The diner has a laid-back, hippie vibe, but the countertop pamphlets detailing the horrors of factory farms are a little much.

MAP 5: 1101 N. Beckley Ave., 214/948-4747, www.spiraldiner.com; Tues.-Fri. 11am-10pm, Sat.-Sun. 9am-10pm

WIMPY'S HAMBURGERS $

For a basic burger on the cheap, Wimpy's walk-up stand will suffice, and it's a great way to experience Dallas's old-fashioned kitsch. The hole-in-the-wall hut adorned with zany cartoon murals has been around for decades, off and on. Located in an unattractive but up-and-coming part of town, and lacking the artisan allure of modern burger joints, Wimpy's is often overlooked.

MAP 5: 1802 Singleton Blvd., 214/749-0277; Mon.-Sat. 7am-10pm

MEXICAN

LA CALLE DOCE $$

After more than 35 years, this well-established 12th Street restaurant remains a local favorite for Mexican seafood. Located in a renovated house with a wraparound porch, La Calle Doce's huge menu has something for every palate, from octopus and ahi tuna to fried catfish and shrimp tacos.

MAP 5: 415 W. 12th St., 214/941-4304, www.lacalledoce-dallas.com; Mon.-Thurs. 11am-10pm, Fri.-Sat. 11am-11pm, Sun. 11am-9pm

MESA $$$

Aside from serving one of the best spicy margaritas in town, Mesa specializes in authentic Mexican seafood (read: not Tex-Mex) from the coastal state of Veracruz. The upscale restaurant is almost hidden amid pawnshops and discount stores along Jefferson Boulevard. Despite its location, Mesa has garnered critical acclaim for its ceviche, jicama salad, and lobster enchiladas. Plus, Beyoncé and Jay-Z dined there while passing through town a few years ago.

MAP 5: 118 W. Jefferson Blvd., 214/941-4246, www.mesadallas.com; Tues.-Thurs. 5pm-10pm, Fri.-Sat. 5pm-11pm

TAQUERIA EL SI HAY $

This red and green freestanding taco shack always has a crowd out front. With no seating, people stand, sit on the curb, or tailgate nearby, feasting on one of seven kinds of street tacos for less than $2 each. You might also see a sweet man pushing an *elote* cart, peddling the Mexican cream corn treats. El Si Hay is cash only.

MAP 5: 601 W. Davis St., 214/941-4042; Sun.-Thurs. 10am-10pm, Fri.-Sat. 10am-11pm

TROMPO $

The sign on the burnt-orange building simply reads, "tacos," but this nondescript taqueria stands out as one of the best. Trompo serves Mexican street tacos with rotisserie pork, onions, and cilantro on corn tortillas. Its growing popularity has resulted in long lines and limited seating during peak times. Fortunately, the shop keeps long hours.

MAP 5: 839 Singleton Blvd., 972/809-7950; daily 11am-10pm

MEDITERRANEAN

GREEK CAFÉ & BAKERY $

Tucked amid trendier restaurants in the Bishop Arts District, this quiet, laid-back eatery is a welcome change of pace. Although the service is fast, the Greek owners foster a familial vibe that encourages diners to linger over a bottle of wine (the café is BYOB with no corking fee). The basic menu offers traditional staples like hummus and baba ganoush, gyros and salads, and large sampler platters. The baklava cheesecake is well worth the splurge.

MAP 5: 334 W. Davis. St., 214/943-1887; Sun.-Mon. 11am-3pm, Tue.-Sat. 11am-9pm

SPANISH

★ CASA RUBIA $$$

One of the first and most successful ventures to come out of the Trinity Groves incubator, Casa Rubia specializes in creative Spanish tapas and shareable plates like char-grilled octopus and honey-and-chili-glazed pork ribs. You can also pair your own meats and cheeses from separate menus, but don't hesitate to ask the waiters for recommendations. After just one year of business, Casa Rubia snagged a James Beard Foundation nomination for "Best New Restaurant." It still quietly thrives in its Trinity Groves corner, even as new restaurants come and go year after year.

Map 5: 3011 Gulden Ln., 469/513-6349, www.casarubiadfw.com; Mon.-Thurs. 5-10pm, Fri.-Sat. 5-11pm, Sun. 5-9pm

CUBAN

C. SENOR $

Situated on the north side of the Bishop Arts District, the red and white food stand C. Señor specializes in Cuban sandwiches prepared with ham, Swiss cheese, pickles, and tangy mustard. You'll also find fried mahi tacos, yucca fries, and a hefty beef-and-chorizo burger topped with crispy potato strings. There are a few stone patio tables nearby, great for people-watching.

MAP 5: 330 W. Davis St., 214/941-4766; Mon.-Thurs. 11am-9pm, Fri.-Sat. 11am-9:30pm

DESSERT

COCOANDRÉ CHOCOLATIER $

Operated by a mother-daughter team, CocoAndré stands out for its novelty chocolates that come in all shapes and sizes, literally. Molds include everything from cowboy boots to ice cream cones to sugar skulls. The shop also makes chocolate-dipped strawberries, figs, and *paletas*. Serious chocoholics can find an array of truffle flavors like lavender, chili, and sea salt, with new combinations being created all year long.

MAP 5: 508 W. 7th St., 214/941-3030, www.cocoandre.com; Tues.-Sat. 11am-7pm, Sun. noon-5pm

EMPORIUM PIES $

No matter where they begin their day, visitors to the Bishop Arts District will all end up at the same sweet destination: "that cute little pie shop." Housed in a charming cottage with a communal patio space, Emporium Pies often has a line extending to the sidewalk, and for good reason. The homemade pies contain no corn syrup, dyes, or other fake stuff. The flavors change with the seasons, but the year-round staples include the Smooth Operator (chocolate with a pretzel crust) and Lord of the Pies (deep-dish apple).

MAP 5: 314 N. Bishop Ave., 469/206-6126, www.emporiumpies.com; Mon.-Thurs. 11am-9pm, Fri.-Sat. 11am-11pm, Sun. 11am-8pm

JOY MACARONS $

Macarons are so hot right now. (Figuratively, that is.) These meringue treats have seen a subtle rise in popularity at Dallas bakeries, and Joy Macarons is among the first specialty shops to arrive. The colorful cookies are almost too beautiful to eat, but the flavors are enticing. Favorites include honey lavender, rose and lychee, and butter pecan.

MAP 5: 839 W. Davis St., 214/434-1922, www.joymacarons.com; Mon.-Thurs. 10am-6pm, Fri.-Sat. 10am-8pm, Sun. noon-5pm

PANADERÍA VERA'S $

This tiny Mexican bakery is neighborhood-famous for its beautiful birthday cakes, but don't overlook the selection of doughnuts, churros, pan de dulce, and melt-in-your-mouth Mexican wedding cookies (*ojarascas*) made fresh daily. With its large Hispanic population, Oak Cliff is full of these little bakeries, but most locals agree that Vera's is the best.

MAP 5: 932 W. Davis St., 214/943-2167; Tues.-Sat. 6am-7pm, Sun. 6am-4pm

COFFEE

BOLSA MERCADO $

Not to be confused with the restaurant by the same owners, Bolsa Mercado's unpretentious atmosphere and friendly staff bring out the regulars. With its spacious interior, long wooden tables, and dependable Wi-Fi, it has become a go-to spot for Oak Cliff neighbors working remotely. The locally roasted coffee is strong and refreshing, particularly the iced espresso mixed with Topo Chico. The shop also serves some of the best breakfast tacos around.

MAP 5: 634 W. Davis St., 214/942-0451, www.bolsadallas.com/bolsa-mercado; daily 7am-7pm

DAVIS STREET ESPRESSO $

Located on the recently revitalized block of Tyler and Davis, the baristas here operate under a different philosophy. They want to reduce waste and encourage human interaction. That's why you won't find any to-go cups or Wi-Fi. So, workaholics and hurried caffeine addicts should look elsewhere. The shop uses beans from the local Oak Cliff Coffee Roasters, and pulls shots from the very precise Alpha Dominche Steampunk espresso machine. The rustic atmosphere is full of reclaimed wood and industrial lighting, and the back patio features a converted vintage bus with more secluded seating.

MAP 5: 819 W. Davis St., 214/941-0381, www.davisstreetespresso.com; Mon.-Fri. 6am-3pm, Sat. 7am-6pm

Downtown Fort Worth **Map 6**

BARBECUE

BAILEY'S BAR-B-QUE $

A tiny red frame house sandwiched between two beige office buildings, Bailey's is the most underrated barbecue joint in the city. That might be because it's only open for weekday lunch, making it a popular spot for downtown employees. But if you're around during that brief window, grab a sliced beef or spicy pulled pork sandwich on the cheap.

MAP 6: 826 Taylor St., 817/335-7469; Mon.-Thurs. 10:30am-4pm, Fri. 10:30am-3pm

RISCKY'S BAR-B-Q $$

With about 75 years of barbecue business under its belt, Riscky's has become a Fort Worth empire. It has four outposts, including a steak house, a deli, and a burger joint, but Riscky's Bar-B-Q in downtown is perhaps the superior of the lot. For the best deal, go for the $12.99 all-you-can-eat beef ribs.

MAP 6: 300 Main St., 817/877-3306, www.risckys.com; Sun.-Mon. 11am-9pm, Tues.-Thurs. 11am-10pm, Fri.-Sat. 11am-11pm

Trinity Groves: A Foodie Oasis

The new dining and entertainment district known as **Trinity Groves** (3011 Gulden Ln., www.trinitygroves.com) seemed to sprout up overnight right after the construction of the Margaret Hunt Hill Bridge in 2012. However, it was an idea decades in the making. The Trinity Groves restaurant incubator program, owned and operated by Phil Ramno (founder of Macaroni Grill and Fuddruckers) and his two partners Stuart Fitts and Butch McGregor, encourages chefs and entrepreneurs to create and test new concepts. This is why you'll find just about every kind of cuisine clustered in one walkable strip with large, tree-shaded courtyards. The popularity of Trinity Groves has made it a crowded weekend destination, so make reservations and allow plenty of time to park.

Among the splurges for diners at Trinity Groves, the modern Spanish tapas restaurant **Casa Rubia** has national awards piling up, including the James Beard Foundation's 2014 "Best New Restaurant" and "Best Chef Southwest." The creative charcuterie and cheese boards have complex flavor combinations. If a casual burger joint is more your style, head to **Off-Site Kitchen,** which unites hefty Angus beef patties with a wide variety of toppings and sauces. You can try to burn off the brick in your stomach with a heated game of Ping-Pong. **Chino Chinatown** serves Asian dishes with Latin American influences starting with duck egg rolls made with Thai basil, agave, and Oaxaca cheese. There's plenty of time to let your food settle while in line at **Cake Bar,** a specialty bakery that sells three-layer cakes by the slice.

One of several local craft breweries to burst onto the Dallas scene, **Four Corners Brewery** began in an Oak Cliff garage before joining the Trinity Groves landscape. Favorite beers include the Local Buzz golden ale, and the El Chingón IPA. Tours run at noon and 1:30pm Saturdays, and the taproom opens every evening, pouring $5 brews. You'll also find Four Corners sold in cans all over the city.

AMERICAN

BIRD CAFÉ $$

Located in a historic Victorian building in Sundance Square, Bird Café is known for its small, shareable plates prepared with locally sourced ingredients. Order the "moth balls" made with ricotta and fried sage. Feeling more adventurous? Try the rabbit potpie.

MAP 6: 155 E. 4th St., 817/332-2473, www.birdinthe.net; Mon.-Thurs. 11am-midnight, Fri. 11am-1am, Sat. 10am-1am, Sun. 10am-10pm

REATA $$$

The rooftop patio at Reata offers stunning views of downtown Fort Worth, making it a prime spot for a dining splurge. The upscale steak house incorporates Mexican specialties to create popular dishes like the tenderloin tamales, jalapeno and cheese elk sausage, and a pretty solid bone-in rib eye. You'll also find wild game on the weekend menu.

MAP 6: 310 Houston St., 817/336-1009, www.reata.net; Sun.-Thurs. 11am-2:30pm and 5pm-10pm, Fri.-Sat. 11am-2:30pm and 5pm-10:30pm

YOLK $$

This bright and open space, complete with a skylight at the center, will wake you up on a dreary morning. Yolk is one of the best spots for an indulgent breakfast. For something sweet, there's red velvet French toast or Nutella crepes. If you're keeping it healthy, go for the quinoa bowl or the kale scrambler.

MAP 6: 305 Main St., 817/730-4000, www.eatyolk.com; Mon.-Fri. 6am-3pm, Sat.-Sun. 7am-3pm

COFFEE

BUON GIORNO $$

Inspired by European coffee culture, Buon Giorno specializes in espresso and French press coffee roasted on-site. The pastries are not an afterthought, especially the warm almond croissant. The shop, which offers free Wi-Fi and outlet plugs, is a great place to slow down during a busy day.

MAP 6: 915 Florence St., 817/698-9888, www.bgcoffee.net; Mon.-Fri. 6:30am-9pm, Sat. 7am-10pm, Sun. 8am-8pm

West Fort Worth

Map 7

BARBECUE

★ ANGELO'S $$

A mounted bear greets visitors at the entrance, and ominous animal trophies line the walls of this local institution. Angelo's is not for the faint of heart, but just go with it, because it's perhaps the greatest example of Texas barbecue in this region. Here, three generations of pit masters have been serving hickory-smoked meats, seasoned with the family's own dry-rub recipe, to diners who casually devour it at cafeteria-style tables. No meal is complete without a Shiner Bock served in an ice-cold schooner.

MAP 7: 2533 White Settlement Rd., 817/332-0357, www.angelosbbq.com; Mon.-Wed. 11am-9pm, Thurs.-Sat. 11am-10pm

AMERICAN

FRED'S TEXAS CAFÉ $$

While many "Texas" themed restaurants feel downright corny, Fred's actually does justice to the often-bungled aesthetic. The wood grain interior is lined with neon beer signs, local art, a modest collection of mounted antlers, and only one giant longhorn head. At any rate, you come to Fred's for the burgers—among the best in the Dallas-Fort Worth dining scene. You can't go wrong with the basic Fredburger, made with a half-pound, Texas-raised beef patty. Feeling more ambitious? There's also a chicken-fried steak burger.

MAP 7: 915 Currie St., 817/332-0083, www.fredstexascafe.com; Mon.-Sat. 10:30am-midnight, Sun. 10am-9pm

MONTGOMERY STREET CAFÉ $

This no-frills, 1950s-era diner is packed with locals every morning, offering a glimpse of Fort Worth life—cattle ranchers, white-haired retirees, leather-clad bikers, and millennial hipsters. They're all united by buttery homemade biscuits and bottomless coffee. For just over $5, you can get two eggs, three strips of bacon, hash browns, and a biscuit with gravy. The tiny restaurant gets crowded, especially on weekend mornings, so be prepared to wait for a table.

MAP 7: 2000 Montgomery St., 817/731-8033; Mon.-Fri. 6am-2pm, Sat. 7am-noon

RIGHTEOUS FOODS $$

Not every restaurant in Fort Worth induces a food coma. Righteous Foods focuses on unprocessed, organic, whole ingredients and humanely raised meats. You'll find creative concoctions like coconut and quinoa porridge, pistachio smoked guacamole, poblano-asparagus soup, and plenty of sandwich and pita options. The menu also includes cold-pressed juices and refreshing "detox" drinks.

MAP 7: 3405 W. 7th St., 817/850-9996, www.eatrighteously.com; Mon.-Fri. 7am-9pm, Sat. 9am-9pm

GERMAN

EDELWEISS $$

Perhaps the most surprising Forth Worth find, this charming and homey restaurant serves up authentic German fare and live accordion music every night. While it may seem like a stereotypical year-round Oktoberfest, the food's legit. The German-born chef prepares a variety of wursts and schnitzels, along with other staples like potato pancakes, goulash, Black Forest cake, and Bavarian apple strudel.

MAP 7: 3801 Southwest Blvd., 817/738-5934, www.edelweissgermanrestaurant.com; Wed.-Thurs. 5pm-9:30pm, Fri.-Sat. 5pm-10:30pm, Sun. noon-9pm

MEDITERRANEAN

TERRA MEDITERRANEAN GRILL $$

The same brothers who opened Dallas's much-lauded Ali Baba also claim Terra Mediterranean Grill in Fort Worth's West Seventh neighborhood. The lunch buffet is the best bang for your buck. Pile your plate with feta cheese bread, dolmas, roasted cumin cauliflower, lamb and saffron chicken kebabs, and hummus with just the right consistency.

MAP 7: 2973 Crockett St., 817/744-7485, www.terramedgrill.com; Mon.-Fri. 11am-2:30pm, Mon.-Thurs. 5pm-10pm, Fri. 5pm-11pm, Sat. 11am-11pm, Sun. 11am-3pm and 5pm-9pm

COFFEE/DESSERT

CURLY'S FROZEN CUSTARD $

At this locally famous food stand, you can build your own custard cup or cone with a few base flavors (vanilla, chocolate, or lemon) and a long list of toppings. For something different, like peach, cappuccino, or mint chocolate chip, ask for the flavor of the month.

MAP 7: 4017 Camp Bowie Blvd., 817/763-8700, www.curlysfrozencustard.com; Sun.-Thurs. 11am-9pm, Fri.-Sat. 11am-10pm

Northside

Map 8

AMERICAN

CATTLEMEN'S STEAKHOUSE $$

A fixture of the Fort Worth Stockyards since 1947, Cattlemen's serves up aged, charbroiled steaks in a traditional, down-home atmosphere. This isn't the fancy steak house you take your significant other to for an intimate anniversary dinner. The casual digs reflect the Stockyards vibe—a bit touristy, but still authentic. The enormous menu can be daunting, but you can't go wrong with one of the sirloin or rib eye steaks, with a buttery baked potato. Try not to fill up on the delicious dinner rolls beforehand.

MAP 8: 2458 N. Main St., 817/624-3945, www.cattlemenssteakhouse.com; Mon.-Thurs. 11am-10:30pm, Fri.-Sat. 11am-11pm, Sun. noon-9pm

LONESOME DOVE WESTERN BISTRO $$$

For a more upscale experience in the Stockyards' dusty Old West setting, Lonesome Dove has a nearly 20-year history of fine dining in Fort Worth, with local celebrity chef Tim Love at the helm. This is where you'll find adventurous, gamey dishes like elk, wild boar, rabbit, and rattlesnake, served with creative pairings. Start with the kangaroo carpaccio nachos with avocado salsa and habanero-fig glaze.

MAP 8: 2406 N. Main St., 817/740-8810, www.lonesomedovefortworth.com; Tues.-Sat. 11:30am-2:30pm, Mon.-Thurs. 5pm-10pm, Fri.-Sat. 5pm-11pm

LOVE SHACK $$

Another Tim Love offering in the middle of the Fort Worth Stockyards, this narrow two-story burger joint is more patio than restaurant, making it a nice spot for outdoor dining and live music. The burgers combine ground prime tenderloin and brisket made to order. The famous "Dirty Love Burger" comes with crispy bacon and a fried quail egg. Love Shack is cash only, but there's an ATM on site.

MAP 8: 110 E. Exchange Ave., 817/740-8812, www.loveburgershack.com; Mon.-Wed. 11am-8pm, Thurs. 11am-9pm, Fri.-Sat. 11am-midnight, Sun. 11am-8pm

MEXICAN

JOE T. GARCIA'S $$

Known for its gorgeous garden-style patio that wraps around the entire block, Joe T. Garcia's is a Fort Worth institution. You will almost always have to wait for a table, but you can at least enjoy the digs while sipping a margarita. The menu is small with very basic Mexican dishes done right. The restaurant is cash only with an ATM on site.

MAP 8: 2201 N. Commerce St., 817/626-4356, www.joets.com; Mon.-Thurs. 11am-2:30pm and 5pm-10pm, Fri.-Sat. 11am-11pm, Sun. 11am-10pm

Southside/TCU

Map 9

AMERICAN

ELLERBE FINE FOODS $$$

For a romantic night out, complete with white tablecloths and multiple forms of silverware, Ellerbe Fine Foods is worth the splurge. The farm-to-table menu focuses on local, seasonal ingredients. Spring for a seat on the gorgeous patio enclosed with curtains and soft string lighting. The requested attire is "dressy casual," so save the worn-out jeans and cowboy boots for the Stockyards.

MAP 9: 1501 W. Magnolia Ave., 817/926-3663, www.ellerbefinefoods.com; Tues.-Thurs. 11am-2pm and 5:30pm-9pm, Fri. 11am-2pm and 5:30pm-10pm, Sat. 5:30pm-10pm

JESUS BBQ $

Many lifelong locals don't even know about this hole-in-the-wall. Jesus BBQ defies all food genres with its menu of cheese enchiladas, chicken-fried steak, barbecue ribs, catfish, and fried pies. It may not be the best food in town, but it's pretty good. Plus, it's a nice escape from the crowded trendy restaurants. Play some Johnny Cash on the jukebox and enjoy this local "secret."

MAP 9: 810 S. Main St., 817/332-0168; Mon.-Sat 10am-10pm

LILI'S BISTRO ON MAGNOLIA $$

With its brick-lined interior and low lighting, Lili's Bistro is a comfy spot for an intimate, relaxed dinner. The eclectic and underhyped menu features small plates like Gorgonzola fries and Thai-spiced dumplings, along with a decent selection of seafood and a whole section of creative vegetable plates. Make reservations on busy weekend nights.

MAP 9: 1310 W. Magnolia Ave., 817/877-0700, www.lilisbistro.com; Mon. 11am-2:30pm, Tues.-Thurs. 11am-2:30pm and 5pm-9:30pm, Fri.-Sat. 11am-2:30pm and 6pm-10pm

★ OL' SOUTH PANCAKE HOUSE $$

The best thing about Ol' South Pancake House? Any pancake, any time of day. After a long, red-eye flight, this 24-hour diner is a godsend. Known for its wide variety of pancakes, you can choose from buttermilk, buckwheat, or corn cakes, plus toppings. For something extra-sweet, the German pancake, or "Dutch baby," comes filled with lemon juice and powdered sugar. That's just one section of the huge menu. Don't be surprised if your server recommends an order of fried pickles at 5am (no thanks).

MAP 9: 1509 S. University Dr., 817/336-0311, www.olsouthpancakehouse.com; 24 hours

PARIS COFFEE SHOP $

This no-frills 90-year-old diner serves up a traditional hearty breakfast in huge portions. You can't go wrong with the reasonably priced combo special of eggs, hash browns, bacon or sausage, and biscuit or toast. The cheese grits reign as one of the most popular dishes, along with the homemade pies available on the lunch menu.

MAP 9: 704 W. Magnolia Ave., 817/335-2041, www.pariscoffeeshop.net; Mon.-Fri. 6am-2:30pm, Sat. 6am-11am

MEXICAN

HOT DAMN, TAMALES! $$

After its initial success as a strictly vegan and vegetarian tamale company, Hot Damn, Tamales! added meat to the menu. It now offers up to 16 lard-free varieties of the Mexican food staple, including beef slow-roasted with Shiner Bock and jalapenos, and barbecue brisket inspired by Angelo's BBQ, a Fort Worth favorite. Its vegan beginnings gave birth to some offbeat options like the Greek tamale made with spinach, feta, and kalamata olives; and the wild mushroom and goat cheese tamale with chipotle peppers.

MAP 9: 713 W. Magnolia Ave., 817/523-1836, www.hotdamntamales.com; Mon.-Thurs. 11am-7pm, Fri.-Sat. 11am-8pm, Sun. 11am-4pm

YUCATAN TACO STAND $$

As its name suggests, this corner restaurant specializes in flavors from the Yucatan region of Latin America (although it is, in fact, a brick-and-mortar building, not a taco stand). The standout dish isn't even a taco: It's the tenderloin tamale wrapped in banana leaf, or the yucca fries with aioli sauce, or the nachos piled high with three kinds of cheese, purple cabbage, lettuce, tomatoes, red onions, jalapenos, sour cream, and guacamole.

MAP 9: 909 W. Magnolia Ave., 817/924-8646, www.yucatantacostand.com; Mon.-Thurs. 11am-10pm, Fri. 11am-midnight, Sat. 10am-midnight, Sun. 10am-10pm

MIDDLE EASTERN

CHADRA MEZZA & GRILL $$

The Southside is home to some great Middle Eastern fare. The $10 lunch buffet at Chadra Mezza & Grill doesn't disappoint with its wide selection of meat and vegetarian dishes, including salads, hummus, and kebabs. You could gorge on the garlic knots all day. The drink menu includes Lebanese sodas and Turkish coffee along with local craft beer, wine, and cocktails.

MAP 9: 1622 Park Place Ave., 817/924-2372, www.chadramezza.com; Mon.-Tues. 11am-3pm, Wed.-Sat. 11am-10pm

DESSERT

★ FUNKYTOWN DONUTS $

Someone somewhere decided to put bacon on top of a glazed doughnut, and since then the traditionally basic morning pastry has been supercharged with Butterfinger pieces, potato chips, and edible glitter. The family-owned FunkyTown Donuts embraces the trend with its made-from-scratch dough and glazes. Flavors of the day might include a glazed doughnut topped with

Fruity Pebbles and Pop Rocks, or a blackberry lemonade glaze with fresh blackberries and lemon zest. Purists needn't worry; there are still plain old glazed, chocolate, and sprinkles, too.

MAP 9: 1000 8th Ave., Suite 101, 817/862-9750, www.funkytowndonuts.com; Tues.-Sat. 6am-1pm, Sun. 8am-1pm

MELT $

It doesn't get more local than Melt, an adorable ice cream shop that partners with an array of Fort Worth purveyors. Key ingredients include doughnuts from Blue Bonnet Bakery for the coffee-and-doughnut ice cream; a black lager from Rahr & Sons Brewing Company to make dark chocolate fudge; and cookies, pies, and brownies from Stir Crazy Baked Goods. Melt's own creations are made from scratch, resulting in impressive rotating flavors like lavender honey, coconut mint, and miso pecan butterscotch.

MAP 9: 1201 W. Magnolia Ave., Suite 115, 817/886-8365, www.melticecreams.com; Tues.-Thurs. noon-10pm, Fri.-Sat. noon-11pm, Sun. noon-10pm

COFFEE

AVOCA COFFEE $

Roasting its own coffee beans in-house, Avoca has become one of the best places in Fort Worth for a caffeine buzz. It has a spacious interior with exposed ductwork, but unlike many hip, artisanal coffee shops, Avoca maintains a cozy and unpretentious atmosphere. If you don't make it into the shop, look for Avoca at other local stores and restaurants. It's also sold at Whole Foods and Central Market. Each bag includes information about where the beans are sourced (mostly Africa and Latin America) and at what altitude, along with a detailed description of the flavor profile.

MAP 9: 1311 W. Magnolia Ave., 682/233-0957, www.avocacoffee.com; Mon.-Sat. 7am-10pm, Sun. 7am-6pm

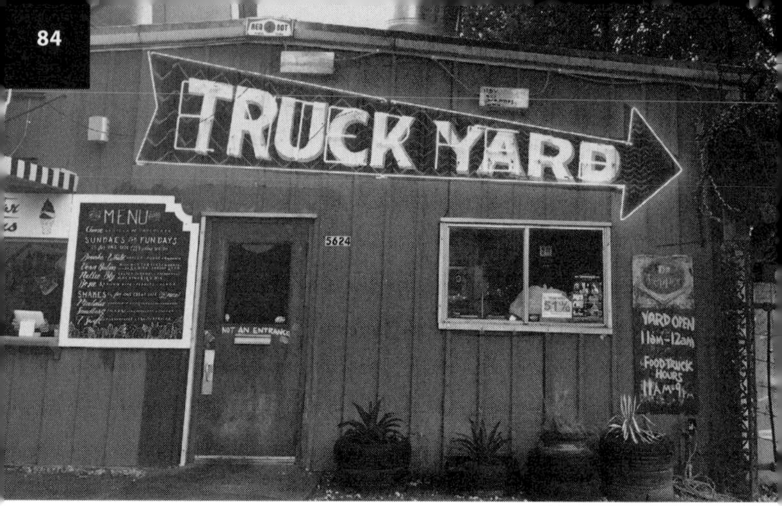
TRUCK YARD
MENU
5624
NOT AN ENTRANCE
YARD OPEN
11am-12am
FOOD TRUCK HOURS

Nightlife

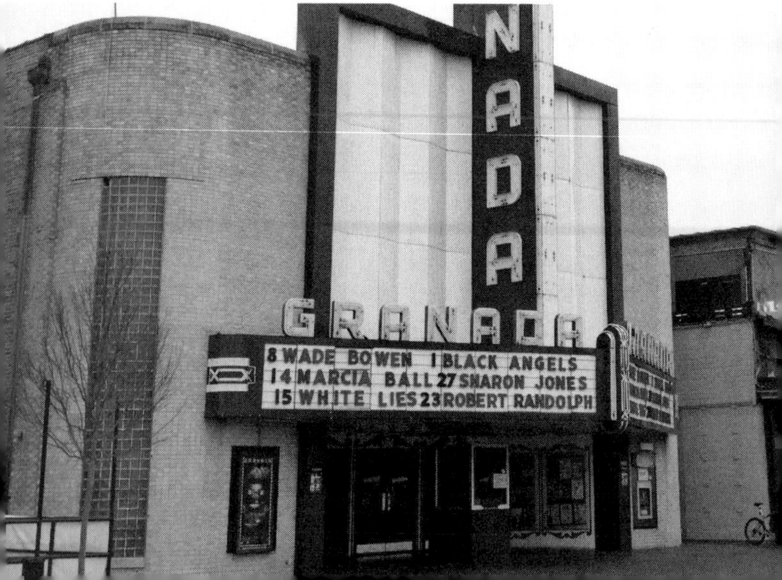
GRANADA
8 WADE BOWEN 1 BLACK ANGELS
14 MARCIA BALL 27 SHARON JONES
15 WHITE LIES 23 ROBERT RANDOLPH

Nightlife in Dallas and Fort Worth runs the gamut, from country-western dance clubs in The Stockyards to basement jazz lounges in Sundance Square to local sketch comedy in Deep Ellum. Quality craft brews and artful cocktails abound at these after-dark establishments.

Deep Ellum draws huge crowds of discerning music lovers almost every night. Sounds of punk rock, New Orleans jazz, hip-hop beats and everything in between fill the streets of Main and Elm. You'll find dingy dive bars, breezy rooftop patios, classy cocktail dens, and warehouse dance floors. Parking isn't easy, so opt for public transit or a rideshare app. The place is crawling with Ubers.

The LGBT community is concentrated in Oak Lawn just north of Downtown Dallas. The walkable Strip on Cedar Springs is lined with long-time dance clubs featuring professional drag shows along with eclectic DJs. Options are more limited and sparse elsewhere in the region. The nearby Uptown neighborhood features swankier establishments and refined sports bars that attract high-earning young professionals. The free McKinney Avenue Trolley makes barhopping safe and easy.

For the quintessential country-western experience, Billy Bob's Texas is a must. Billed as "the world's largest honky-tonk," it has expansive dance floors, bull riding (both mechanical and real) and big-name musical acts. At the other end of the spectrum, Fort Worth is home to low-key jazz lounges, comedy clubs and bars featuring more intimate live music stages.

The wide range of nightlife in Dallas-Fort Worth is just more proof of the region's diversity.

Previous: Truck Yard; The Granada anchors the Lower Greenville area.

Look for ★ to find recommended Nightlife

Highlights

★ **Best Restored Music Venue:** A multi-million-dollar redesign brought the **Bomb Factory** back to its former 1990s glory as the heart the Deep Ellum music scene (page 88).

★ **Best Laughs:** For inexpensive amusement, off-the-wall improv shows run several nights a week at **Dallas Comedy House** (page 89).

★ **Best Patio:** Picnic tables, lawn chairs, a tree house and trailers peddling booze and tacos make the **Truck Yard** perfect on a summer night (page 91).

★ **Best Gay Club:** Well-established in the Oak Lawn gay scene, **Station 4** features multi-level dance floors and one of the best drag shows in town (page 93).

★ **Best Speakeasy:** Beneath the bustling Downtown Fort Worth streetscape, you'll find **Scat Jazz Lounge,** a 1920s time capsule with live jazz music every night (page 96).

★ **World's Largest Honky-Tonk:** Serving as home base for touring country music icons, **Billy Bob's Texas** features 30 bars and 100,000 square feet with ample space for two-stepping and bull-riding (page 98).

★ **Best Craft Beer:** A fixture of Fort Worth's revitalized Magnolia Avenue, the **Bearded Lady** serves rotating taps of local craft beers found only in DFW (page 99).

Downtown Dallas

Map 1

BARS

ANGRY DOG

Open since 1990, this Deep Ellum dive has seen the neighborhood change dramatically over the past couple of decades. Trendy restaurants and bars have come and gone, but Angry Dog's longevity makes it one of the most reliable (and reasonably priced) spots to have a drink and some of the best late-night bar food in town. You'll find more than 20 beers on tap, along with gourmet burgers and wings.

MAP 1: 2726 Commerce St., 214/741-4406, www.angrydog.com; Mon.-Thurs. 11am-midnight, Fri.-Sat. 11am-2am

BLACK SWAN SALOON

You might walk past this hidden bar a few times before wandering inside. Black Swan Saloon's brick façade has no signage but still manages to draw huge crowds on weekends. As evidenced by the endless array of liquors behind the bar, the focus here is artisan cocktails. Pick your poison, and the mixologist will whip up a better version of your favorite drink.

MAP 1: 2708 Elm St., 214/749-4848; Tues.-Sun. 7pm-2am

DOUBLE WIDE

Located on the eastern end of Commerce Street, Double Wide occupies its own corner away from the Deep Ellum barhoppers. This "trashy" dive attracts more of a neighborhood crowd; everyone here seems to know each other. On weekends, the bar hosts an eclectic lineup of live music from metal to Motown and reggae to punk rock.

MAP 1: 3510 Commerce St., 214/887-6510, www.double-wide.com; Mon.-Fri. 5pm-2am, Sat.-Sun. 7pm-2am

OFF THE RECORD

The small vinyl collection is mostly just for show at this bar/record store, but it's enough to spark conversations among music lovers. Off the Record, which specializes in local craft beer, feels bright and spacious compared to other dark Deep Ellum haunts. Live DJs spin a range of genres on any given night, including hip-hop, soul, and techno.

MAP 1: 2716 Elm St., 214/745-1402; Mon.-Fri. 5pm-2am, Sat.-Sun. noon-2am

TRUTH & ALIBI

You might wonder why the "Original Deep Ellum Candy Company" is never open during the day. That's because it's not an old-fashioned candy store; it's a glamorous, password-protected nightclub. Although Truth & Alibi doesn't quite fit into the neighborhood's gritty vibe, it offers an experience all its own with its dim purple lighting, velvet couches, and vintage décor. You can reserve a table in advance and find the password on the club's Facebook page.

MAP 1: 2618 Elm St., www.thruthandalibi.com; Thurs.-Sat. 9pm-2am

TWILITE LOUNGE

With glowing chandeliers and a jukebox full of old jazz, country, and soul music, Twilite Lounge has a vintage yet polished vibe. It's particularly pleasant early in the evenings before the noisy nightlife invades the spacious bar. The small stage hosts live music, and the large patio features TV screens in heavy use during football season.

MAP 1: 2640 Elm St., 214/741-2121, www.thetwilitelounge.com; Mon.-Fri. 4pm-2am, Sat.-Sun. noon-2am

LIVE MUSIC

All Genres

★ THE BOMB FACTORY

This early-20th-century building manufactured bombs and ammo during World War II. Now, the Bomb Factory is a legendary Deep Ellum music venue. The 50,000-square-foot space peaked during the 1990s, hosting bands like Radiohead, Sonic Youth, the Ramones, and Fugazi. It recently underwent a multimillion-dollar renovation and made a dramatic return to the music scene in 2015. Thousands of concertgoers still flood the massive floor for '90s icons as well as current indie rock and hip-hop. You can splurge on balcony tickets for excellent views of the performers and the venue. If you get hungry, Wiles Barbecue is usually smoking meats on-site at most shows.

MAP 1: 2713 Canton St., 214/932-6501, www.thebombfactory.com; hours vary

CLUB DADA

This intimate, standing-room-only venue books mostly small acts under $20 a ticket, as well as some bigger-name performers with cult followings. While the venue is tiny, the back patio is huge—a great place to grab some fresh air and a drink during a packed show.

MAP 1: 2720 Elm St., 214/748-5150, www.dadadallas.com; hours vary

TREES

Owned by the team behind the Bomb Factory, Trees is another survivor of Deep Ellum's 1990s heyday. Its neon green sign has beckoned music fans for decades, making it one of the most well-known venues in the city. Trees is perhaps most remembered for Kurt Cobain's infamous brawl with a security guard during a sold-out Nirvana show in 1991. The club closed in 2005 and, after renovations, reopened four years later.

MAP 1: 2709 Elm St., 214/741-1122, www.treesdallas.com; doors open at 7pm

THREE LINKS

This open garage-turned-bar offers quite the spectacle for passersby, with live music blaring from the stage inside throughout the week. The curious art and décor at Three Links pays tribute to the Independent Order of Odd Fellows, of which the owners are members.

MAP 1: 2704 Elm St., 214/653-8228, www.threelinksdeepellum.com; Mon.-Thurs. 2pm-2am, Fri.-Sun. 11am-2am

Honky-Tonk

ADAIR'S SALOON

This dim and hazy honky-tonk is a Deep Ellum institution, known for its live old-school country music, blues, and everything in between. The most memorable feature at Adair's is probably the Sharpie marks completely covering walls and furniture. The saloon has been open since the 1980s, so there's bound to be stories in there somewhere. Don't leave without trying the gourmet (yet inexpensive) hamburger.

MAP 1: 2624 Commerce St., 214/939-9900, www.adairssaloon.com; Mon.-Sat. 11am-2am, Sun. noon-2am

DANCE CLUBS

THE CHURCH

Located inside an old trolley car repair station built in 1899, this dark, industrial-style nightclub offers a different kind of vibe. The venue brings out the Goths and misfits, featuring two kinds of DJs in two rooms. The rooftop patio provides a beautiful view of the downtown Dallas skyline. Arrive early for $3 well drinks until 11pm.

MAP 1: 2424 Swiss Ave., 214/826-4768, www.thechurchdallas.com; Thurs. and Sun. 9pm-2am

COMEDY CLUBS

★ DALLAS COMEDY HOUSE

With live shows nearly every night of the week, the Dallas Comedy House showcases mostly improv and sketch along with some stand-up acts from local and touring comedians. The shows are adult-themed, except for the family-friendly comedy show on Saturdays at 6pm. If you're feeling more adventurous, the club offers a free improv class on the last Wednesday of every month at its training center where its performers cut their teeth.

MAP 1: 3025 Main St., 214/741-4448, www.dallascomedyhouse.com; hours vary

Lakewood/East Dallas

Map 2

BARS

THE BALCONY CLUB

Tucked above the historic Lakewood Theatre, the Balcony Club features live jazz music every night in an intimate lounge that feels like someone's 1920s living room. The art deco details mirror those of the nearly 80-year-old movie palace below. The theater recently became an official Dallas landmark but remains closed as a venue. Meanwhile, the upstairs Balcony Club, open since 1988, presses on while attracting a mostly over-30 crowd. Arrive early for a good seat in the tiny, speakeasy-style den.

MAP 2: 1825 Abrams Rd., 214/826-8104, www.balconyclub.com; daily 5pm-2am; $5 cover Fri.-Sat., free Sun.-Thurs.

BARCADIA

Part bar, part arcade, this late-night spot emanates with vintage video game nostalgia. You'll find old-school games like Ms. Pacman, Frogger, Mario Bros., Donkey Kong, Space Invaders, and more, along with Skee-Ball and life-sized Jenga on the patio. Barcadia also boasts a wide selection of craft beers and ciders.

MAP 2: 1917 N. Henderson Ave., 214/821-7300, www.barcadiabars.com/barcadiadallas; Mon.-Thurs. 4pm-2am, Fri.-Sat. 3pm-2am, Sun. 11am-2am

THE GOAT

This White Rock Lake-area bar is rather ordinary, except for its blues jam sessions and karaoke nights. Stop by at 10pm Monday or Thursday to see professionals perform and at 9pm Sunday for less-than-perfect renditions of the oldies. The drinks are cheap and strong, and the bartenders start serving bright and early at 7am.

MAP 2: 7248 Gaston Ave., 214/327-8119, www.thegoatdallas.com; Mon.-Sat. 7am-2am, Sun. noon-2am

LAKEWOOD LANDING

The dark and cozy Lakewood Landing has all the necessary trappings of a true neighborhood dive: wood-paneled walls, worn-out sofas, snarky bartenders, and a jukebox full of every kind of great music, from Willie Nelson to David Bowie. The wall-to-wall memorabilia pays tribute to decades of regulars, including the beloved barkeep Lucille, who poured drinks there for over 30 years. Come hungry; the kitchen serves one of the best burgers in town.

MAP 2: 5818 Live Oak St., 214/823-2410; daily 3pm-2am

SHIPS LOUNGE

There isn't anything quite like Ships. The 70-year-old, nautical-themed dive bar recently closed and reopened under new management. Besides the updated plumbing and nixing of the BYOL (bring your own liquor) policy, the iconic Dallas bar has remained much the same. The quiet, unpretentious, cash-only dive draws an old, long-standing clientele with jukebox tunes to match it.

MAP 2: 1613 Greenville Ave., 972/707-7234, www.shipslounge.com; Mon.-Sat. 10am-midnight, Sun. noon-midnight

★ TRUCK YARD

During patio season, Truck Yard's trashy-hipster vibe attracts constant crowds to its huge outdoor space, accented with vintage beat-up trucks, old lawn chairs, and other junkyard accessories. The "tree house" balcony is the most coveted spot to enjoy a local craft beer. Rotating food trucks park at the back of the patio, and there's live music on the weekends.

MAP 2: 5624 Sears St., 469/500-0139, www.texastruckyard.com; daily 11am-midnight

LIVE MUSIC

Rock

THE GRANADA

Built in 1946 as a movie theater, and renovated in 2004 as a music venue, the Granada is a fixture of Lower Greenville Avenue. The space contains a standing-room-only floor, balcony seating, and an art deco interior adorned with a massive mural of a mythological goddess. The theater books big-name acts and obscure indie bands in mostly rock, blues, and country genres. Sundown at Granada next door is great for a pre- or post-concert dinner, serving a local, farm-to-table menu.

MAP 2: 3524 Greenville Ave., 214/824-9933, www.granadatheater.com

DANCE CLUBS

BEAUTY BAR

On weekends, this glammed-up, salon-style club is so packed you'll spend most of the night inching your way through dancing bodies to find anything—the bar, the restrooms, or the patio. Still, it's where the bar-hopping hipsters of Henderson Avenue end up by closing time to catch some of the city's best DJs.

MAP 2: 1924 Henderson Ave., 214/841-9600, www.thebeautybar.com; Tues., Wed., and Sat. 7pm-2am, Thurs.-Fri. 4pm-2am

IT'LL DO CLUB

People go to It'll Do Club to do one thing: dance. True to its name, the small club consists of a colorful, light-up dance floor, a local DJ, and not much else. There's also a special family-friendly event, Disco Kids, every other Friday night where parents can bring their kiddos out dancing.

MAP 2: 4322 Elm St., 214/827-7236; Sat. 10pm-2am

Uptown

BARS

BOWEN HOUSE

Bowen House dispels the unfortunate myth that Uptown's nightlife is obnoxious and superficial. Built 1874, the Victorian-style house is a cozy time capsule updated with a subtly modern vibe—an ideal spot for a fancy cocktail. The top-notch mixologists create innovative drinks from fresh ingredients.

MAP 3: 2614 Boll St., 214/484-1385, www.bowenhousetx.com; Sun.-Tues. 4pm-midnight, Wed.-Sat. 4pm-2am

BOWLOUNGE

After 9pm on weekends, this vintage bowling alley turns into a 21-and-up late-night lounge. The 12 wooden lanes and first-generation electronic scoring system were salvaged from an old bowling alley in East Texas and moved to the Dallas Design District to create Bowlounge's fun, retro vibe. Bowling rates are $6.80 per game per person, plus $2.75 shoe rentals. The full bar has 40 beers on tap, and the restaurant serves dishes that are far superior to your typical bowling alley fare—including some nostalgic frozen treats like Lemon Chills and Bomb Pops.

MAP 3: 167 Turtle Creek Blvd., 214/741-7737, www.bowlounge.com; Sun.-Thurs. 11am-midnight, Fri.-Sat. 11am-2am

KATY TRAIL ICE HOUSE

The runners, cyclists, puppies, and other colorful characters of the Katy Trail all funnel into this popular bar. Katy Trail Ice House features a huge communal patio perfect for people watching. There are plenty of shade trees and misting fans to keep the place cool during the summer, and several heaters and fire pits to get through Dallas's brief winter. Plus, there's nothing better than throwing back a craft beer and a half-pound burger after a good workout. Expect things to get rowdy when the Cowboys are playing, or if the Highland Park High School football team makes the playoffs.

MAP 3: 3127 Routh St., 214/468-0600, www.katyicehouse.com; Mon.-Fri. 11am-2am, Sat.-Sun. 10am-2am

GAY AND LESBIAN

GRAPEVINE BAR

This kitschy yet comfy dive doesn't seem to carry the label of "gay bar," based on its diverse crowd. It's a nice, laid-back spot for pool and cheap drinks. There's also a small basketball court outside where people often play a pickup game. Climb a set of steep wooden stairs to the rooftop patio, which offers a good-enough view of the Dallas skyline.

MAP 3: 3902 Maple Ave., 214/522-8466, www.grapevinebar.com; Mon.-Sat. 3pm-2am, Sun. 1pm-2am

ROUND-UP SALOON

For almost 35 years, the Round-up Saloon has embraced country-and-western culture. Although here, there are tighter jeans and fewer shirts. A fixture of the Dallas LGBT scene, the club draws a mixed crowd—young and old, gay and straight. Besides country, you'll hear a variety of dance music. In fact, Lady Gaga has been known to stop here during her tours through Dallas, having performed here before she became famous. Of the club's six bars, make your way up to the Horseshoe Bar; it's quicker, less crowded, and offers a nice overlook of the dance floor.

MAP 3: 3912 Cedar Springs Rd., 214/522-9611, www.roundupsaloon.com; Mon.-Fri. 3pm-2am, Sat.-Sun. noon-2am

★ STATION 4

Known by its patrons as simply S4, this huge multilevel nightclub covers 24,000 square feet, including an expansive patio for when you need a breather from the crowded, laser-filled dance floor. The best thing about S4 is its weekly drag shows—perhaps the finest you'll see in Dallas. Performers like Cassie Nova are local celebrities. Shows begin at 11pm and 12:30am Friday, Saturday, and Sunday in the club's Rose Room upstairs.

MAP 3: 3911 Cedar Springs Rd., 214/526-7171, www.station4dallas.com; Thurs.-Sun. 8pm-4am

West Dallas/Oak Cliff Map 5

BARS

BARBARA'S PAVILLION

Hidden on a nondescript side street, this gay dive bar draws a mixed crowd of locals. The bartenders will know you're a newbie and offer a warm welcome. The dark, retro-mod ambience and colored lights set the stage for some killer karaoke—the kind you can actually enjoy. The regulars have serious talent, belting out heartfelt '80s ballads and high-energy pop songs. Don't worry, though: They can still accommodate the drunken butchering of beloved tunes. Catch karaoke on Thursday and Saturday nights.

MAP 5: 325 Centre St., 214/941-2145; daily 4pm-2am

THE FOUNDRY

As the family crowds at Chicken Scratch thin out, the adults start settling in at the Foundry, which shares the lot. This laid-back bar is known for its large courtyard adorned with string lights and old shipping containers converted into seating areas. The outdoor stage, built from hundreds of artfully arranged wooden pallets, hosts an eclectic variety of live music on the weekends, from alternative rock to big band ensembles.

MAP 5: 2303 Pittman St., 214/749-1112, www.cs-tf.com; Mon.-Fri. 4pm-2am, Sat.-Sun. noon-2am

Top: Truck Yard's patio and door; **Bottom:** Hayes Carll performs at Billy Bob's Texas.

NOVA

Only an offbeat establishment like Nova would have pizza, ribs, enchiladas, and pho all on the same menu. The mid-century modern gastropub places special attention on food (served until midnight), but it's primarily a late-night neighborhood bar. You'll find a wide range of cocktails like vodka with fresh berries and thyme, or tequila with pineapple juice and ginger beer, along with craft brews on tap.

MAP 5: 1417 W. Davis St., 214/484-7123, www.novadallas.com; Mon.-Sun. 4pm-2am

PARKER BARROWS

Named for Dallas's notorious Depression-era outlaws, Bonnie Parker and Clyde Barrow, this speakeasy-themed bar and deli recently took over a prominent corner of the Bishop Arts District, becoming one of the area's only signs of life after midnight. The barkeep makes an outstanding old-fashioned, and the tap list features local craft beer selections you don't often see. One drawback, though, is the loud atmosphere, which makes conversation difficult.

MAP 5: 338 W. Davis St., 214/943-1269; daily 11am-2am

SMALL BREWPUB

This airy Jefferson Boulevard bar brews its own beer in small batches with 10 rotating drafts. You'll also find Lonestar on tap along with creative cocktails. Small Brewpub is a great spot to chill before a movie or event at the nearby Texas Theatre.

MAP 5: 333 W. Jefferson Blvd., 972/863-1594, www.smallbrewpub.com; Tues.-Sat. 4pm-midnight

Downtown Fort Worth — Map 6

BARS

FLYING SAUCER

Flying Saucer is heaven for beer lovers looking to try something new. Its endless row of taps extends down the entire bar, with a selection representing nearly all 50 states. The patio has large picnic tables ideal for group outings. The bar features live music on the outdoor stage and hosts lots of offbeat events like the paper football tournament. Stop by on a Sunday when Texas pints are only $3 all day.

MAP 6: 111 E. 3rd St., 817/336-7470, www.beerknurd.com; Mon.-Thurs. 11am-1am, Fri.-Sat. 11am-2am, Sun. noon-midnight

LOUNGES

SILVER LEAF CIGAR LOUNGE

Here, you can catch the comforting aroma of cigars without sitting in a thick cloud of smoke. Silver Leaf Cigar Lounge features an air filtering system that keeps the place well ventilated, so your nonsmoking friends won't mind tagging along and sharing a bottle of wine. There's an extensive list of cigars, plus a large walk-in humidor. If a dark, smoky hideout is what you're looking for, however, Silver Leaf may disappoint with its bright and modern ambience.

MAP 6: 426 Commerce St., 817/887-9535, www.silverleafcigar.com; Sun.-Thurs. 10am-midnight, Fri.-Sat. 10am-2am

LIVE MUSIC

Jazz

★ SCAT JAZZ LOUNGE

Peek into the narrow alley behind Simply Fondue, and look for the neon sign pointing the way down into the basement of the historic Woolworth Building. Scat Jazz Lounge re-creates the dark, speakeasy vibe of the 1920s and manages to avoid the kitsch. With its art deco curves and minimal indoor signage, the lounge feels like a secret hangout for jazz lovers. Local and touring bands perform every night. That includes the free Black Dog Jam every Sunday, one of the city's longest-running weekly shows.

MAP 6: 111 W. 4th St., Suite 11, 817/870-9100, www.scatjazzlounge.com; Tues.-Thurs. 7pm-2am, Fri. 5pm-2am, Sat. 6pm-2am, Sun. 7pm-2am

COMEDY CLUBS

FOUR DAY WEEKEND

Every Friday and Saturday, the comedy troupe Four Day Weekend performs an off-the-wall improv show based on audience suggestions. The 7:30pm act is usually pretty clean while the 10pm version gets a little edgier. Even after 20 years, shows still sell out almost every weekend, so buy tickets in advance. Eat dinner before you go, too, because the club does not serve food. On the upside, there's no drink minimum like at most comedy clubs.

MAP 6: 312 Houston St., 817/226-4329, www.fourdayweekend.com; Fri-Sat. 7:30pm and 10pm; $20

HYENA'S COMEDY CLUB

While Four Day Weekend is strictly improv, Hyena's Comedy Club is where you'll find stand-up comedians spitting jokes in front of a redbrick wall. The club hosts local and nationally touring comedians who perform several shows in a weekend. Thursday nights are free.

MAP 6: 425 Commerce St., 817/877-5233, www.hyenascomedynightclub.com; Thurs. 8:30pm, Fri. 8:30pm and 10:30pm, Sat. 8pm and 10:30pm, $12

West Fort Worth

Map 7

BARS

THE ABBEY PUB

This classic Irish pub has TVs mounted throughout the bar, making it a popular spot to watch sports—especially soccer. Aside from World Cup season, the bar never seems to get too noisy for decent conversation over a nice craft beer. There's no food menu, but you can order tacos or Greek food delivered from the restaurants next door.

MAP 7: 2710 W. 7th St., 817/810-9930, www.abbey-pub.com; daily 3pm-2am

DANCE CLUBS

FORT WORTH SWING DANCE SYNDICATE

If you find yourself restless on a Thursday night, drop by a beginner swing dancing class held 8pm-9pm each week at this local nonprofit. After an hour-long $7 lesson, stick around for the social dance 9pm-11:30pm to practice your moves while a DJ spins tunes.

MAP 7: 1300 Gendy St., 817/738-1938, www.fwsds.org; Mon.-Fri. 9am-5pm, Sat. 10am-5pm; Thurs. 8-11:30pm

LIVE MUSIC

Rock/Country

CAPITAL BAR

The $1.50 PBRs at Capital Bar are a magnet for the college-aged crowd. The venue features a laid-back rooftop patio with a view of the Fort Worth skyline. The dance floor and outdoor stage host local country and party bands most nights of the week, so you can avoid the weekend rush and cover charge.

MAP 7: 3017 Morton St., 817/820-0049, www.capital-bar.com; daily 4pm-2am

MAGNOLIA MOTOR LOUNGE

For an Americana, acoustic vibe, Magnolia Motor Lounge has a decent lineup every night in its indoor-outdoor, garage-like setting. The bar also tends to bring out a wider age range, so if you're trying to avoid drunken college kids, Magnolia is a good bet. Plus, the appetizers, sandwiches, and burgers are a step above your typical bar food.

MAP 7: 2005 Morton St., 817/332-3344, www.mmlbar.com; Mon.-Sat. 11am-2am, Sun. 10:30am-2am

LOLA'S SALOON

The gritty trailer park ambience is what locals love about Lola's. The intimate venue books a range of genres, including indie rock, folk, punk, and electronic. It opened in 2007, filling a hole left by the Wreck Room, a pioneer of today's Fort Worth music scene. One of this dive bar's drawbacks is that you can smoke inside, but the bathrooms are surprisingly clean.

MAP 7: 2736 W. 6th St., 817/877-0666, www.lolassaloon.com; Mon.-Fri. 2pm-2am, Sat.-Sun. noon-2am

Northside

Map 8

LIVE MUSIC

★ BILLY BOB'S TEXAS

This massive honky-tonk isn't the most historic venue in Fort Worth, but it might be the most famous. Since its opening weekend 35 years ago, Billy Bob's has hosted country music legends like Willie Nelson, Waylon Jennings, and George Jones, along with every star that rose thereafter. The concrete Wall of Fame immortalizes them with their handprints—everyone from Johnny Cash and Conway Twitty to Gretchen Wilson and Miranda Lambert. Billy Bob's 100,000 square feet includes 30 individual bars, bull riding, and a huge dance floor. If you're feeling insecure about your honky-tonk skills, swing by at 7pm on a Thursday night for free line-dancing lessons.

MAP 8: 2520 Rodeo Plaza, 817/624-7117, www.billybobstexas.com; Mon.-Tues. 11am-10pm, Wed. 11am-10:30pm, Thurs. 11am-10pm, Fri.-Sat. 11am-2am, Sun. noon-10pm

THE BASEMENT BAR

A neon sign directs visitors downstairs below Star Café to what is cheekily called "the world's smallest honky-tonk," in response to the massive Billy Bob's nearby. The not-so-Stockyards-y Basement Bar hosts a more eclectic mix of live music and DJs every Friday and Saturday night. It's a cheap, dark, and smoke-filled dive.

MAP 8: 105 W. Exchange Ave., 817/624-2770, www.the-basementbar.com; Mon.-Thurs. 3pm-2am, Fri.-Sun. noon-2am

THE THIRSTY ARMADILLO

Established in 1990, this live music mainstay offers one of the best windows into the Texas music scene. The Thirsty Armadillo has seen the beginnings of several country music careers, claiming homegrown acts like Casey Donahew, Eli Young, and Randy Rogers, who all got their starts on the Stockyards-area stage.

MAP 8: 120 W. Exchange Ave., 817/624-2770, www.thirstyarmadillo.biz; Fri. 7pm-2am, Sat.-Sun. 3pm-2am

WHISKEY GIRL SALOON

Known for hosting some of the best local music in town, Whiskey Girl Saloon features an indoor stage and dance floor, and a few tables and chairs. The place can get pretty cramped on a Saturday night, so expect limited personal space. The drinks here are decently priced compared to other Stockyards hotspots.

MAP 8: 2413 Ellis Ave., 817/945-2055; Wed.-Sat. 7pm-2am, Sun. 4pm-2am

Southside/TCU

Map 9

BARS

★ THE BEARDED LADY

Set inside a Craftsman-style house with minimal signage, it's easy to miss this late-night haunt. The Bearded Lady is known for its craft beer selection, featuring brews from around the country but with some extra attention paid to the local industry. Most draughts are from Texas breweries, many of them in Dallas and Fort Worth. The warm, homey atmosphere accommodates chatty groups right alongside the workaholic on a laptop.

MAP 9: 1229 7th Ave., 817/349-9832; Tues.-Sat. 11am-2am, Sun. 11am-midnight

CHIMERA BREWING COMPANY

You won't find an endless row of beers on tap at this local brewery, but what's here is top-notch. About 4 of the 16 taps are brewed in-house while the rest are carefully selected from other local and national craft breweries. Soccer fans can count on seeing England's Chelsea F.C. matches broadcast on the bar's flat-screen TVs. Find your way back to the bar in the morning to feast on crab cake eggs Benedict.

MAP 9: 1001 W. Magnolia Ave., 817/923-8000, www.chimerabrew.com; Mon.-Fri. 11:30am-midnight, Sat. 10am-midnight, Sun. 10am-10pm

LIVE MUSIC

Alternative Rock

THE AARDVARK

If you don't mind mingling with a rowdy college crowd, the Aardvark hosts an interesting lineup of local live music near the TCU campus. One of the regulars, Holy Moly, plays something called "cowpunk," a genre that mixes country and punk. In years past, the bar has claimed some bigger names, too, like Bowling for Soup and Cross Canadian Ragweed.

MAP 9: 2905 W. Berry St., 817/926-7814, www.the-aardvark.com; Tues.-Sun. 11am-2am, Mon. 6pm-2am

Rock, Blues, and Jazz

SHIPPING AND RECEIVING BAR

Located in an old, nondescript warehouse building, Shipping and Receiving features an eclectic lineup of musicians with an underground vibe. Local bands perform on a small outdoor stage in front of a large patio with communal seating. Jazz ensembles take the stage every Thursday night. The rest of the week you'll hear everything from blues to trap music.

MAP 9: 201 S. Calhoun St., 817/887-9313, www.shippingandreceiving.bar; Mon.-Wed. 4pm-midnight, Thurs.-Fri. 4pm-2am, Sat. 2pm-2am, Sun. 2pm-midnight

Arts and Culture

Nothing squashes Dallas stereotypes more than the city's robust arts scene. Spanning 19 acres through the heart of downtown, the Dallas Arts District is the largest contiguous arts district in the country.

Wealthy collectors helped thrust Dallas into the international spotlight decades ago. In fact, major museums grew from the private collections of prominent real estate moguls like Raymond and Patsy Nasher of the Nasher Sculpture Center; and Trammel and Margaret Crow of the Crow Collection of Asian Art. The beginnings of the Dallas Museum of Art date back more than a century when the city's earliest cultural leaders formed the Dallas Arts Association, holding exhibits at the public library. The museum has since amassed thousands of significant pieces along with a $200 million endowment to become a pillar of the Dallas arts community.

The scene is as diverse as it is large. Performing arts far outnumber visual arts, featuring a variety of beautifully designed venues hosting a wide range of companies. The Dallas Symphony Orchestra's powerful sound fills an intimate shoebox-style concert hall inside the Meyerson Symphony Center while the 40-year-old Dallas Black Dance Theatre brings its energetic choreography to stages all over the city.

In addition, the Dallas arts scene is incredibly accessible. Many museums have free admission, public transportation is a breeze, and it's all centered around a vibrant community park built over a former freeway deck.

The Fort Worth Cultural District is just as impressive. The Kimbell Art Museum, renowned for its Louis Khan-designed building, houses a rare Michelangelo painting along with Piscassos, Monets, and other big names. American art is left to the Amon Carter Museum, and post-World War II works fill the Modern Art Museum of Fort Worth, creating a harmonious balance of art and culture throughout the district.

Previous: Dallas Museum of Art; Perot Museum of Nature and Science

Highlights

Dallas Museum of Art

★ **Best Bang for Your Buck:** Admission to the **Dallas Museum of Art** is always free, which makes viewing the nearly 4,000-piece collection feel like a steal (page 103).

★ **Best Kid-Friendly Events:** The creative performances at the **Dallas Children's Theater** bring new life to traditional stories in ways that appeal to children and adults alike (page 106).

★ **Best Historic Art-House Cinema:** Built in the 1930s, the beautifully restored **Texas Theatre** screens curated selections for film aficionados in the space where Lee Harvey Oswald was apprehended (page 112).

★ **Best Performing Arts Center:** *Travel + Leisure* named **Bass Performance Hall** in Fort Worth one of the 10 best opera houses in the world when it opened 20 years ago—and it still lives up to the ranking (page 113).

★ **Best Art Museum:** At the **Kimbell Art Museum**, the building itself is a work of art, designed by Louis Khan, housing a small but significant collection of ancient and contemporary works (page 116).

Downtown Dallas

Map 1

MUSEUMS

CROW COLLECTION OF ASIAN ART

Stemming from the private collection of Dallas developer Trammel Crow, the Crow Collection of Asian Art features a sculpture garden and galleries full of ancient and contemporary artworks in a variety of mediums from China, Japan, India, and Southeast Asia. Besides the rotating exhibitions, the museum includes a focus on wellness, offering free yoga and meditation classes in the gallery.

MAP 1: 2010 Flora St., 214/979-6430, www.crowcollection.org; Tues.-Thurs. 10am-9pm, Fri.-Sat. 10am-6pm, Sun. noon-6pm; free

★ DALLAS MUSEUM OF ART

Ever since the Dallas Museum of Art switched to free admission, attendance has skyrocketed. One of the 10 largest art museums in the country, its permanent collection includes more than 24,000 pieces of art from all over the world. You could spend an entire day exploring each gallery, from contemporary American paintings to ancient African sculptures. You'll also find works by major artists like Rothko, Andy Warhol, and Van Gogh. The special exhibitions are usually worth the added admission fee, showing significant works rarely seen elsewhere in the country. Recently, the DMA featured Mexican modern art from icons like Diego Rivera and Frida Kahlo. A free guided tour of the museum is offered at 2pm Saturdays, and you can reserve a group tour in advance.

MAP 1: 1717 N. Harwood St., 214/922-1200, www.dma.org; Tues.-Wed. 11am-5pm, Thurs. 11am-9pm, Fri.-Sun. 11am-5pm; free

NASHER SCULPTURE CENTER

Across the street from the Dallas Museum of Art, the Nasher Sculpture Center houses more than 300 modern artworks, originating from the collection of local real estate magnates Raymond and Patsy Nasher. Several major artists are well represented. You'll find nine sculptures by Henri Matisse, seven by Pablo Picasso, and seven by Henry Moore. Spend plenty of time outside strolling the beautifully manicured grounds. The museum stays open late once a month for Til Midnight at the Nasher, where families can enjoy an outdoor concert and a movie screening.

MAP 1: 2001 Flora St., 214/242-5100, www.nashersculpturecenter.org; Tues.-Sun. 11am-5pm; adults $10, seniors and military $7, students $5, children under 12 and first responders free

PEROT MUSEUM OF NATURE AND SCIENCE

With its bold modern architecture that features a glass-enclosed escalator jutting out from the side of the building, the Perot Museum of Nature and Science is the most interesting structure you'll spot from Woodall Rodgers Freeway. The daring design is one clue that this is not your typical science

Arts After Dark

The only downside of a trip to the museum is planning your day around the 5 p.m. closing time. Museums are a daytime activity, but not always.

The **Dallas Museum of Art** hosts Late Nights on the third Friday of each month. The museum stays open until midnight, featuring special programs, concerts and tours in addition to the permanent collection. While admission to the DMA is usually free, Late Nights costs $15 per person, but you gain access to more than you would on a typical day.

In conjunction with the DMA next door, the **Nasher Sculpture Center** offers its own late-night event, 'til Midnight at The Nasher, with outdoor concerts, film screenings and live music. Bring a blanket to lounge on the lawn. Admission is free, but no outside food and drinks are allowed.

Each month, the **Perot Museum of Nature and Science** features Social Science, a 21-and-up night where adults can participate in experiments and enjoy thought-provoking discussions with a cocktail in hand. The event routinely sells out, so buy tickets ($25, www.perotmuseum.org) online as soon as possible.

museum. Dedicated to igniting kids' curiosities in STEM subjects, the museum gets children to participate in the exhibits, not just look at them. The 180,000-square-foot building includes 11 permanent exhibit halls with themed, hands-on activities. You can learn about the origins of the universe through an immersive multimedia experience, examine fossils and modern animal behavior, or design and build a robot. Teens can even don a lab coat, gloves, and goggles to perform real experiments, such as studying their own cheek cells.

The admission price is steep, but worth it if you carve out an entire day to explore the museum. Reserve tickets online in advance to avoid the long lines. Field trips clear out by 2:30pm on weekdays.

MAP 1: 2201 N. Field St., 214/428-5555, www.perotmuseum.org; Mon.-Sat. 10am-5pm, Sun. noon-5pm; adults $19, youth $12, seniors $13

PERFORMING ARTS

AT&T PERFORMING ARTS CENTER

This 10-acre artistic epicenter encompasses four major venues: Winspear Opera House, Wyly Theatre, Annette Strauss Square, and Sammons Park. Each has a distinct architectural design, from the red, ribbon-like rooftop of the Winspear to the stark vertical lines of the Wyly. The center's completion in 2009 signaled the birth of the Dallas Arts District, bringing the city's cultural powerhouses to one home. That home includes the Dallas Theater Center, Dallas Opera, Dallas Black Dance Theater, Texas Ballet Theater, and the Anita N. Martinez Ballet Folklorico.

MAP 1: 2403 Flora St., 214/880-0202, www.attpac.org

DALLAS CITY PERFORMANCE HALL

Smaller than its neighboring venues, the 750-seat proscenium theater at Dallas City Performance Hall provides an intimate experience with impeccable acoustics—whether you're absorbing each distinct sound of chamber orchestra or delighting in a one-man play. The modern architecture employs linear pavilions and a glass façade that seems to blend into the surrounding Arts District scene.

MAP 1: 2520 Flora St., 214/671-1450, www.dallasartsdistrict.org

MORTON H. MEYERSON SYMPHONY CENTER

Home to the Dallas Symphony Orchestra, the Meyerson Symphony Center boasts superior sound quality thanks to a design by acoustician Russell Johnson, who's engineered the world's finest concert halls. Although not used often enough, the massive Lay Family Organ serves as the stunning focal point, the largest of its 4,535 pipes reaching 32 feet. You can see the instrument in action during the spring Opus 100 organ series.

MAP 1: 2301 Flora St., 214/849-4376, www.mydso.com

CONCERT VENUES

ANNETTE STRAUSS SQUARE

Framed by skyscrapers but shielded from city noise, this laid-back open-air venue hosts concerts, theater performances, and other Dallas Arts District events. The pavilion's design incorporates patterns that are especially beautiful when illuminated at night. Strauss Square is the kind of place where no matter who is performing, the setting is reason enough to pack a blanket and chill on the lawn. Plus, it's BYOB.

MAP 1: 2403 Flora St., 214/880-0202, www.dallasartsdistrict.org

HOUSE OF BLUES DALLAS

Located in the historic White Swan industrial building constructed in 1925, the House of Blues hosts a wide range of local and touring musical acts as well as recurring events like burlesque, DJs, and a monthly gospel brunch. The performance space is not too big, not too small; balcony seats offer sufficient views of the stage. For something more exclusive after the show, upgrade to the VIP Foundation Room upstairs, which features personalized drink service in a ultra-fancy Renaissance-style setting.

MAP 1: 2200 N. Lamar St., 214/978-2583, www.houseofblues.com/dallas

MAJESTIC THEATER

Built in 1921, the Majestic is the last remaining piece of "Theater Row," Dallas's strip of ornate movie palaces popular during the vaudeville era. In its early days, the Majestic hosted major acts like Bob Hope, Mae West, and Houdini. After closing in 1973, the theater was restored inside and out, preserving its original Renaissance Revival architecture and landing it a spot in the National Register of Historic Places. Today, the Majestic books big-name musicians and comedians.

MAP 1: 1925 Elm St., 214/670-3687, www.majestic-theater.com

CINEMA

ALAMO DRAFTHOUSE

The Dallas outpost of this trendy Austin-based chain does the dinner-and-a-movie atmosphere best—by making the dinner part as unobtrusive as possible. You'll use a pen and paper to place your order, and don't even think about using your phone during the movie; Alamo Drafthouse has a strict policy against it. The theater caters to film nerds with special series and premiere events. Plus, the patio bar offers a great skyline view.

MAP 1: 1005 S. Lamar St., 214/914-4443, www.drafthouse.com/dfw

Lakewood/East Dallas Map 2

CULTURAL CENTERS

AFRICAN AMERICAN MUSEUM OF DALLAS

This Fair Park facility is the only museum in the southwestern United States that specializes in preserving and exhibiting African American art, culture, and history. The folk art collection is particularly impressive, and the permanent Freedman's Cemetery exhibit should be required viewing for every Dallasite. It tells the story of North Dallas's post-Civil War community, featuring artifacts, archival photos, oral histories, and documents, including slave transactions.

MAP 2: 3536 Grand Ave., 214/565-9026, www.aamdallas.org; Tues.-Fri. 11am-5pm, Sat. 10am-5pm; free admission, $5 docent-guided tour

BATH HOUSE CULTURAL CENTER

After a hot day exploring the enormity of White Rock Lake, the Bath House Cultural Center offers a welcome reprieve from the elements. The art deco-style shoreline building features visual and performing arts in a 116-seat black-box theater and three galleries. The center hosts the Festival of Independent Theatres each summer, the One Thirty Productions matinee series, and scores of gallery shows all year long. It also houses the White Rock Lake Museum, which features the history of the area along with rotating art exhibitions inspired by the lake.

MAP 2: 521 E. Lawther Dr., 214/670-8749, www.dallasculture.org/bathhouseculturecenter; Tues.-Sat. noon-6pm; free

THEATER

★ DALLAS CHILDREN'S THEATER

Over the past few decades, the Dallas Children's Theater has worked to shed the stereotype attached to its name—that "children's theater" means silly, superficial performances. Every season, you'll find familiar stories told in rich and creative adaptations that challenge young audiences to consider big ideas without dumbing down the material.

MAP 2: 5938 Skillman St., 214/978-0110, www.dct.org

MUSIC HALL AT FAIR PARK

Built in 1925 with a Spanish Baroque design, the historic Music Hall at Fair Park seats over 3,400 people on multiple levels that surround the orchestra pit. The nonprofit organization Dallas Summer Musicals (DSM) hosts six touring productions each year, sometimes including popular recurring shows like Wicked and The Lion King. About two hours before each show, the Dining Room restaurant offers a $25 buffet, often serving food that fits the theme of the evening's production. Outside of the DSM, the Music Hall also books concerts, ballet performances, and other events.

MAP 2: 1121 First Ave., 214/421-9998, www.liveatthemusichall.com

POCKET SANDWICH THEATER

Looking for a break from pesky social norms? Catch a show at Pocket Sandwich Theater. Tucked away in a strip shopping center, this live dinner theater features locally produced comedies and melodramas with a twist: during some shows, guests can boo and throw popcorn at the "bad guys" on stage. Despite the ragtag vibe of the small, dive-y venue, Pocket Sandwich usually delivers high-quality, polished performances.

MAP 2: 5400 E. Mockingbird Ln., Suite 119, 214/821-1860, www.pocketsandwich.com; $12-25

CINEMA

ANGELIKA FILM CENTER

The eight-screen Angelika Film Center shows independent films and big-budget releases and has easy public transit access at DART's Mockingbird Station. You can catch special screenings such as the "crybaby matinee" for parents with babies, and watch parties for popular TV shows. The theater also hosts the annual Dallas International Film Festival in April.

MAP 2: 5321 E. Mockingbird Ln., 214/841-4713, www.angelikafilmcenter.com/dallas

Uptown

Map 3

GALLERIES

DALLAS CONTEMPORARY

If you're into the weird, the shocking, and the irreverent, the Dallas Contemporary does not disappoint. The party gallery draws a lot of young hipsters as well as longtime local arts patrons. Look for the gallery's outdoor installation "Playboy Marfa," a sculpture that was too controversial for its namesake West Texas arts community. The Dallas Contemporary has also left a mark miles from its own building: In 2012, the owners commissioned the famous street artist Shepard Fairey, known for the 2008 Obama "Hope" poster, to produce murals around West Dallas.

MAP 3: 161 Glass St., 214/821-2522, www.dallascontemporary.org; Tues.-Sat. 11am-6pm, Sun. noon-5pm; free

GOSS-MICHAEL FOUNDATION

This contemporary British art gallery features mid-career and emerging artists from across the pond. Kenny Goss and his former partner, the late pop singer George Michael, established the Goss-Michael Foundation in 2007. The two carefully selected about 500 pieces for the collection, which includes avant-garde artists. Look for Tracey Emin's neon piece, *George Loves Kenny*.

MAP 3: 1305 Wycliff Ave., Suite 120, 214/696-0555, www.g-mf.org; Mon.-Fri. 10am-4pm; free

MUSEUM OF GEOMETRIC AND MADI ART

Inspired by the international abstract art movement known as MADI, the Museum of Geometric and MADI Art is one of the most underrated art museums in Dallas. Most locals may not even know it exists, which is strange since it's the only museum of its kind in North America. The permanent collection features colorful mind-bending art from across the globe. You can see the entire museum in about an hour if you take your time. Admission is free, but donations are appreciated.

MAP 3: 3109 Carlisle St., 214/855-7802, www.geometricmadimuseum.org; Tues.-Sat. 11am-5pm, Thurs. 11am-7pm, Sun. 1pm-5pm; free

THEATER

KALITA HUMPHREYS THEATER

One of the last buildings—and the only theater—that Frank Lloyd Wright designed, the Kalita Humphreys Theater opened in 1959 and became a historic landmark in 2007. For 50 years, it was home to the Dallas Theater Center, which has since moved to the Dallas Arts District downtown. Today, the building houses smaller performing arts groups like the Uptown Players and Second Thought Theatre, which produce unique, thought-provoking plays. The intimate space provides excellent sound and a clear view of the stage from any seat. Get there early to fully appreciate the architecture and the heavily wooded Turtle Creek landscape.

MAP 3: 3636 Turtle Creek Blvd., 214/219-2718, www.attpac.org

CINEMA

MAGNOLIA THEATER

Part of the Landmark Theatres chain of art-house cinemas, the Magnolia features a consistently good lineup of limited-release independent films as well as big Hollywood movies. If you arrive early, swing by the Magnolia Bar, a chic and somewhat hidden lounge. You can order a cocktail and take it with you into the theater. The concessions go way beyond buttered popcorn and Milk Duds. The menu includes gourmet pizza from the Dallas-based Campisi's, steak empanadas, and hummus plates.

MAP 3: 3699 McKinney Ave., 214/520-0394, www.landmarktheatres.com

Park Cities

MUSEUMS

MEADOWS MUSEUM AT SMU

Housed on the Southern Methodist University campus, the Meadows Museum boasts one of the finest Spanish art collections outside of Spain. The museum recently expanded its collection, acquiring significant paintings by 18th-century artist Francisco de Goya along with modern works of Salvador Dali and Pablo Picasso. Don't miss the outdoor sculpture exhibit, which includes *Wave* by Santiago Calatrava, the same artist who designed Dallas's new signature bridges.

MAP 4: 5900 Bishop Blvd., 214/768-2516, www.meadowsmuseumdallas.org; Tues.-Sat. 10am-5pm, Sun. 1pm-5pm; adults $10, seniors $8, students $4, children under 12 free

MUSEUM OF BIBLICAL ART

With a focus on Jewish and Christian themes, the Museum of Biblical Art features a stunning array of ancient and contemporary works in 11 galleries. From rare, handwritten Bible passages to modern figurative sculptures, there's much to take in. Don't miss the chance to watch preservationists at work in the art conservation lab. Plus, the Via Dolorosa outdoor sculpture garden offers a place for reflection amid the 14 stations of the cross.

MAP 4: 7500 Park Ln., 214/368-4622, www.biblicalarts.org; Tues.-Sat. 10am-5pm, Sun. 1pm-5pm; adults $12, seniors and students $10, children $8, children 5 and under free

CINEMA

INWOOD THEATRE

Built in 1947, the historic, art deco-style Inwood Theatre still features the aquatic-themed murals it had when it opened. The three-screen theater sends moviegoers back in time while showing the newest blockbusters and limited-release independent films. On weekends, you can catch campy cult classics from the comfort of plush sofas during "Midnight Madness" screenings. Grab a drink in the Inwood Lounge, known for its creative martini selection.

MAP 4: 5458 W. Lovers Ln., 214/352-5085, www.landmarktheatres.com

HIGHLAND PARK VILLAGE THEATRE

The Village Theatre opened in 1935 as Texas's first luxury movie theater, just a few years after the upscale Highland Park Village shopping center developed, showcasing Spanish-style architecture. Today, two of the four screens feature an intimate space that feels more like your own home theater. You can watch new releases in a small, 10-seat room with large, comfortable recliners.

MAP 4: 32 Highland Park Village, 214/443-6035, www.hpvillagetheatre.com

Top: AT&T Performing Arts Center; **Bottom:** Magnolia Theater

West Dallas/Oak Cliff

Map 5

MUSEUMS

OAK CLIFF CULTURAL CENTER

The city-owned Oak Cliff Cultural Center is a big part of the neighborhood art scene, featuring exhibits in photography, mixed media, and local street art as well as music and poetry performances. The community center doesn't exactly top the list of Dallas arts destinations, so travelers with a tight schedule shouldn't make a special trip here. But it's definitely worth popping into on the way to the historic Texas Theatre next door.

MAP 5: 223 W. Jefferson Blvd., 214/670-3777, www.dallasculture.org/oakcliffculturalcenter; Tues.-Fri. 3pm-9pm, Sat. 10am-6pm; free

TURNER HOUSE

Dallas isn't known for preservation. So any time a building lasts more than 100 years, local historians and architecture buffs work hard to keep it that way. Built in 1912 for just $55,000, the Turner House mansion is a terrific example of the modified Prairie style of American foursquare architecture. Today, it's home to the Oak Cliff Society of Fine Arts, which presents art exhibits, classical music performances, and talks with local preservation luminaries. The house offers tours by appointment and opens to the public for events.

MAP 5: 401 Rosemont Ave., 214/946-1670, www.turnerhouse.org

GALLERIES

BASEMENT GALLERY

Located beneath a historic building that once housed the Oak Cliff Masonic Lodge, the Basement Gallery's DIY artist community showcases local graffiti and pop art. With its hip-hop-infused opening events, the gallery provides a dedicated space for underground artists to roam free. For a hands-on experience, check the calendar for low-cost evening arts workshops that welcome people of all skill levels.

MAP 5: 115 S. Beckley Ave., www.facebook.com/diybasement; hours vary

ERIN CLULEY GALLERY

The Dallas Contemporary's former director opened her own gallery, riding the wave of West Dallas's new entertainment district taking shape in the shadow of the Margaret Hunt Hill Bridge. The industrial, light-filled space focuses on contemporary artists from Dallas and the East Coast, where Cluley has ties. Her artists are also the minds behind some of the neighborhood's striking public art.

MAP 5: 414 Fabrication St., 214/760-1155, www.erincluley.com; Wed.-Sat. noon-5pm or by appointment

THEATER

BISHOP ARTS THEATRE CENTER

Behind the walls of an unassuming marquee, TeCo Theatrical Productions operates a vibrant and diverse lineup of plays, jazz performances, and educational programs at the Bishop Arts Theatre Center in the fall and spring. The nonprofit organization is perhaps best known for its annual holiday production, *Black Nativity*, and the recurring LGBT PlayPride Festival.

MAP 5: 215 S. Tyler St., 214/948-0716, www.bishopartstheatre.org

CONCERT VENUES

THE KESSLER THEATER

Known by locals as simply "the Kessler," this historic 1940s movie theater sat vacant for decades until it reopened as a music venue in 2010. Fans also describe the intimate, low-lit space as a "listening room," where every seat offers an excellent perspective. The Kessler books classic and indie rock, blues, and R&B as well as comedians and writers including the likes of Amy Sedaris, John Waters, and the girls from *Broad City*.

MAP 5: 1230 W. Davis St., 214/272-8346, www.thekessler.org; Thurs.-Sat. 6pm-close

CINEMA

★ TEXAS THEATRE

This historic building is much more than the site of Lee Harvey Oswald's arrest. For locals, that's merely a footnote to what the Texas Theatre has become: the epicenter of the Dallas film community. The Oak Cliff Film Festival occurs every June and has garnered national acclaim for its indie film lineups. Every other time of year, the art-house theater screens cult classics, experimental work, limited-release documentaries, and blockbusters.

MAP 5: 231 W. Jefferson Blvd., 214/948-1546, www.thetexastheatre.com; $10 movie ticket, other event prices vary

Downtown Fort Worth

Map 6

GALLERIES

MILAN GALLERY

Most visitors wander into Milan Gallery while strolling through Sundance Square. The warm and inviting space houses more than 600 works of art from local and national artists, including paintings, photography, and sculpture. You'll see Fort Worth and other Texas artists represented, especially during the summer Discovery Exhibit.

MAP 6: 505 Houston St., 817/338-4278, www.milangallery.com; Mon.-Thurs. 11am-7pm, Fri. 11am-9pm, Sat. noon-9pm, Sun. 1pm-5pm; free

SID RICHARDSON MUSEUM

Required viewing for any Fort Worth traveler, the Sid Richardson Museum features permanent exhibitions from legendary artists Frederic Remington and Charles Russell, whose paintings depict life in 19th-century western America. The museum offers free docent-guided tours at 2pm Tuesday and Saturday along with several children's programs and studio activities.

MAP 6: 309 Main St., 817/332-6554, www.sidrichardsonmuseum.org; Mon.-Thurs. 9am-5pm, Fri.-Sat. 9am-8pm, Sun. noon-5pm; free

CINEMA

COYOTE DRIVE-IN

The drive-in movie theater exists mostly in memories of a bygone era, but Coyote Drive-In offers a rare opportunity to recapture that retro all-American night out—without any price gouging. The only venue of its kind in Dallas-Fort Worth, Coyote has three screens that show double features at dusk against the backdrop of the Fort Worth city skyline. You can see two full movies with one $7 ticket. The large outdoor patio sells snacks and alcohol, and hosts food trucks. The wildly popular venue opens at 5:30pm every day, so arrive at least an hour before showtime to snag a good parking spot.

MAP 6: 23 NE 4th St., 817/717-7767, www.coyotedrive-in.com; adults $7, children $5, under 4 free

PERFORMING ARTS

★ BASS PERFORMANCE HALL

Two 48-foot-high limestone angels overlook the sidewalk alongside Bass Performance Hall, which covers an entire city block. Inside, the stunning piece of European-style architecture features a painted dome 80 feet in diameter. This world-class opera house serves as the performing venue for the Fort Worth Symphony Orchestra, Texas Ballet Theater, Fort Worth Opera, and the famous Van Cliburn International Piano Competition. Constructed in 1998, Bass Hall is one of the most celebrated concert halls in the country. But to locals, it's much more than that. It symbolizes the rebirth of downtown Fort Worth as Sundance Square transformed the area into a walkable urban community.

Arrive early to order drinks and explore the architectural details of the building. Venture up to the mezzanine balcony for a perfect view of the downtown skyline, from the perspective of those towering limestone angels you saw on your way in.

MAP 6: 525 Commerce St., 817/212-4200, www.basshall.com

CIRCLE THEATRE

For an intimate theater experience, duck into the Circle Theatre, a 125-seat venue set in the basement of the historic Sanger building. This regional theater specializes in contemporary plays you've probably never seen before. It has no actual stage; the seats are level with the performance area, giving the plays a more personal vibe.

MAP 6: 230 W. 4th St., 817/877-3040, www.circletheatre.com; $25-38

JUBILEE THEATRE

Specializing in works that highlight the African American experience, Jubilee Theatre routinely receives critical acclaim from the local press. The season lineups feature a variety of theatrical styles, from solemn one-woman shows to high-energy musicals.

MAP 6: 506 Main St., 817/338-4411, www.jubileetheatre.org; $19-30

West Fort Worth — Map 7

MUSEUMS

AMON CARTER MUSEUM OF AMERICAN ART

Works from two of the greatest artists of the American West—Frederic Remington and Charles Russell—are on display under the same roof in the Amon Carter's permanent collection. The museum opened in 1961 to house the Fort Worth philanthropist's paintings and bronze sculptures depicting the real-life cowboys and Indians of the late 19th century. But the museum isn't stuck in the past. The rotating exhibitions of photography, multimedia, and abstract art illustrate the forward-thinking artists of this century, too.

MAP 7: 3501 Camp Bowie Blvd., 817/738-1933, www.cartermuseum.org; Tues.-Wed. 10am-5pm, Thurs. 10am-8pm, Fri.-Sat. 10am-5pm, Sun. noon-5pm, free

FORT WORTH MUSEUM OF SCIENCE AND HISTORY

Known for its paleontology exhibits and IMAX theater experience, the Fort Worth Museum of Science and History houses more than 150,000 historical and scientific objects in interactive exhibits. The recently renovated DinoLab features fossils and full-scale replicas that tell the stories of prehistoric species. It's a great way to entertain kids for a couple of hours. If you're not traveling with children, though, skip this one and head to Dallas's much more impressive Perot Museum of Nature and Science, which does a better job of engaging adults and kids alike.

MAP 7: 1600 Gendy St., 817/255-9300, www.fwmuseum.org; Mon.-Sat. 10am-5pm, Sun. noon-5pm; adults $15, youth $12, seniors $14

Top: Bass Performance Hall; **Bottom:** *Walking Flower (La fleur qui marche)* by Fernand Léger, on the grounds of the Kimbell Art Museum

★ KIMBELL ART MUSEUM

Of all the Cultural District attractions, the nationally renowned Kimbell Art Museum should top your list. It's regarded as the best art museum in the Southwest, housing significant works from 3,000 BC to the mid-20th century. The permanent collection is small, containing fewer than 350 pieces, but it's carefully curated. It features art from ancient Egypt, Greece, and Rome, Italian Renaissance paintings, pre-Colombian ceramics, African terra-cotta sculptures, and more. Designed by Louis Kahn and erected in 1972, the building itself is a work of modern art.

MAP 7: 3333 Camp Bowie Blvd., 817/332-8451, www.kimbellart.org; Tues.-Thurs. 10am-5pm, Fri. noon-8pm, Sat. 10am-5pm, Sun. noon-5pm; adults $18, seniors and students $16, children $14

MODERN ART MUSEUM OF FORT WORTH

Known to locals as simply "the Modern," this museum features a stunning collection of post-World War II art, covering major movements from abstract expressionism to pop and minimalism. Contemporary art fans will find all their favorite iconoclasts like Mark Rothko, Andy Warhol, and Philip Guston, just to name a few. Arrive by 2pm Tuesday-Saturday for a docent-led tour of the museum.

MAP 7: 3200 Darnell St., 817/738-9215, www.themodern.org; Tues.-Thurs. 10am-5pm, Fri. 10am-8pm, Sat.-Sun. 10am-5pm; general $10, students and seniors $4, children under 12 free

NATIONAL COWGIRL MUSEUM AND HALL OF FAME

This small museum's permanent and traveling exhibitions feature thousands of artifacts that showcase women's contributions to cowboy culture. The Hall of Fame honors hundreds of influential cowgirls—not just rodeo champions and cattle ranchers. You'll find artists, writers, public servants, and entertainers who helped shape the American West, from sharpshooter Annie Oakley to retired Supreme Court justice Sandra Day O'Connor. Some of the most fascinating honorees are the lesser-known women like Mollie Taylor Stevenson, who ran one of the oldest African American-owned ranches in the United States during segregation, establishing a school for black children to learn the trade.

MAP 7: 1720 Gendy St., 817/336-4475, www.cowgirl.net; Tues.-Sat. 10am-5pm, Sun. noon-5pm; adults $10, children, seniors, and military $8, children under 3 free

PERFORMING ARTS

CASA MAÑANA

Many Dallas-Fort Worth natives fondly remember their grade-school field trips to the children's theater at Casa Mañana, which has endured for more than 80 years. There's not a bad seat in the intimate performing space, and the actors stick around to chat and take pictures after the shows. Basically, kids love Casa Mañana, but the theater also features full seasons of Broadway plays for general audiences, usually garnering critical acclaim locally.

MAP 7: 3101 W. Lancaster Ave., 817/332-2272, www.casamanana.org; Tues.-Fri. 10am-4pm, Sat. noon-5pm

FORT WORTH COMMUNITY ARTS CENTER

Its name sounds quaint considering this community arts center offers two theaters and seven galleries under one roof. You'll find local art on display in the form of film festivals, dance shows, visual art exhibits, and theater performances. While it may not top the list of cultural attractions, it offers a worthwhile glimpse into the Fort Worth community arts scene.

MAP 7: 1300 Gendy St., 817/738-1938, www.fwcac.com; Mon.-Sat. 9am-5pm, free

CINEMA

MOVIE TAVERN

The West Fort Worth location of this national chain screens major new releases in a comfortable dinner-theater setting. The extensive menu offers more than your basic burger or chicken finger basket. You'll find flatbreads, sliders, salmon, salads, and sandwiches. Plus, there's a breakfast menu if you catch a movie before 10:30am on weekends, which is a pretty good reason to wake up early after a night of barhopping along 7th Street.

MAP 7: 2872 Crockett St., 682/503-8101, www.movietavern.com

Northside

Map 8

MUSEUMS

TEXAS COWBOY HALL OF FAME

Housed in a 25,000-square-foot warehouse that was built in 1888 as a horse and mule barn, the Texas Cowboy Hall of Fame features exhibits on its more than 100 inductees—people who have "excelled in the sport and business of rodeo, and the western lifestyle." That includes names like legendary Rangers pitcher Nolan Ryan, actor Tommy Lee Jones, and country music star George Strait. Spanning several generations of cowboys, the museum claims the world's largest collection of lifestyle wagons as well as the 1933 Cadillac that belonged to Fort Worth entrepreneur Amon G. Carter. For an extra $30, you can dress up as a gunfighter or saloon girl for a sepia-toned souvenir print at the Jersey Lilly Old Time Photo Parlor.

MAP 8: 128 E. Exchange Ave., 817/626-7131, www.texascowboyhalloffame.org; Mon.-Thurs. 9am-5pm, Fri.-Sat. 10am-7pm, Sun. 11am-5pm; adults $6, seniors $5, children $3

A Day in the Fort Worth Cultural District

While the glittering Dallas Arts District offers museumgoers a scenic, big-city experience, the less flashy **Fort Worth Cultural District** (www.fw-culture.com) takes it down a notch. But don't let Dallas's dominating culture deter you from this understated gem to the west. Fort Worth's museums contain some of the finest art collections in the world. Before you go, visit www.fortworth.com, click on the map section, and download the Cultural District walking map. Here are a few tips for seeing it in one day.

To prepare for the busy museum day ahead, find some Zen at the **Fort Worth Botanic Garden,** which opens at 9am. If it's springtime, head straight to the Japanese Garden and follow the winding wooden paths to see cherry trees in full bloom. Next, make your way to the opposite side of the district where most of the museums are clustered. Start at the **Kimbell Art Museum,** known for its distinctive modern architecture, featuring barrel-vault buildings with skylights down the center. The permanent collection features major works from 3,000 BC to the mid-20th century, from the medieval Italian painter Duccio to surrealist Pablo Picasso. The temporary exhibits, such as the recent focus on Monet's early career, are always impressive.

For strictly contemporary art, the **Modern Art Museum of Fort Worth** takes the lead, focusing on post-World War II works across all mediums. It doesn't take long to view the museum's entire collection of pop art, photography, minimalism, figurative sculpture, and multimedia. You'll find works from significant artists like Philip Guston, Francis Bacon, Dan Flavin, and Roy Lichtenstein. For lunch, the museum's **Café Modern** is worth the splurge, and its floor-to-ceiling windows offer a lovely view of the building's glassy, serene pond.

If it's nearing 5pm, and you can make just one more stop, hit the **Amon Carter Museum of American Art.** Admission is free, so it's hard not to justify a quick visit. Aside from its famous Remington and Russell paintings, of particular note is the museum's collection of more than 45,000 prints that illustrate the history of photography from haunting daguerreotypes of the 1800s to Richard Avedon's striking portraiture of western life.

The Cultural District has plenty to offer after the museums close. Just down the street from Amon Carter, **Piola Restaurant and Garden** (3700 Mattison Ave., 817/989-0007, www.fwpiola.com) serves upscale Italian fare in a tiny 1940s cottage. For something cheaper and more laid-back, **The Ginger Man** (3716 Camp Bowie Blvd., 817/886-2327, www.thegingerman.com) has great bar food and an endless selection of decently priced craft beers from all over the world.

Southside/TCU

Map 9

PERFORMING ARTS

STAGE WEST

With nearly 40 years of productions, this intimate, 150-seat theater has garnered consistently rave reviews from local and regional critics. Recently, Stage West has won over millennial audiences with edgy dramas and dark comedies that premiered off Broadway within the last few years. Spring for Prix Fixe Fridays when a $45 ticket includes dinner before the show. Or, if you're on a tight budget, you can preview a play before its official opening for $17.

MAP 9: 821 W. Vickery Blvd., 817/784-9378, www.stagewest.org; general $31-35

Festivals and Events

Winter

FORT WORTH STOCK SHOW AND RODEO

For 23 days in January and February, visitors flock to Fort Worth for the annual **Fort Worth Stock Show and Rodeo**. Dating back to 1896, the event celebrates the western heritage and still vibrant ranching industry that shaped the city. Nearly 30,000 animals are shown off for top prizes, and cowboys compete in bull riding and other rodeo events. There are also carnival rides, children's exhibits, live music, and shopping. On the first Saturday, the Stock Show Parade is held in Downtown Fort Worth, drawing more than 100,000 spectators. By the end of its annual run, the show pulls in over one million guests.

Northside: 3400 Burnett-Tandy Dr., 817/877-2400, www.fwssr.com

Spring

DEEP ELLUM ARTS FESTIVAL

The **Deep Ellum Arts Festival** (3414 Elm St., 214/855-1881, www.deepellumartsfestival.com) covers three blocks of Deep Ellum, focusing on three main areas of creativity: art, music, and food. Hundreds of visual artists showcase their work in a variety of mediums. In keeping with the neighborhood's roots, around 150 bands perform on six stages spanning all genres. The festival also features the best of Deep Ellum's culinary scene, including barbecue, Tex-Mex, craft beer and wine, and off-the-wall food trends. The event is held in April each year, headquartered at Sons of Herman Hall.

Downtown Dallas: 3414 Elm St., 214/855-1881, www.deepellumartsfestival.com

GREENVILLE AVENUE ST. PATRICK'S DAY PARADE

Billed as the largest event of its kind in the Southwest, the **Greenville Avenue St. Patrick's Day Parade** (www.dallasstpatricksparade.com)

draws over 125,000 people to the two-mile stretch just east of Southern Methodist University. More than 90 themed parade floats proceed south, slinging beads, candy, and other goodies. The family-friendly vibe doesn't last long as shirtless debauchery and portable sound systems fill the streets. The official parade and festival run during the late morning and early afternoon, but celebrations continue well into the night at Lower Greenville Avenue bars.

Dallas: Greenville Ave., www.dallasstpatricksparade.com

FAN EXPO DALLAS

Formerly known as Dallas Comic-Con, the **Fan Expo Dallas** () is the largest comics, sci-fi, horror, anime, and gaming event in Texas. Over 50,000 costumed connoisseurs descend upon the Kay Bailey Hutchison Convention Center during the star-studded three-day festival to catch a glimpse of guests like Stan Lee, Mark Hamill, Tim Curry, and Catherine Tate. Other attractions include panel discussions, gaming rooms, movie screenings, and retro dance parties. Visit the event website for a slew of special ticket packages and coupons.

Downtown Dallas: 650 S. Griffin St., www.fanexpodallas.com

Summer

VAN CLIBURN INTERNATIONAL PIANO COMPETITION

Named for one of the great pianists in history, the quadrennial **Van Cliburn International Piano Competition** (201 Main St., Fort Worth, 817/738-6536, www.cliburn.org) is one of the most significant classical music competitions in the world. A screening jury travels the globe observing the best pianists. Thirty of the best are invited to perform at Bass Performance Hall in Fort Worth, competing for cash prizes and the chance to embark on a professional career. For discerning concertgoers, the competition offers a rare view of the future icons of classical music. The competition runs in May and June.

Fort Worth: 201 Main St., Fort Worth, 817/738-6536, www.cliburn.org

Fall

STATE FAIR OF TEXAS

With the exception of a few years during World Wars I and II, the **State Fair of Texas** (www.bigtex.com) has been held every year since 1886. It began when a group of Dallas businessmen secured 80 acres on the east side of town for an exposition park. Now covering 277 acres, it's one of the largest and longest-running state fairs in the country. Every year, locals gear up for the debut of the next fried food sensation. Thousands of students from across the state compete in the Youth Livestock Auction, earning millions of dollars in scholarships. Most visitors simply wander through the fair until they stumble on the most popular attractions like the pig races, the chili cook-off, new and vintage car shows, and, of course, the chance to capture the perfect selfie with Big Tex himself. The state fair runs for 24 days in September and October.

East Dallas: Fair Park, www.bigtex.com

AT&T RED RIVER SHOWDOWN

This historic college football rivalry turns Fair Park and much of Dallas into a sea of crimson and burnt orange. In the annual game known as the **AT&T Red River Showdown** (www.fairpark.org), the Texas Longhorns and Oklahoma Sooners face off at the Cotton Bowl Stadium during the State Fair of Texas. The event dates back to 1900, with Dallas providing neutral turf halfway between Austin and Norman, Oklahoma. Alumni from both schools often settle in Dallas, creating a lively mix of passionate Longhorns and Sooners.

East Dallas: Fair Park, www.fairpark.org

dogs enjoying the State Fair of Texas

Sports and Activities

Home to some of the most iconic teams in sports, Dallas-Fort Worth is a mecca for fans.

The Dallas Cowboys are worshiped like gods. AT&T Stadium known as "Jerry's World" after the team's billionaire owner, Jerry Jones, is their megachurch. The massive dome can be seen on the horizon from neighboring suburbs 20 miles away. The Texas Rangers reside nearby, filling Globe Life Park with red-and-blue-clad baseball buffs. The Dallas Mavericks and the Dallas Stars pack the American Airlines Center with boisterous basketball and hockey fanatics.

Even more fast-paced, Texas Motor Speedway attracts NASCAR enthusiasts to its 1.5-mile racing track and massive entertainment center—one of the largest sports venues in the country. Diehard fans pitch tents and park RVs overnight for the full experience. If you prefer real horsepower, place your bets at the Lone Star Park horseracing track.

Part of the western heritage of Fort Worth, the rodeo is more than a tourist attraction. Death-defying bull-riders compete for cash every weekend in the Stockyards. These young men hold their own as serious athletes, outmaneuvering the 1,500-pound beasts.

Even in this flat, landlocked region, you can find a surprising number of nature activities like hiking, biking, kayaking, canoeing, fishing, and bird watching. Local organizations like the Trinity River Audubon Center and the Fort Worth Wildlife Refuge have worked hard to preserve important animal species, native plants and grasses.

Whether you want to join a rowdy crowd of sports fans or escape the noise for nature, Dallas-Fort Worth can meet your needs.

Previous: AT&T Stadium; The Texas Rangers play ball at Globe Life Park in Arlington.

Look for ★ to find recommended Sports and Activities

Highlights

★ **Best Urban Oasis:** Spanning more than 1,000 acres east of downtown Dallas, **White Rock Lake Park** offers serene shoreline vistas along with exhilarating water sports (page 126).

★ **Best Hike-and-Bike Trail:** The **Trinity Trails** system winds through Fort Worth, following the Trinity River's west fork. The best stretch begins at tree-canopied Trinity Park near the Fort Worth Cultural District (page 130).

★ **Best Daredevil Sport:** People spend the longest eight seconds of their lives gripping the back of an angry bucking bull at **Fort Worth Stockyards Championship Rodeo** every weekend (page 131).

★ **Best-Loved Sports Team:** Even though they haven't won a Super Bowl since the 1990s, the **Dallas Cowboys** will always be "America's Team," as far as locals are concerned (page 131).

★ **Best Wildlife Haven:** Once an illegal dumpsite in southern Dallas, the **Trinity River Audubon Center** is now home to one of the region's best bird-watching sites (page 133).

Downtown Dallas

Map 1

SPECTATOR SPORTS

Basketball

DALLAS MAVERICKS

Ever since local celebrity businessman Mark Cuban bought the team in 2000, the NBA's Dallas Mavericks have soared in both popularity and win percentage. It also helps to have one of the league's most valuable and adored players in Dirk Nowitzki. Not a basketball fan? Go for the halftime shows, which are often more entertaining than the actual game with stunts, acrobatics, and, of course, the Mavericks Dancers.

MAP 1: American Airlines Center, 2500 Victory Ave., 214/467-8277, www.mavs.com; regular season Oct.-Apr.

Hockey

DALLAS STARS

Hockey and Texas may not seem like a winning combination in professional sports, but Dallas proves otherwise. The NHL's Dallas Stars attract passionate fans who routinely pack the American Airlines Center clad in their festive green and white garb. The team's ranking goes up and down—from securing the Stanley Cup in 1999 to missing the playoffs for five straight seasons—but the energy remains electric. Arrive early during warm-ups for a closer view of the players.

MAP 1: American Airlines Center, 2500 Victory Ave., 214/467-8277, www.nhl.com/stars; regular season Oct.-Apr.

BIKING

LOCAL HUB BICYCLE CO.

No matter your skill level, this Deep Ellum shop offers a comfortable and neighborly atmosphere for anyone who wanders in perusing the selection of gorgeous bikes, including cruisers, commuters, and road bikes. Rentals are $10 an hour or $35 a day, and you can reserve online. Plus, you can't beat the location, a perfect starting point for exploring downtown, Deep Ellum, and beyond. Local Hub also hosts themed group rides, and in-store yoga sessions, so check the calendar for upcoming events.

MAP 1: 2633 Main St., Suite 130, 214/484-1019, www.localhubbc.com; Tues.-Sat. 10am-7pm, Sun. noon-6pm

Lakewood/East Dallas

SPECTATOR SPORTS

College Football

COTTON BOWL STADIUM

The original home of the Dallas Cowboys, the historic Cotton Bowl Stadium at Fair Park now hosts major college football games, the biggest being the annual Texas-Oklahoma Red River Showdown. Dallas becomes a sea of red and burnt orange as fans flock to the stadium to watch the matchup between the Texas Longhorns and Oklahoma Sooners. The Cotton Bowl is also home to the slightly less competitive powder-puff football game, Blondes versus Brunettes, which raises money for the Alzheimer's Association every August.

MAP 2: 3750 Midway Plaza, 214/670-8400, www.bigtex.com/fun/football

Rodeo

TEXAS BLACK INVITATIONAL RODEO

Held annually on Juneteenth weekend, the Texas Black Invitational Rodeo celebrates the little-known contributions of African American cowboys and cowgirls. The event usually begins with a motorcycle parade followed by a series of events such as bull riding, barrel racing, and steer wrestling at Fair Park's State Fair Coliseum. A nearly 30-year-old tradition, the rodeo attracts thousands of spectators. For more festivities, visit the African American Museum of Dallas, the nonprofit organization that sponsors the event.

MAP 2: 1438 Coliseum Dr., 214/565-9026, www.aamdallas.org; $10-35

PARKS

★ WHITE ROCK LAKE PARK

Covering more than 1,000 acres, White Rock Lake Park is the crown jewel of the Dallas park system. The man-made reservoir at its center was built in 1911 as the city's main water source. Today, it's a prime spot for outdoor recreation, from sailing and kayaking to hiking and bird-watching. Serious cyclists and marathon maniacs pound the pavement of the 9.5-mile hike-and-bike trail that follows the lake's shoreline. The public park is also home to an array of wildlife, softly swaying native prairie grasses, and wildflowers that bloom in spring. At the White Rock Lake Dog Park, eager pups plunge into the water after wayward tennis balls. Winfrey Point, located on the lake's southeast side, offers a stellar sunset view against the backdrop of the city skyline. The only drawback of White Rock Lake? Its popularity. It is notoriously crowded on weekends.

MAP 2: 8300 Garland Rd., 214/670-4100, www.dallasparks.org

Top: Cotton Bowl Stadium; **Bottom:** White Rock Lake Park

HIKING AND BIKING

SANTA FE TRAIL

Named after the old rail line on which the path was built, the 4.2-mile Santa Fe Trail is one of the best ways to experience Lakewood and East Dallas by bike. The concrete path extends from the Deep Ellum area to White Rock Lake, winding through popular entertainment spots and quaint, tree-lined neighborhoods, eventually connecting to the White Rock Lake Loop Trail. Between the two destinations, however, things can look a little sketchy and nondescript. Bring plenty of water and avoid the trail at night.

MAP 2: Winsted Dr. and Garland Dr., S. Hill Ave., www.dallascounty.org

WATER SPORTS

WHITE ROCK PADDLE CO.

Operating during the spring, summer, and early fall months, White Rock Paddle Co. reveals a side of Dallas that visitors don't often see: true outdoor adventure. Though it's surrounded by miles of concrete, White Rock Lake feels like it's a world away from the urban jungle—especially when you get out onto the water. The paddle company rents canoes, kayaks, and stand-up paddleboards for around $20 an hour, including paddles and life jackets. You can take a relaxing trip through the calm waters of White Rock Creek or tackle the waves near the center of the lake. Make reservations in advance; weekends are often booked solid.

MAP 2: 389 E. Lawther Dr., 469/888-0620, www.whiterockpaddle.com; Wed.-Thurs. 10am-6pm, Fri.-Sun. 8am-6pm

Uptown

Map 3

HIKING AND BIKING

KATY TRAIL

One of the most popular trails in Dallas, the 3.5-mile Katy Trail follows picturesque Turtle Creek and continues up to the busy Knox Street shopping and retail area. Much of the wide concrete path is lined with lush trees that provide plenty of shade on a scorching day. You'll spot all kinds of characters here: marathon runners, spandex-clad cyclists, in-line skaters, kids in strollers, groups of yogis, and the hippest pets in the city. The path gets very crowded, so be sure to brush up on trail etiquette. To access the trail, leave your car at Reverchon Park on the southern end (2505 Maple Ave.).

MAP 3: 2505 Maple Ave. to Travis St. and Knox St., 214/303-1180, www.katytraildallas.org

TRINITY SKYLINE TRAIL

Stretching 4.6 miles, the paved Trinity Skyline Trail follows the Trinity River under several West Dallas roadways, providing a ground-level view of downtown. The scenery ranges from vast green spaces to the industrial Union Pacific Railroad Bridge to the bustling street festivals happening

near the Margaret Hunt Hill Bridge. There are three access points. Of those, the parallel parking is rarely full at the Commerce Street trailhead.
MAP 3: 3700 Sylvan Ave., 109 Continental Ave., and 110 W. Commerce St., www.trinityrivercorridor.com

West Dallas/Oak Cliff

Map 5

PARKS AND GARDENS

LAKE CLIFF PARK/FOUNDERS PARK

These separate but adjoining city parks are popular picnicking spots, offering expansive lawns and downtown views. The 45-acre Lake Cliff features a nice shoreline scene, a paved trail circling the park, and a charming pineapple fountain framed by rosebushes. Don't mind the folks walking around in formal wear; the park is a prime location for prom pictures and wedding photography. In Founders Park to the north, you'll find more active groups tossing Frisbees on the Roger Lytle Disc Golf Course. Steer clear of these areas after dark.

MAP 5: Zang and Colorado Blvd., www.friendsofoakcliffparks.org

TWELVE HILLS NATURE CENTER

It's hard to believe that such a beautiful place was once covered in crime-ridden apartments. The product of neighborhood activism, Twelve Hills Nature Center offers a small respite from city life. On just five acres, the property's grassy path makes a short loop around native prairies, wildflowers, and a monarch butterfly habitat. The area also serves as an outdoor classroom for the public elementary school next door.

MAP 5: 817 Mary Cliff Rd., 469/249-2817, www.twelvehills.org

HIKING AND BIKING

OAK CLIFF NATURE PRESERVE

The 121 acres of hilly trails within the Oak Cliff Nature Preserve make the surrounding apartments and warehouses almost disappear. Maintained by the Texas Land Conservancy, the park has eight miles of trails that wind through wooded areas and large wildflower fields. The park attracts mostly mountain bikers, which can be a slight inconvenience to those wandering the same paths on foot.

MAP 5: 2875 Pierce St., 512/301-6363

Downtown Fort Worth

Map 6

WATER SPORTS

PANTHER ISLAND PAVILION

Located on the banks of the Trinity River, against the backdrop of the Fort Worth skyline, Panther Island hosts huge outdoor concerts and festivals year-round. But its biggest attraction is the sandy beach, offering direct access to the water—something unfathomable on Dallas's side of the Trinity. No one can dispute that Fort Worth has far surpassed Dallas in its transformation of the Trinity into a true recreational park. **Backwoods Paddle Sports** (817/403-6906, www.backwoodspaddlesports.com) operates during the spring, summer, and early fall months, renting out stand-up paddleboards, canoes, and kayaks. Swimming and tubing are also permitted; you can float right in front of the waterfront stage during a concert. Check water-quality reports before heading into the river. For daily reports, call the Tarrant Regional Water District at 817/335-2491, or visit www.trwd.com and click on "Water Supply."

MAP 6: 395 Purcey St., 817/698-0700, www.pantherislandpavilion.com

West Fort Worth

Map 7

PARKS AND TRAILS

★ TRINITY PARK

At the southern end of the Fort Worth Cultural District, this pristine piece of green space provides access to a range of outdoor recreation. A small fishing pier juts into the Trinity River; anglers can catch and release trout, which are stocked each spring. The park is also a great starting point for exploring the Trinity Trails system, more than 40 miles of hike-and-bike paths that follow the riverbanks as they zigzag through the city center. Ride north to Panther Island Pavilion or head south toward the Fort Worth Zoo and refuel at the super-hip Woodshed Smokehouse, located right off the trail.

MAP 7: 2401 University Dr., www.trinitytrails.org

Northside

Map 8

SPECTATOR SPORTS

Rodeo

★ FORT WORTH STOCKYARDS CHAMPIONSHIP RODEO

Witness the most dangerous eight seconds of a cowboy's life at 8pm every Friday and Saturday night in the Fort Worth Stockyards' historic Cowtown Coliseum. Professional bull riders compete to stay anchored atop a 2,000-pound bucking beast, earning points to advance. You'll also see barrel racing, calf roping, and other events. Arrive early for a pre-rodeo party at 6:30pm, featuring food, drinks, and live music. Plenty of tickets are available at the door, but reserve box seats in advance.

MAP 8: 121 E. Exchange Ave., 817/625-1025, www.stockyardsrodeo.com; adults $19, seniors $14, children $10

Greater Dallas and Fort Worth

Map 10

SPECTATOR SPORTS

Football

★ DALLAS COWBOYS

"America's Team" made history in the mid-1990s, winning three consecutive Super Bowls—and then never won again. Fans now have a conflicted relationship with their beloved/hated Cowboys, hoping every year the team returns to its former glory. The closer they get, the harder it hurts. The team is no less iconic, however, and visiting AT&T Stadium is an experience all its own. The 300-foot-high dome can be seen from hilly suburbs 30 miles away, maybe farther. As the world's largest domed stadium, it's the epitome of Big D excess, although it's not actually in Dallas.

If you're in town for a game, schedule an extra day just to see the stadium. You can truly understand its magnitude on a self-guided tour (about $20-30 a ticket), where you can access the field, toss a ball around, and walk through the cheerleaders' locker rooms.

MAP 10: 1 AT&T Way, Arlington, 817/892-4000, www.stadium.dallascowboys.com; Mon.-Sat. 10am-5pm, Sun. 11am-4pm

Baseball

TEXAS RANGERS

Many a Dallasite plays hooky from work every year at the beginning of April. Why? It's opening day for the Texas Rangers' Major League Baseball season. Dedicated fans attend every home game at Globe Life Park in Arlington, which includes more than 48,000 seats. Bring plenty of sunscreen, a personal fan, and a hat to the open-air facility.

MAP 10: 1000 Ballpark Way, Arlington, 817/273-5222, www.texas.rangers.mlb.com

Top: Texas Motor Speedway; **Bottom:** Trinity River Audubon Center

Golf

AT&T BYRON NELSON CHAMPIONSHIP

Named for the legendary pro golfer who won a record 11 straight tournaments in 1945, the AT&T Byron Nelson Championship tees off every spring, in April or May, at the Four Seasons Resort Dallas at Las Colinas. A major stop on the PGA Tour, the Nelson attracts the best players from around the world. Daily grounds admission for the weeklong competition is $45, which includes access to postgame concerts. Grey Goose 19th Hole tickets will set you back about $100.

MAP 10: 3400 N. Walton Walker Blvd., 214/943-9700, www.attbyronnelson.org

Horse Racing

LONE STAR PARK

If you're the betting type, the 36,000-square-foot Lone Star Park horse track is open daily, attracting serious gamblers as well as first-time spectators. The park's two main live racing events are the annual spring Thoroughbred season, which usually begins in April and runs for 50 days; and the quarter horse season, which runs September through November. Pay an extra $3 for the climate-controlled grandstand seats; it's worth it to avoid Dallas's unpredictable weather. Block out an entire day, and prepare for crowds and long lines.

MAP 10: 1000 Lone Star Pkwy., Grand Prairie, 972/263-7223, www.lonestarpark.com; $5

NASCAR

TEXAS MOTOR SPEEDWAY

Four times the size of AT&T Stadium, the 1,500-acre Texas Motor Speedway is its own racecar city within a city. The major races, NASCAR and IndyCar, convene in April, June, and November, drawing thousands of fans that camp in one of the venue's vast tent cities. Newbies should know to arrive about three hours before the first race, bring earplugs, and wear comfortable shoes.

MAP 10: 3545 Lone Star Cir., 817/215-8500, www.texasmotorspeedway.com

PARKS AND GARDENS

★ TRINITY RIVER AUDUBON CENTER

Transformed from an illegal dump site into a vibrant wildlife habitat, the Trinity River Audubon Center in south Dallas provides access to the 6,000-acre Great Trinity Forest, the largest urban hardwood forest in the country. Educational opportunities abound, especially for bird lovers. Sixty resident species and more than 200 migrants fly through the area during the spring and fall, following the Central Flyway between Canada and Mexico.

Watch the pollination of six beehives and taste some local honey; see reptiles and amphibians inside the exhibit hall; take a group camping trip overnight; or tour the Audubon center's eco-friendly building, designed by architect Antoine Predock, known for his Southwest modernism. Visit during late spring to see a lusher and greener landscape. Admission is free every third Thursday of the month.

MAP 10: 6500 Great Trinity Forest Way, 214/309-5801, www.trinityriver.audubon.org; Tues.-Sat. 9am-4pm, Sun. 10am-5pm; adults $6, children $3, seniors $4

CEDAR RIDGE NATURE PRESERVE

Located near Dogwood Canyon, the Cedar Ridge Preserve offers a bit more for hikers, making it a popular training ground for trail runners and backpackers preparing for a big trip. With about nine miles of trails weaving through 600 acres, the nature center comprises a variety of scenes, from thick forests to open prairies. Take the one-mile Cattail Pond Trail to a small wooden observation tower for a vast view of Joe Pool Lake and surrounding treetops. There's heavy weekend trail traffic; go on a weekday for a more tranquil experience.

MAP 10: 7171 Mountain Creek Pkwy., Cedar Hill, 972/709-7784, www.audubondallas.org/cedar-ridge-preserve; Tues.-Sun dawn-dusk, free

FORT WORTH NATURE CENTER AND REFUGE

Watch the bison roam and spot adorable prairie dogs eyeing you with suspicion at one of the largest city-owned nature centers in the country. The Fort Worth Nature Center and Refuge covers more than 3,600 acres of forests, prairies, and wetlands. This urban oasis manages to stay surprisingly serene without too much traffic crowding the 20 miles of trails that meander along the Trinity River's west fork and around Lake Worth. The best time to see active wildlife is late spring to early summer.

MAP 10: 9601 Fossil Ridge Rd., 817/392-7410, www.fwnaturecenter.org; Oct.-April daily 8am-5pm, May-Sept. Mon-Fri. 7am-5pm, May-Sept. Sat.-Sun. 7am-7pm; adults $5, children $2, seniors $3

DOGWOOD CANYON

An easy 20-minute drive south of downtown Dallas, Dogwood Canyon extends across 200 acres of wildlife habitat ideal for bird-watching. The red-tailed hawk, great horned owl, and hairy woodpecker are just a few of the many birds that call the canyon home. Hikers will find only two trails: an easy half-mile stroll you can take with a toddler or your grandma, and one moderately difficult 1.65-mile trek to a panoramic view of the southern Dallas greenbelt.

MAP 10: 1206 W. F.M. 1382, Cedar Hill, 469/526-1980, www.dogwoodcanyon.audubon.org; Tues.-Sun 9am-5pm, free

Shops

Look for ★ to find recommended Shops

Highlights

treasures at Curiosities

★ **Best High-End Fashion:** It's hard to beat **Neiman Marcus,** first on the scene in upscale fashion. Although locations exist around Dallas, the downtown flagship is a destination for discerning shoppers (page 138).

★ **Best Oddball Finds:** You never know what you'll find while inching your way through **Curiosities**, a tiny Lakewood gift shop packed with weird and often spooky objects (page 139).

★ **Best Souvenir Shop:** More creative than your typical souvenir store, screen printing shop **Bullzerk** is known for tongue-in-cheek T-shirts that poke fun at Dallas with original one-liners (page 140).

★ **Best Shopping Mecca:** If you only have time to visit one shopping mall in Dallas, make it **NorthPark Center.** The design, art installations, and green space make it a community gathering space (page 145).

★ **Best Literary Buzz:** A blend of bookstore, coffee shop and bar, **The Wild Detectives** is hard to categorize. But the small, curated collection of books and regular author events have made waves in the literary community (page 146).

★ **Best Antiques:** The largest store of its kind in Fort Worth, **Montgomery Street Antique Mall** features a warehouse full of more than 200 antique dealers, plus the adorable Secret Garden Tea Room (page 149).

In Dallas, shopping isn't just a necessity; it's a way of life as old as the city itself.

Established as a riverside trading post in the mid-1800s, Dallas eventually became a retail engine, fueled by immigrant craftsmen and later by the arrival of the railroads. Then in 1907, Neiman Marcus debuted its luxury clothing store in downtown, launching the fashion industry fixture that we know today. In fact, it's the oldest department store that still operates under the same name and is still headquartered in the same city.

Shopping centers and malls sprouted all over Dallas throughout the 20th century. Those still thriving today include the high-end Highland Park Village, the artfully designed NorthPark Center, and the gigantic Galleria Dallas.

While they're certainly worth the visit, don't let the major retail players distract you from the delightful neighborhood shops peppered throughout the city. In Oak Cliff, the historic Bishop Arts District has been revitalized with vibrant specialty shops peddling jewelry, handmade clothing, art, paper goods, and other odds and ends. In East Dallas, antique furniture markets and fashion boutiques line the streets of Greenville and Henderson Avenues. Uptown's more modern West Village shopping center offers a blend of independently owned stores and popular chains.

When it comes to shopping, Dallas definitely outdoes Fort Worth. However, Cowtown offers a few gems in Sundance Square and West Seventh Street. Plus, no visit to the Fort Worth Stockyards is complete without browsing the western-themed souvenir shops.

Previous: The Wild Detectives; NorthPark Center

Downtown Dallas

BOOKS AND MUSIC

BILL'S RECORDS

Located on the up-and-coming south side of downtown, Bill Wisener's old-school record shop is a little messy and unorganized, but it's worth the hunt for quality vintage vinyl at a fair price. Stop by on Saturday afternoons for live music and free beer.

MAP 1: 1317 S. Lamar St., 214/421-1500; Mon.-Thurs. 10:30am-10pm, Fri.-Sat. 10:30am-midnight, Sun. noon-10pm

CLOTHING

FORTY FIVE TEN

Where Neiman Marcus offers a chic, old-world charm, Forty Five Ten presents a modern, eclectic style open to interpretation. In 2016, after 15 years on the luxury fashion scene, the company's 37,000-square-foot flagship store opened in its new downtown digs and quadrupled in size. Here, you can shop among unconventional designer brands, admire the contemporary art, or just relax at the champagne bar.

MAP 1: 1615 Main St., 214/559-4510, www.fortyfiveten.com; Mon.-Sat. 10am-6pm

★ NEIMAN MARCUS

This piece of Dallas history is more than just a high-end department store. Neiman Marcus is a multilevel museum dedicated to the fashion and retail industry. This is the second location of the company's flagship store; it was constructed after the first iteration, built in 1907 at Elm and Murphy Streets, burned down in 1913. You'll find designer-brand clothes, luxurious dressing rooms, art installations, and framed artifacts from the store's beginnings. If you visit Dallas during the holidays, Neiman Marcus is a must-see for its extravagant window displays.

MAP 1: 1618 Main St., 214/741-6911, www.neimanmarcus.com; Mon.-Wed. 10am-6pm, Thurs. 10am-7pm, Fri.-Sat. 10am-6pm

WILD BILL'S WESTERN STORE

A fixture of downtown's West End, Wild Bill's is an experience all its own with over 50 years in the local boot-making business. Rows of boots line the walls inside the historic redbrick building along with hats, belts, buckles, and bolo ties. From the saddle barstools and longhorn armchairs, you can watch the craftsmen steam cowboy hats to a custom fit. Wild Bill's is also a great spot for unique Texas-themed T-shirts and other souvenirs.

MAP 1: 311 N. Market St., 214/954-1050, www.wildbillwestern.com; Mon.-Tues. 10am-7pm, Wed.-Sat. 10am-9pm, Sun. noon-6pm

Lakewood/East Dallas

Map 2

ANTIQUES AND VINTAGE

★ CURIOSITIES

Having endured for more than a decade in the Lakewood neighborhood, Curiosities is covered wall-to-wall with the weird fascinations of its owners. The mother-son team has a knack for collecting macabre objects like mounted gators and snakes, creepy dolls, vintage medical tools and posters, animal bones, and ghostly daguerreotype photography.

MAP 2: 2025 Abrams Pkwy., 214/828-1886, www.getcuriosities.com; Mon.-Thurs. 10am-6pm, Fri.-Sat. 10am-7pm, Sun. noon-5pm

DOLLY PYTHON

Known for its creative collection of vintage cowboy boots, Dolly Python is also Dallas's institution for the hip and the nostalgic. You could easily spend at least an hour browsing booths from about 30 dealers. The shop showcases mid-century modern furniture and light fixtures, vintage clothing, antique posters, books and records, and handmade statement jewelry fashioned from animal bones and gems. You'll also find watercolor paintings of satirical skeletons from local artist Pinky Diablo, and plenty of inappropriate greeting cards.

MAP 2: 1916 N. Haskell Ave., 214/887-3434, www.dollypythonvintage.com; Tues.-Sat. 11am-6pm, Sun.-Mon., noon-5pm

VOODOO CHILE

Located off the beaten path of Lower Greenville's vibrant nightlife, Voodoo Chile's small, redbrick house calls out to curious shoppers with its absurd assortment of vintage clothing, artwork, creepy masks, and old records and VHS tapes. The eccentric Japanese owner, a former Jimi Hendrix cover artist, curates the shop himself without much explanation. Beware the provocative art pieces; they're likely to offend the faint of heart, but they're an unsurprising fit for the shop's irreverent vibe.

MAP 2: 5643 Bell Ave., 214/752-0266; daily 5pm-midnight

BOOKS AND MUSIC

HALF-PRICE BOOKS

Despite the valiant efforts of local literary minds, the indie bookstore scene in Dallas has yet to flourish beyond a couple of tiny shops. Still, we don't mind boasting about our beloved chain, Half-Price Books, and its flagship store in East Dallas. In fact, it often feels like an indie bookstore, hosting neighborhood poetry readings, art shows, live music, and acclaimed authors. There's plenty of room to roam and lounge. Get a quick buzz at the adjoining Black Forest Coffee, which makes a delicious chai latte.

MAP 2: 5803 Northwest Hwy., 214/379-8000, www.hpb.com; daily 9am-11pm

GOOD RECORDS

Aside from its impressive selection of new and vintage vinyl, Good Records has gained more of a reputation for its in-store performances, signings, and listening parties—a place to be seen. The shop has brought in everyone from indie pop artists like Sylvan Esso to hip-hop sensation Killer Mike. A couple of years ago, it made local headlines for hosting a surprise concert by Alice Cooper.

MAP 2: 1808 Greenville Ave., 214/752-4663, www.goodrecords.com; Mon.-Thurs. 10am-11pm, Fri.-Sat. 10am-midnight, Sun. 11am-9pm

CLOTHING

★ BULLZERK

If you're journeying around Dallas in search of the perfect souvenir T-shirt, then Bullzerk is your mecca. The Greenville Avenue shop specializes in graphic tees with original and very specific one-liners like "Keep Dallas Better Than Austin," and "Dallas: It's What Everyone in Dallas Is Talking About." You'll also find more basic designs featuring the iconic Pegasus, the city skyline, and the Texas state outline.

MAP 2: 1909 Greenville Ave., 972/677-7705, www.bullzerk.com; Sun.-Wed. 11am-7pm, Thurs. 11am-8pm, Fri.-Sat. 11am-10pm

GYPSY WAGON

The Gypsy Wagon looks like the dreamy living room of a free-spirited, bohemian cowgirl. The charming local boutique boasts quirky (but pricey) designs in apparel, gifts, and home décor, making it a great stop for Dallas- and Texas-themed souvenirs. You'll find wide selections of denim, vintage boots, and other fashion accessories.

MAP 2: 2928 N. Henderson Ave., 214/370-8010, www.the-gypsy-wagon.com; Mon.-Wed. 10am-6pm, Thurs. 10am-7pm, Fri.-Sat. 10am-6pm, Sun. noon-5pm

GIFTS

TALULAH BELLE

Located on a charming strip of mom-and-pop shops, Talulah Belle has a wide selection of gifts that can accommodate almost any occasion. You'll find designer fragrances, minibar accessories, embellished panties and thongs, and gardening gifts, to name a few. Shoppers can also enjoy complimentary champagne and sweets.

MAP 2: 2011 Abrams Rd., 214/821-1927, www.talulahbelle.com; Sun.-Wed. 10am-6pm, Thurs.-Sat. 10am-8pm

THE T SHOP

This neighborhood florist is also a go-to gift shop for locals. The T Shop carries cute greeting cards and framed graphic art along with handmade jewelry, stationery, textiles, home accents, and bath and body products. Monogrammed gifts are a hit here, and the shop owners are also highly sought-after wedding stylists.

MAP 2: 1908 Abrams Pkwy., 214/821-8314, www.thetshoplakewood.com; Mon.-Fri. 10am-6pm, Sat. 11am-5pm

Uptown

Map 3

ANTIQUES AND VINTAGE

AGAIN & AGAIN

You can't miss the pink door and the chic furniture sitting out front of an otherwise drab building. There's a lot more where that came from. Again & Again salvages discarded furniture from local estate sales, and repairs and reupholsters it to sell in the bright and cheery consignment store in the Design District. The shop also features unique light fixtures and modern artwork.

MAP 3: 1202 N. Riverfront Blvd., 214/746-6300, www.againandagain.com; Mon.-Sat. 10am-5:30pm, Sun. noon-5pm

UNCOMMON MARKET

This homegrown shop started 45 years ago with a couple of neighborhood guys selling antiques in an old house. Now, Uncommon Market operates from a huge warehouse in the Design District, specializing in European antiques found in England, France, Belgium, and the Netherlands. You'll see lots of architectural salvage, ornate chandeliers, and solid wood furniture. The artisans don't just sell the stuff; they restore the pieces to their original glory.

MAP 3: 100 Riveredge Dr., 214/871-2775, www.uncommonmarketdallas.com; Mon.-Sat. 10am-5:30pm

GIFTS AND HOME DÉCOR

GRANGE HALL

Even if you can't afford to buy anything, Grange Hall is worth a visit just to admire its dark oddities and otherworldly home design. The luxury retailer showcases designers from around the world, featuring pieces that are more artsy than functional, such as skeletal sconces and porcelain egg-shaped vases. Spend some time in the delicious bath and body section, and see if you don't leave with a $95 candle.

MAP 3: 4445 Travis St., Suite 101, 214/443-0600, www.grangehall.com; Mon.-Sat.10am-6pm

SHOPPING CENTERS

WEST VILLAGE

Located on the northern edge of Uptown, the West Village open-air shopping center is a fun place for a stroll even if you don't have a destination in mind. You'll pass a plethora of brand-name shops, local boutiques, and popular restaurants and bars. From high-end clothing stores to sophisticated wine bars, the West Village has a decidedly upscale vibe. Take in a movie at the five-screen Magnolia Theatre, or swing by on a Wednesday night when the Dallas Film Society offers free outdoor screenings with a cash bar. It's free and easy to park in one of the three garages, or valet. The McKinney Avenue Trolley also runs around the village.

MAP 3: 3699 McKinney Ave., 214/219-1144, www.westvillagedallas.com

Park Cities

Map 4

ANTIQUES

JACKSON ARMORY

Specializing in rare antique firearms and collectibles, this Snider Plaza shop is a hub for gun enthusiasts and history buffs. Jackson Armory's impressive inventory includes vintage shotguns, rifles, handguns, and edged weapons dating back to the 1800s. Stop by on a Saturday to see gunsmiths at work, and don't leave without checking out the shop's room full of rare first-edition books.

MAP 4: 3416 Rosedale Ave., 214/363-2767, www.jacksonarmory.com; Tues.-Sat. 10am-5pm

CLOTHING AND ACCESSORIES

CANARY

Look for a boxy, bone-white building with no sign and only a hint of yellow around the entrance. That's the first intriguing feature of Canary, a contemporary women's clothing boutique that showcases English designers with a focus on color. The styles are more classic compared to the beachy, bohemian looks found in its sister store, **Cabana** (4711 Lovers Ln., 469/917-7606, Mon.-Fri. 9am-5pm). Canary's lesser-known labels make it an interesting addition to Dallas's high-fashion scene.

MAP 4: 4609 W. Lovers Ln., 214/351-4400, www.shopcanarydallas.com; Mon.-Fri. 9am-5pm

CASTLE GAP JEWELRY

Known for its wide selection of sterling silver, Castle Gap Jewelry commissions Native American artists to handcraft one-of-a-kind rings, necklaces, bracelets, charms, and earrings. Family-owned since 1976, you can find its 97-year-old proprietor, Maxine, working in the shop every day.

MAP 4: 8300 Preston Rd., Suite 500, 214/361-1677, www.castlegap.com; Mon.-Sat. 10am-6pm

DRAPER JAMES

Dallas recently added another big name to Highland Park Village: Reese Witherspoon. To much fanfare, the actress opened Draper James, a clothing and gift shop inspired by her southern roots. Decked in blue and white floral décor with sweet tea on tap, the shop features the word "y'all" on almost everything, plus all the tailgating accessories you might need for game day.

MAP 4: 6 Highland Park Village, 214/780-0960, www.draperjames.com; Mon.-Sat. 10am-6pm, Sun. noon-5pm

Top: Wild Bill's Western Store; **Bottom:** Draper James

ELEMENTS

On the Dallas map since 1999, this upscale women's clothing boutique features designer labels, including those from several up-and-coming artists. You'll find a wide selection of denim along with cocktail dresses and other special-occasion wear that looks relaxed and effortless.

MAP 4: 4400 Lovers. Ln., 214/987-0837, www.elementsclothing.com; Mon.-Sat. 10am-6pm

YLANG 23

The husband-and-wife team behind Ylang 23 has been specializing in designer jewelry since the 1980s. From large, clunky statement pieces to fine, delicate designs, the collection includes styles that appeal to a variety of tastes. The boutique carries the latest trends from Jennifer Meyers, Ten Thousand Things, and Cathy Waterman.

MAP 4: 8300 Preston Rd., 214/234-0002, www.ylang23.com; Mon.-Sat. 10am-7pm, Sun. noon-5pm

GIFTS AND HOME DÉCOR

ANTEKS CURATED

With a modern-day Lewis and Clark aesthetic, Anteks Curated showcases rustic designs including hand-painted canoe paddles, Aztec art, and a wide selection of Native American-inspired Pendleton brand blankets. You'll find plenty of manly gifts like pocketknives, flasks, and barbecue cookbooks. The shop also features Brackish bow ties, handcrafted with vibrantly colored feathers of peacocks and other birds.

MAP 4: 4004 Villanova St., 214/706-6983, www.antekscurated.com; Mon.-Sat. 10am-6pm, Sun. noon-5pm

SWOOZIE'S

Fans of stationery and anything personalized will have a field day inside Swoozie's. The locals' go-to gift shop specializes in party décor and accessories along with other random trappings for holidays and everyday celebrations. You'll probably score a few Dallas-themed souvenirs not found in typical tourist shops.

MAP 4: 8417 Preston Center Plaza Dr., 214/890-0433, www.swoozies.com; Mon.-Sat. 10am-7pm, Sun. noon-6pm

THE URBAN MANOR

Carefully curated by a father-daughter duo, the Urban Manor blends modern and traditional styles of home décor and accessories. Their collection includes designer furniture and lighting along with locally made bath and body products. Venture to the back of the store to "the garden," a full-service florist and all-around beautiful space.

MAP 4: 6817 Snider Plaza, 469/802-6848, www.theurbanmanor.com; Mon.-Sat. 10am-6pm

SHOPPING CENTERS AND MALLS

HIGHLAND PARK VILLAGE

To witness high fashion in the flesh, take a stroll down the tree-lined cobblestone paths of Highland Park Village, which is packed with the kind of designer boutiques that give Dallas its shopping cred. You'll find outposts for Alexander McQueen, Chanel, Dior, Ralph Lauren, Tom Ford, and Tory Burch, just to name a few. The village even has personal shoppers for hire. Sample artisan cheeses at Molto Formaggio or swing by the Royal Blue Grocery for a glass of wine on the sidewalk patio.

MAP 4: 47 Highland Park Village, 214/443-9898, www.hpvillage.com

★ NORTHPARK CENTER

The small-scale shopping plazas peppered around Dallas are just precursors to the main attraction: NorthPark Center. As the locals say, it's "more than a mall." Sure, you'll find all the high-end department stores like Nordstrom and Neiman Marcus, but you'll also find a garden, a public library, art installations, and locally owned restaurants—all the things that create community. The mid-century modern architecture and carefully manicured landscape make NorthPark an inviting space to lounge and roam.

MAP 4: 8687 N. Central Expy., 214/361-6345, www.northparkcenter.com; Mon.-Sat. 10am-9pm, Sun. noon-6pm

SNIDER PLAZA

Despite the metropolis that has mushroomed around it, the historic Snider Plaza feels frozen in time. Built in 1927, the shopping center houses every mom-and-pop business a small town would need: hair salon, pharmacy, dentist office, coffee shop, you name it. There's even a gun store that also sells rare first-edition books spanning seven centuries. Longevity is the theme at Snider Plaza; even the restaurants have lasted for generations.

MAP 4: Snider Plaza and Milton Ave., www.sniderplaza.net

West Dallas/Oak Cliff

Map 5

ANTIQUES AND VINTAGE

LULA B'S ANTIQUES SHOP

The antiques stalls are surprisingly organized at Lula B's, a longtime Dallas dealer that recently opened a newer, bigger space in Oak Cliff. The shop carries mid-century modern furniture, both classy and kitschy, as well as retro lamps, housewares, classic pop-culture posters, and lots of vintage clothing and accessories. Located away from the Design District's antiques row, Lula B's is a little inconvenient for the typical traveler, but still worth visiting.

MAP 5: 1982 Fort Worth Ave., 214/824-2185, www.lulabsdallas.com; Mon.-Sat. 11am-7pm, Sun. noon-7pm

BOOKS AND MUSIC

LUCKY DOG BOOKS

This large but humble bookstore has struggled to stay afloat over the years, yet always seems to keep on kicking. Lucky Dog Books accommodates anyone who loves thumbing through used titles to pass the time. There's even a living room setup with leather sofas and recliners. Don't forget to check the cart outside containing free books.

MAP 5: 911 W. Jefferson Blvd., 214/941-2665, www.luckydogbooks.com; Mon.-Sat. 10am-9pm, Sun. noon-7pm

SPINSTER RECORDS

In addition to selling new and vintage records, Spinster aims to spread the gospel of vinyl any way that it can. The store has several different turntables playing on the floor with an expert available to convert MP3 music fans. Most new releases adorn the walls while discounted records are stocked near the front. You might also catch a local band performing live in the store.

MAP 5: 829 W. Davis St., 972/598-0814, www.spinsterrecords.com; daily 10am-10pm

TOP TEN RECORDS

According to the shop's former owner, Mike Polk, police officer J. D. Tippit hurried into this storefront on November 22, 1963, and used the telephone just before he was allegedly shot and killed by Lee Harvey Oswald. The building's supposed connection to the JFK assassination is just one of the things that makes Top Ten Records worth a visit. Full of vintage vinyl and cassette tapes and covered wall-to-wall in concert posters. The Texas Theatre owners recently bought the shop, planning to incorporation a non-profit media library with help from SMU archivists.

MAP 5: 338 W. Jefferson Blvd., 214/942-7595; Sun. 1pm-5pm, Wed.-Sat. 11am-6pm

★ THE WILD DETECTIVES

This bookstore/bar/coffee shop has been making headlines since it opened in 2014. Located in a renovated house near the Bishop Arts District, The Wild Detectives has a carefully curated selection of new books, plus a few records. Author readings occur regularly, and the large back patio hosts local arts and culture events, as well as live music. The venue also fosters a strong sense of community, shutting down its Wi-Fi on the weekends. To further incentivize talking to your neighbor, The Wild Detectives will serve your new friend a drink on the house.

MAP 5: 314 W. 8th St., 214/942-0108, www.thewilddetectives.com; Sun. 10:30am-11pm, Mon. 2pm-midnight, Tues.-Sat. 8:30am-midnight

GIFTS, ART, AND HOME DECOR

SET & CO.

Essentially an art gallery for high-end home goods, you're almost afraid to touch anything in Set & Co. A card accompanies each handcrafted bowl, cutting board, or teacup, detailing its material and origin. Items come from all over the world, including pieces from England, Italy, and Japan. The shop also sells home fragrances, bath and body goods, and pretty greeting cards.

MAP 5: 841 W. Davis St., 214/948-1000, www.setandco.com; Tues.-Sat. 10am-6pm, Sun. noon-5pm

WE ARE 1976

The walls of this adorable letterpress studio are covered in original graphic art prints. Some pay homage to the city of Dallas and touring indie rockers, but mostly, We Are 1976 is a random collection of oddities, from Japanese-inspired ceramics to knitted animal figurines to striking geometric jewelry. Stock up on some cute, off-the-wall greeting cards and stationery. Behind a curtain at the back of the shop, you can catch a glimpse of artists at work in the printmaking studio.

MAP 5: 313 N. Bishop Ave., 214/821-1976, www.weare1976.com; Sun. 11am-5pm, Mon.-Fri. 11am-7pm, Sat. 10am-8pm

CLOTHING

EPIPHANY

This Bishop Arts District boutique carries Bohemian-style dresses and blouses, fun graphic tees, and a wide selection of purses and jewelry—there are lots of chunky beaded necklaces and bracelets as well as delicate, understated designs. Directly across the street is Epiphany for Men, where you'll find vintage-style T-shirts, cuff links, underwear, and socks with quirky designs.

MAP 5: 412 N. Bishop Ave., 214/946-4411, www.epiphanystores.com; Sun.-Mon. 11am-5pm, Tues.-Thurs. 11am-7pm, Fri.-Sat. 11am-10pm

HOUSE OF MACGREGOR

In a small, sun-filled studio above the restaurant Bolsa, Oak Cliff fashion designer Cassie MacGregor crafts custom hats, using traditional millinery techniques she learned while apprenticing for Albertus Swanepoel (whose work appears in major designer stores). Styles include sun hats, cocktail hats, fedoras, newsboys, and elaborate creations for the Kentucky Derby. No two hats are alike, and the prices reflect a lifelong investment. Plus, the fitting process is an experience all its own.

MAP 5: 614 W. Davis St., Suite 203, 214/942-1966, www.thehouseofmacgregor.com; Mon., Wed., and Fri. 10:30am-4pm, Sat. noon-5pm

THE LAUGHING WILLOW

From the vibrant chalk art to the live music shows, passersby can't help but wander into the Laughing Willow, a vintage women's clothing boutique at the southern end of the Bishop Arts District. You'll find breezy sundresses and blouses, T-shirts and tanks with cheeky one-liners, shabby-chic jewelry, and some clever accessories for new moms.

MAP 5: 301 N. Bishop Ave., 972/849-9764, www.thelaughingwillow.com; Mon.-Wed. 11am-4pm, Thurs.-Fri. 11am-9pm, Sat. 10am-10pm, Sun. noon-5pm

Top: We Are 1976; Bottom: Bishop Arts District

West Fort Worth

Map 7

ANTIQUES AND VINTAGE

★ MONTGOMERY STREET ANTIQUE MALL

Carve out a few hours to browse the 61,000-square-foot space at Montgomery Street Antique Mall. The massive warehouse features more than 200 booths from different dealers, and these aren't random junk collectors. Most of the vendors have a distinct specialty. You'll find collections of 1950s "TV lamps," vintage trunks, old-school slot machines, industrial décor, shabby-chic furniture, and die-cast toys, just to name a few. Luckily, the mall's Secret Garden café offers a much-needed lunch break from an afternoon of shopping.

MAP 7: 2601 Montgomery St., 817/735-9685, www.montgomerystreetantiques.com; Mon.-Sat. 10am-6pm, Sun. noon-6pm

CLOTHING

REVINT BOUTIQUE

This adorably chic consignment shop carries vintage designer party dresses, jewelry, and handbags with a hip western flair. The store is neatly organized by color, including vibrant hues as well as blacks and neutrals. You'll find accessories like bags and clutches along the perimeter of the store. Be sure to explore the boot selection on the back wall.

MAP 7: 931 Foch St., 817/882-8223; Tues.-Sat. 11am-3pm

Northside

Map 8

BOOKS AND MUSIC

CHIEF RECORDS

Named after country music icon Ray Price and the Cherokee Cowboys, Chief Records boasts the largest country music vinyl collection in the Dallas-Fort Worth area, including swing, bluegrass, honky-tonk, and more. The family-owned shop has been in business for decades, formerly as the Ernest Tubb Record Shop, and is a local hangout for touring musicians. You'll find new and vintage records, and there are in-store performances most weekends. You might also score a complimentary craft beer while you browse.

MAP 8: 140 E. Exchange Ave., Suite 135, 817/624-8449, www.chiefrecordsonline.com; Mon.-Sat. 10am-7pm, Sun. noon-6pm

CLOTHING

M. L. LEDDY'S

The large boot-shaped sign on the corner advertises one of M. L. Leddy's specialties, and it's not for the casual shopper. These stunning handmade boots showcase the trade as a true art form. You'll find a variety of materials

A Day in the Bishop Arts District

Once a neighborhood secret, this tiny, walkable district packs more than 50 independent shops and restaurants into less than one mile, offering a slice of small-town life in the big city—from the adorable florist to the manly antiques store to the little pie shop that seems to have jumped off the page of a storybook. The name Bishop Arts District came along during the 1970s and '80s when local artists began moving into the neighborhood's abandoned storefronts, signifying the earliest efforts to revitalize the area. It would take another 20 years to finally turn it around, as local developers worked to preserve the historic architecture and encourage mom-and-pop business owners to take a chance on the budding retail district. To top it off the **Oak Cliff Streetcar** has returned, running from downtown to Bishop Arts. Although it lacks old-school charm, it's efficient (and free) transportation. Here's how to spend a few hours.

Grab some java and an empanada at the Latin coffee shop **Espumoso Caffe** (408 W. Davis St., Suite 105, 214/948-2055, www.espumosocaffe.com; Mon. 9am-6pm, Tues. 8am-8pm, Wed.-Thurs. 8am-8:30pm, Fri. 8am-10pm, Sat. 9am-10pm, Sun. 9:30am-6pm). However, if it's a Sunday, make reservations at **Hattie's** (418 N. Bishop Ave., 214/942-7400, www.hatties.com; Mon.-Sat. 11:30am-2:30pm, Tues.-Sun. 5:30pm-10pm, Sun. 11am-2:30pm) for a classic southern-style brunch. If you're on a budget, keep it low-key at **El Jordan** (416 N. Bishop Ave., 214/941-4451, Sun-Mon. 7am-2:30pm, Wed.-Sat. 7am-2:30pm) with *migas* or breakfast tacos. Stop in to **M'Antiques** (424 W. Davis St., 214/941-4195, www.dfwmantiques.com; Tues.-Wed. 11am-6pm, Thurs. 11am-8pm, Fri.-Sat. 11am-9pm, Sun. noon-5pm), which *Antiques Roadshow* dubbed "Where Indiana Jones Would Shop." Sip some free beer while you browse vintage swords, action figures, old issues of Playboy, and other manly treasures. Head down Bishop Avenue to **Ginger Fox Gallery** (408 N. Bishop Ave., Suite 102, 214/914-4126, www.gingerfoxgallery.com; Mon.-Tues.

such as ostrich, gator, and calf skins, and intricate, one-of-a-kind designs, all fashioned into the perfect fit. If you're serious about buying some real cowboy boots, and you're willing to drop a thousand bucks or so, spend an afternoon at Leddy's.

MAP 8: 2455 N. Main St., 817/624-3149, www.leddys.com; Mon.-Sat. 9am-6pm

GIFTS

THE CANDY BARREL

With kids in tow, it's hard not to get dragged into this shop of colorful confections. As its name suggests, you'll find an array of sweets piled into wooden barrels throughout the store. Most of the selection is pretty standard, except for the gold mine of saltwater taffy, including more than 50 different flavors like cayenne and maple bacon. The Candy Barrel is just one of the 25 specialty shops in the open-air market known as Stockyards Station.

MAP 8: 140 E. Exchange Ave., 817/624-4424, www.stockyardsstation.com; Sun.-Thurs. 10am-8pm, Fri.-Sat. 10am-9pm

by appointment, Wed.-Thurs. 11am-6pm, Fri.-Sat. 11am-10pm, Sun. noon-4pm) to view contemporary realism and catch the artist in action, painting her next piece. Next, hit **Neighborhood** (411 N. Bishop Ave., 214/943-5650; Tues.-Wed. 11am-6pm, Thurs. 11am-8pm, Fri.-Sat. 11am-10pm, Sun. 11am-5pm), part gift shop and part gallery, featuring modern art exhibits.

For lunch or dinner, the delicious thin-crust pies at **Eno's Pizza Tavern** (407 N. Bishop Ave., 214/943-9200, www.enospizza.com; Tues.-Thurs. 11:30am-10pm, Fri.-Sat. 11:30am-midnight, Sun.11:30am-10pm) never disappoint. Snag a table on the 2nd floor for a lovely view of the district. Take in the aromas at **Society** (403 N. Bishop Ave., 214/942-4600, www.shopatsociety.com; Mon.-Tues. 11am-5pm, Wed.-Sat. 11am-10pm, Sun. 11am-6pm), a candle shop with traditional and unusual scents. Across the street, the well-established **Artisan's Collective** (410 N. Bishop Ave., 214/943-5892, www.artisanscollective.net; Wed.-Thurs. 11am-7pm, Fri.-Sat. 11am-10pm, Sun. 11am-4pm) represents more than 150 Dallas artists, having operated in the neighborhood for more than 10 years. And no visit to the Bishop Arts District is complete without a stop at the adorable **Emporium Pies** (314 N. Bishop Ave., 469/206-6126, www.emporiumpies.com; Mon.-Thurs. 11am-9pm, Fri.-Sat. 11am-11pm, Sun. 11am-8pm), a small stand-alone house that offers homemade pies made with seasonal ingredients.

To keep the night going, head over to **The Wild Detectives** (314 W. 8th St., 214/942-0108, www.thewilddetectives.com; Sun. 10:30am-11pm, Mon. 2pm-midnight, Tues.-Sat. 8:30am-midnight), the bookstore/bar that's making waves in the literary community. Finally, **Ten Bells Tavern** (232 W. 7th St., 214/943-2677, www.tenbellstavern.com; Mon.-Fri. 3pm-2am, Fri.-Sat. 11am-2am) stays open late and has a laid-back patio that attracts a mostly local crowd.

THE GENERAL STORE

You'll find a little bit of everything at the General Store in the Fort Worth Stockyards, including Texas-themed souvenirs in the form of magnets, key chains, koozies, mugs, and shot glasses. The shop has an even wider selection of food items like candied popcorn, Rice Krispies treats, salsas, and dips. Don't miss the homemade jams with adventurous flavor combinations such as blackberry jalapeno and peach habanero.

MAP 8: 101 W. Exchange Ave., 817/625-4061, www.generalstorestockyards.com; Mon.-Thurs. 10am-6pm, Fri. 10am-8pm, Sat. 10am-9pm, Sun. 11am-6pm

HOUSE OF BLADES KNIFE ALLEY

Packed into a narrow Stockyards storefront, this specialty shop features every kind of knife from tactical fixed blades to pocketknives to cutlery, along with personalized engravings and a sharpening service. What began as a personal collection over 40 years ago has become a booming local business.

MAP 8: 114 E. Exchange Ave., 817/378-0477, www.houseofblades.com; Sun.-Thurs. 11am-6pm, Fri.-Sat. 11am-7pm

Southside/TCU

Map 9

ANTIQUES AND VINTAGE

BUTLER'S ANTIQUES

Chock-full of vintage knickknacks of varying value, Butler's should be on any antique shopper's to-do list. The fun stuff is out back in "Butler's Alley." The furniture selection is a refurbisher's dream, with high-quality pieces that just need a little love. You'll also find plenty of odds and ends like doors, window frames, and shutters for home improvement projects.

MAP 9: 2221 8th Ave., 817/921-3403; Mon.-Sat. 10am-6pm, Sun. 1pm-5pm

Greater Dallas and Fort Worth

Map 10

SHOPPING CENTERS AND MALLS

GALLERIA DALLAS

Situated at the intersection of two major freeways in North Dallas, the 3.7 million-square-foot Galleria Dallas is the region's largest shopping mall. Its architecture was inspired by the Galleria Vittorio Emanuele II in Milan, Italy, featuring a glass vaulted ceiling above four stories of shops and restaurants, with an ice-skating rink at the center. It's pretty impressive, especially during the holidays; you just have to navigate two busy toll roads and a mazelike parking garage to get there. Kids will have a field day romping around the rain forest-themed Children's Play Place, or having teatime at the American Girl Boutique and Bistro. The ice-skating rink opens at noon on weekends with an $11 admission charge and $3 skate rentals. Group rates are a little easier on the wallet.

MAP 10: 13350 Dallas Pkwy., 972/702-7100, www.galleriadallas.com

Where to Stay

Look for ★ to find recommended Where to Stay

Highlights

★ **Best Historic Hotel:** Built in 1912 as Dallas' first luxury hotel, the Beaux-style **Adolphus Hotel** contains much of the city's entertainment and bootlegging history (page 156).

★ **Best Budget Hotel:** If you're just looking for a place to lay your head at night, **Best Western Cityplace Inn** will suffice. It's located near several neighborhood attractions (page 156).

★ **Best Boutique Hotel:** Situated atop a West Dallas hill, the Art Moderne-style **Belmont Hotel** features white-stucco facades and stellar skyline views (page 158).

★ **Best Splurge:** Located within walking distance of Sundance Square, the **Worthington Renaissance** offers proximity to most Fort Worth sights and large, luxurious rooms (page 159).

★ **Best Bed-and-Breakfast:** The **Texas White House Bed and Breakfast** offers a quiet, tree-filled getaway just steps from Fort Worth's vibrant restaurant scene (page 160).

PRICE KEY

$ Less than $100 per night

$$ $100–200 per night

$$$ More than $200 per night

The choice of hotel can make or break a travel experience. Dallas and Fort Worth have a wide range of accommodations. It just depends on what type of traveler you are.

For a comfortable stay steeped in history, Dallas is home to a number of historic hotels like the Adolphus and Magnolia, constructed in the early 20th century. Travelers can absorb the stories preserved within the hotel walls before even setting foot outside.

Those who don't want their nights to end can book a room at a posh party hotel like The Joule or NYLO Dallas South Side, complete with glowing rooftop pools and lively late-night bar's.

Fort Worth offers more bed-and-breakfast options. From Miss Molly's kitschy Old West vibe to the Texas White House's lush gardens, you'll find distinct decor, home-cooked meals, and attentive innkeepers.

Budget hotels around $75-100 per night are harder to find, unless you stay several miles from the city center. A large cluster of chain hotels line Interstate 35 a few miles from the Design District and Oak Lawn neighborhoods. Most of these options come with bland views of parking lots and busy freeways.

For business travelers with a company expense account, Dallas-Fort Worth has more to offer than what can fit in this guidebook. The region is full of Marriotts, Hiltons, and Holiday Inns, along with Dallas' convention center hotel, the Omni, which illuminates the skyline with its LED light shows.

Previous: The Belmont Hotel; Texas White House Bed and Breakfast

Downtown Dallas

Map 1

★ THE ADOLPHUS HOTEL $$$

Some of the most enchanting Dallas history happened at the Adolphus, the city's first luxury hotel. From big bands and bootlegging to hula girls and fire-knife drumming, the parties here were legendary. Adolphus Busch, the founder of Anheuser-Busch, opened the hotel in 1912. The building was designed in the heavily ornamented beaux arts style. In 2016, the hotel underwent more than $40 million in renovations without diminishing its lavish old-world atmosphere.

MAP 1: 1321 Commerce St., 214/742-8200, www.adolphus.com

THE JOULE, DALLAS $$$

This restored 1920s neo-Gothic building is more than a glitzy hotel with flashy art. For locals, the Joule is a prime spot for a spa day or a posh night out. Booking a room or a penthouse here offers a peaceful escape from the world and convenient access to some of the coolest parties in town. Relax by the heated rooftop pool or head down to the basement for a nightcap at the Midnight Rambler cocktail lounge.

MAP 1: 1530 Main St., 214/748-1300, www.thejouledallas.com

MAGNOLIA HOTEL $$$

Situated at the center of downtown, the Magnolia Hotel also serves as the perch for Dallas's iconic red neon Pegasus. Built in 1922, the 29-story building was the city's first skyscraper, and the first skyscraper in the country to have air-conditioning. The hotel has large, comfortable rooms with nice views of downtown. Plus, there's free milk and cookies every night.

MAP 1: 1401 Commerce St., 214/915-6500, www.magnoliahotels.com/dallas

Lakewood/East Dallas

Map 2

★ BEST WESTERN CITYPLACE INN $

For a budget-friendly option close to Downtown Dallas, this corporate chain is a safe bet. What it lacks in glamour it makes up for in location, with its proximity to restaurants, shopping, and nightlife in Uptown, Knox/Henderson, and Lower Greenville. You'll also find local flavor just outside your doorstep at the 24-hour, pop art-themed diner, BuzzBrews Kitchen, which serves all-day breakfast and bottomless coffee. Explore most of Dallas's top attractions via the nearby DART bus route and train station, or drive five minutes down the freeway. Rooms cost less than $100 with advance purchase.

MAP 2: 4150 N. Central Expy., 214/827-6080, www.bestwestern.com

THE HIGHLAND DALLAS $$

This lavish boutique hotel puts guests on the edge of two prime Dallas neighborhoods—Lakewood and University Park. Located off the North Central Expressway and across the street from DART's Mockingbird Lane rail station, the Highland provides easy access to attractions in either direction, from the museums around SMU to the nightlife on Henderson and Greenville Avenues. The mid-century modern hotel is also home to Knife, the critically acclaimed upscale steak house from celebrity chef John Tesar.

MAP 2: 5300 E. Mockingbird Ln., 214/520-7969, www.curiocollection3.hilton.com

MAGNOLIA HOTEL DALLAS PARK CITIES $$

You can't beat the convenience of the swanky Magnolia Hotel, located off the Central Expressway and within walking distance of the Mockingbird Lane train station, SMU Boulevard, and the George W. Bush Presidential Library. You'll also appreciate the little things, such as hot breakfast and complimentary milk and cookies every night.

MAP 2: 6070 N. Central Expy., 214/750-6060, www.magnoliahotels.com

Uptown

Map 3

HOTEL ST. GERMAIN $$$

A boutique hotel with only seven rooms, this Queen Anne-style house features an antique southern elegance you wouldn't expect in a big city like Dallas. Hotel St. Germain is only a block away from the McKinney Avenue Trolley stop, making it easy to explore Uptown. The hotel restaurant is known for its elaborate special-occasion dinners with wine and champagne pairings.

MAP 3: 2516 Maple Ave., 214/871-2516, www.hotelstgermain.com

ROSEWOOD MANSION ON TURTLE CREEK $$$

Perhaps the most famous hotel in Dallas, the Rosewood Mansion on Turtle Creek is the ultimate place to treat yourself to luxurious massages, poolside service, or an intimate dinner on the terrace. Built in the 1920s, the sprawling estate's architecture showcases an ornate Italian Renaissance style. Many of the original features remain, such as the marble floors and the stained glass windows. The mansion was built as the private residence of a wealthy cotton baron, hosting parties for the rich and famous. Now as a hotel and five-star restaurant and bar, it's still a major scene for the Dallas elite.

MAP 3: 2821 Turtle Creek Blvd., 214/559-2100, www.rosewoodhotels.com

WARWICK MELROSE $$

Built in 1924 as the Melrose Court Apartment Hotel, the Warwick originally marketed its efficiency rooms toward Dallas bachelors. Today, the historic Sullivanesque Chicago-style building offers five types of upscale rooms and suites, inspired by French Empire design, although less gaudy and more classic. The Library cocktail and piano bar draws a local crowd, putting you at the center of Uptown's nightlife.

MAP 3: 3015 Oak Lawn Ave., 214/521-5151, www.warwickhotels.com/dallas

Park Cities

Map 4

HILTON DALLAS/PARK CITIES $

Located in the bustling Preston Center area, Hilton's Park Cities hotel is a short walk from shops and restaurants. Beyond that, you'll need to drive to see any other attractions, and this car-centric neighborhood becomes gridlocked during weekday rush hour. The hotel restaurant, Grain, is worth the splurge, serving dishes with seasonal ingredients sourced in Texas. Another plus? The rooftop pool with a skyline view.

MAP 4: 5954 Luther Ln., 214/368-0400, www3.hilton.com

HOTEL LUMEN $$

This mid-century modern boutique hotel sits right across the street from SMU's Owen Arts Center. Hotel Lumen guests have access to free loaner bikes—great for exploring the university grounds and the historic Snider Plaza shopping center a few blocks up Hillcrest Avenue. Recuperate with cocktail service at the hotel's outdoor heated pool.

MAP 4: 6101 Hillcrest Ave., 214/219-2400, www.hotellumen.com

West Dallas/Oak Cliff

Map 5

★ THE BELMONT HOTEL $$

Built in 1946 along what was then the main highway between Dallas and Fort Worth, the retro-chic Belmont Hotel is a destination all its own. After decades of decay, the building was restored to its original condition, featuring an art moderne, white stucco façade. The hilltop hotel boasts skyline views from the south side of the Trinity River greenbelt. Next door, chef Tim Byres's upscale barbecue restaurant, Smoke, attracts more locals than hotel guests, so you know it's good.

MAP 5: 901 Fort Worth Ave., Dallas, 214-393-2300, belmontdallas.com

COMFORT SUITES WEST DALLAS-COCKRELL HILL $

Situated off the interstate amid chain restaurants and big-box stores, this Comfort Suites is a no-frills, budget hotel away from congestion. While not the prettiest urban landscape, it's only a short drive into downtown, West Dallas, and Oak Cliff. It also offers a straight shot along I-30 to Cowboys Stadium, Six Flags Over Texas, and other Arlington attractions, as well as downtown Fort Worth. The rooms are large and clean, and come with a generous continental breakfast.

MAP 5: 4275 DFW Turnpike/I-30, 214/267-0100, www.choicehotels.com

Downtown Fort Worth Map 6

ETTA'S PLACE BED & BREAKFAST $$

Named for a woman with romantic ties to Butch Cassidy, Etta's Place includes 10 rooms, each named for a member of Cassidy's Hole in the Wall Gang. The hotel puts you right in the action of Sundance Square within walking distance to restaurants and nightlife. Guests receive a home-cooked breakfast that goes way beyond your typical bagel bar: Think eggs Benedict and banana pancakes.

MAP 6: 200 W. 3rd St., 817/255-5760, www.ettas-place.com

SHERATON FORT WORTH DOWNTOWN $

Located near the Fort Worth Convention Center and just steps from the Fort Worth Water Gardens, the Sheraton is the most convenient option for business travelers or those not looking for anything touristy. The rooms are bright and clean, and still offer some nice views of downtown. The indoor pool is a nice retreat after a summer day of sightseeing.

MAP 6: 1701 Commerce St., 817/335-7000, www.sheratonfortworth.com

★ WORTHINGTON RENAISSANCE $$$

Although it has a contemporary design inside and out, the views from the rooms at the Worthington Renaissance take in the historic architecture of downtown Fort Worth, including the century-old Tarrant County Courthouse clock tower. The luxury hotel features cozy bedding, large bathrooms, and Starbucks coffee in the lobby café. Plus, it's within walking distance of Sundance Square and Main Street activity.

MAP 6: 200 Main St., 817/870-1000, www.marriott.com

Northside Map 8

HYATT PLACE FORT WORTH STOCKYARDS $

For a budget-friendly option, Hyatt Place is a good bet while still placing you at the center of the Stockyards action. The hotel's free hot breakfast features an impressive selection of egg sandwiches, pastries, oatmeal, and fruit. Each room includes a work space ideal for business travelers.

MAP 8: 132 E. Exchange Ave., 817/626-6000, www.stockyards.place.hyatt.com

MISS MOLLY'S BED & BREAKFAST $$

This historic bed-and-breakfast puts a speakeasy spin on the traditional western theme of the Stockyards. The building, opened as a boardinghouse in 1910, operated as a brothel throughout the 1940s. The popular Miss Josie Room, named after one of the madams, is covered in extravagant and downright eerie Victorian décor; it also includes a real wood-burning stove and a vintage cast iron bathtub.

MAP 8: 109 W. Exchange Ave., 817/626-1522, www.missmollyshotel.com

STOCKYARDS HOTEL $$

For the ultimate Old West experience, the Stockyards Hotel transports guests back to the early 20th century when the hotel opened. The historic building dates to 1907, when cattle ranchers arrived on horseback or by stagecoach. Today, the hotel maintains a good reputation with tourists and even locals who embrace the Stockyards staycation.

MAP 8: 109 E. Exchange Ave., 817/625-6427, www.stockyardshotel.com

Southside/TCU Map 9

COURTYARD FORT WORTH UNIVERSITY DRIVE $

Most convenient for guests visiting Fort Worth's Texas Christian University, the Courtyard provides easy access to any part of town. It's also right across the street from the Trinity Trails System, which runs along the Trinity River through West Fort Worth and into downtown. The rooms are clean and well stocked with all the essentials—flat-screen TV, reliable Wi-Fi, mini-fridge, and coffeemaker. Plus, the lobby includes a 24-hour convenience store, which is handy for late nights.

MAP 9: 3150 Riverfront Dr., 817/335-1300, www.marriott.com

★ TEXAS WHITE HOUSE BED & BREAKFAST $$

Located within walking distance of Magnolia Avenue's vibrant restaurant scene, Texas White House feels a world away. At the century-old home, guests can sip sangria on the wraparound porch or snooze in a hammock hidden in the sprawling garden. The themed rooms feature private bathrooms with claw-foot tubs and locally made soaps. The farm-to-table breakfast includes eggs laid by the neighbors' hens.

MAP 9: 1417 8th Ave., 817/923-3597, www.texaswhitehouse.com

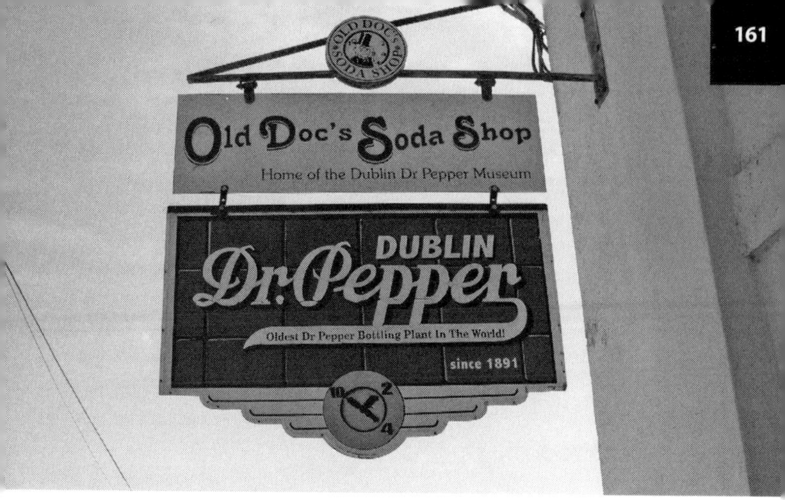

Day Trips

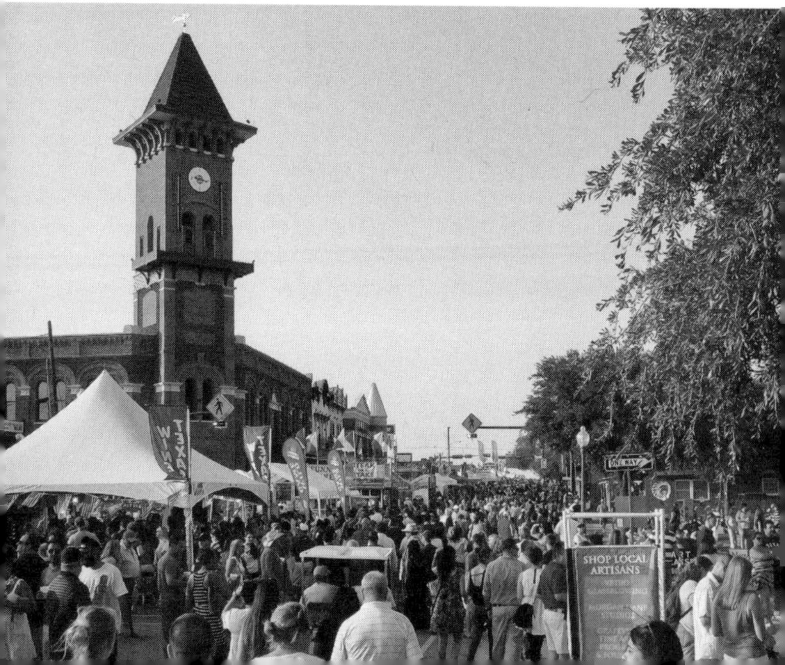

Look for ★ to find recommended Day Trips

Highlights

the Delaney Vineyards and Winery on the Grapevine Urban Wine Trail

★ **Best Book Lover's Paradise:** Browse the dusty shelves of **Booked Up No. 1** and find some literary inspiration courtesy of the shop's proprietor, who happens to be legendary Texas writer Larry McMurtry (page 167).

★ **Best Blast from the Past:** Made with pure cane sugar, the first batch of Dr Pepper was crafted at **Dublin Bottling Works** 120 years ago. Step back in time while touring the old factory, and sip on a "real" root beer float (page 170).

★ **Best Small-Town Theater:** The beautifully restored **Granbury Opera House** showcases superb local talent that far exceeds the expectations for a small-town community theater company (page 173).

★ **Best Place to Pamper your Palate:** A collection of tasting rooms form the **Grapevine Urban Wine Trail,** which offers an in-depth look at the Texas wine industry. Plus, you can indulge in delicious food pairings along the way (page 176).

While rushing to hit every major museum and trendy restaurant in Dallas-Fort Worth, it's easy to overlook the gems that lie just outside the bursting metropolis. Sometimes, you just need to slow down and wander through a new piece of scenery. These day trips are favorites among locals who want to escape the big-city chaos for small-town diversions.

From a beautifully desolate western town to a massive indoor theme park/hotel, the DFW perimeter has much to offer the weary urban traveler. In Archer City, famed Texas author Larry McMurtry (*Lonesome Dove*) runs an antique bookstore adored by the southwestern literary community. Grapevine caters to wine connoisseurs while offering plenty of kid-friendly adventures. Dublin is home to the original Dr Pepper bottling company, which now crafts an exclusive line of pure cane sodas. You can spend an entire day antiquing in Granbury, one of Texas's quintessential small towns full of family-oriented adventures.

PLANNING YOUR TIME

Choosing a day trip from Dallas and Fort Worth depends on a few things: your interests, your comfort level, and, of course, how much time you have to spend.

For seasoned road-trippers with time to kill and an undying appreciation for sleepy western towns, Archer City lies about two hours and 45 minutes from Dallas-Fort Worth. Plan an overnight stay during a weekend to fully experience the place made famous by *The Last Picture Show*. You'll want plenty of daylight to see city landmarks, enjoy a home-cooked meal, and roam the aisles of the antiquarian bookstore. The town all but

Previous: Dublin Bottling Works in Dublin, Texas; downtown Grapevine

goes to sleep by 5pm, except for the neon-lit Royal Theater where the performing arts scene comes alive. Archer City tends to attract older visitors and bookish types.

History buffs, farm-to-table snobs, and anyone in search of a sugar rush can find something to love about Dublin and Hico. The neighboring towns are located about one hour and 50 minutes south of Dallas-Fort Worth and are doable in a day. However, after seeing Dublin's historic Dr Pepper factory and soaking up the Old West charm of Hico, you might want to get a room at the local inn and stay awhile. In the vicinity, on the cusp of the Texas Hill Country, Granbury offers plenty of small-town attractions to fill an overnight trip. You won't want to leave without catching a theater performance at the gorgeous Granbury Opera House.

About 30-45 minutes north of Dallas-Fort Worth, Grapevine is an easy out-and-back excursion. Local commuters make the drive daily. In Grapevine, you can drink and dine your way through top Texas wineries, and keep the kids entertained in life-sized LEGO towns and sprawling water parks.

Archer City

To the untrained eye, Archer City looks like any other blink-and-you'll-miss-it Texas town. But to movie buffs and bibliophiles, it's a bucket-list destination. Spanning about two square miles with a population just over 1,800 people, the sleepy town is the birthplace of Pulitzer Prize-winning novelist Larry McMurtry, who authored famous titles such as the *Lonesome Dove* series and *Terms of Endearment*. The Texas icon once operated a mini-empire of bookstores in Archer City, stemming from his wide-ranging personal library. That has since been whittled down to just one popular outpost, Booked Up.

While it didn't become quite the literary mecca that McMurtry had hoped for, Archer City is still celebrated as the setting for the fictional town of Anarene in his coming-of-age novel *The Last Picture Show*. The 1971 Oscar-winning movie adaptation, preserved in the National Film Registry, was filmed on location and featured the historic Royal Theater, which still operates today.

Don't expect too many touristy thrills in this slow-paced, ghostlike town (i.e., children may get bored). Archer City is ideal for flexible travelers fascinated by history and the desolate western landscape.

SIGHTS

Archer County Courthouse

Built in 1892, the historic **Archer County Courthouse** (100 S. Center St., 940/574-4302, www.archercity.org, Mon.-Fri. 8:30am-5pm) is a beautiful example of the day's Romanesque Revival architecture. Although only three stories high, the imposing façade of quarry-faced sandstone makes the building seem enormous. Today's design differs dramatically from the

Day Trips

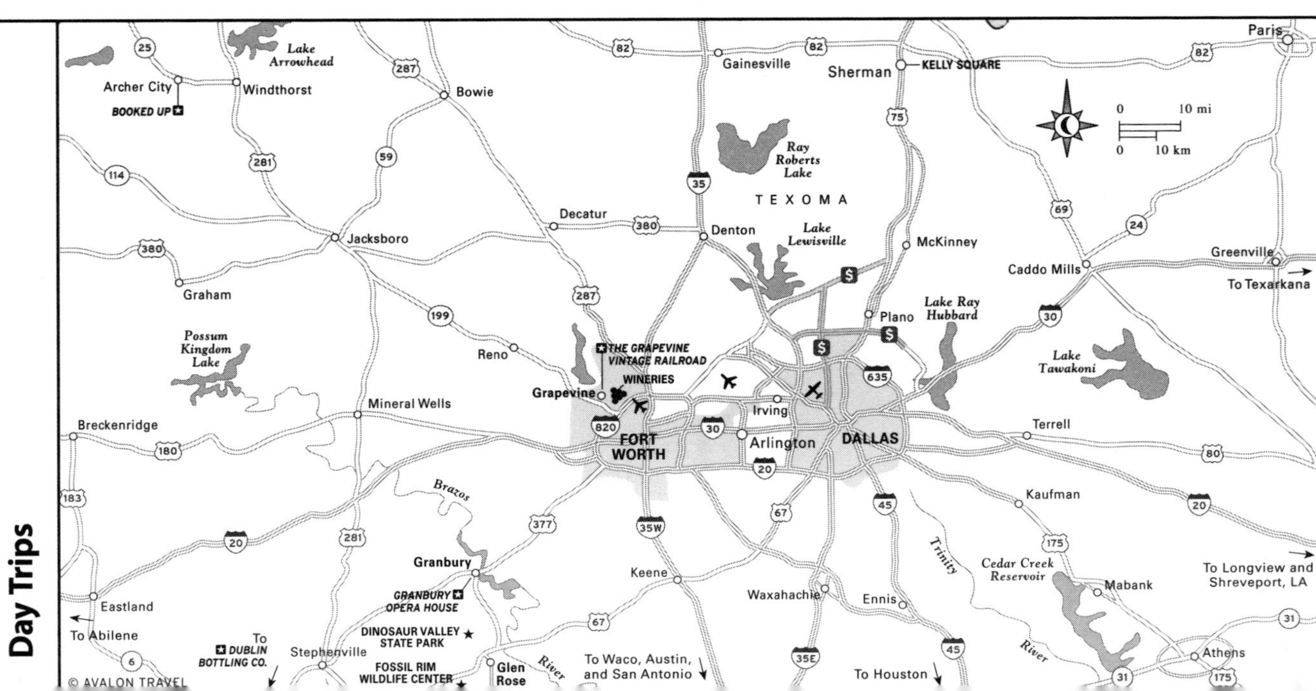

Archer City
BOOKED UP
Windthorst
Lake Arrowhead
Bowie
Gainesville
Sherman
KELLY SQUARE
Paris
0 10 mi
0 10 km
Ray Roberts Lake
TEXOMA
Decatur
Denton
Lake Lewisville
McKinney
Jacksboro
Graham
Caddo Mills
Greenville
To Texarkana
Plano
Lake Ray Hubbard
Reno
Possum Kingdom Lake
THE GRAPEVINE VINTAGE RAILROAD
WINERIES
Grapevine
Lake Tawakoni
Mineral Wells
Irving
Breckenridge
FORT WORTH
Arlington
DALLAS
Terrell
Brazos
Kaufman
Trinity
Cedar Creek Reservoir
Granbury
Keene
Waxahachie
Ennis
Mabank
To Longview and Shreveport, LA
Eastland
To Abilene
GRANBURY OPERA HOUSE
DINOSAUR VALLEY STATE PARK
To DUBLIN BOTTLING CO.
Stephenville
FOSSIL RIM WILDLIFE CENTER
Glen Rose
River
To Waco, Austin, and San Antonio
To Houston
River
Athens
© AVALON TRAVEL

Southfork Ranch

Side-by-side images of glistening skyscrapers, greasy oil rigs, and sprawling cattle ranches scrolled across 1980s TV screens, introducing one of the highest-rated shows of all time. From 1978 to 1991, the nighttime soap opera Dallas captivated audiences with its portrayal of the Ewing family feuds, often ending in dramatic cliffhangers like "Who Shot J. R.?"

The show perpetuated stereotypes that Dallas both embraces and evades. In reality, the Ewing estate known as Southfork Ranch is in the suburb of Parker, about 35 miles away from the distinctly cosmopolitan city where 10-gallon Stetson hats are few and far between. It takes some extra effort to experience the Dallas depicted on TV.

You can spend an afternoon absorbing the lifestyle portrayed by the wealthy oil family. **Southfork Ranch** (3700 Hogge Rd., 972/442-7800, www.southforkranch.com) offers guided tours of the Ewing mansion as longhorns roam the ranch outside. You'll learn everything you ever wanted to know about the making of Dallas. The house appears just as it did in the show, fully furnished and full of artifacts and memorabilia, including Jock Ewing's original 1978 Lincoln Continental.

The ranch is open daily 10am-5pm with tours running every 45 minutes. Admission is $15 for adults, $13 for seniors, $9 for children, and free for kids under 5. Make reservations for groups of more than 10 people.

original, however. The third story was added in 1926 during a remodel that also nixed the octagonal clock tower and four corner domes.

Archer County Museum and Jail

Located a couple of blocks from the courthouse, the **Archer County Museum and Jail** (203 E. Plum St., 940/574-2489, www.archercity.org, Sat. 9am-5pm, Sun. 1pm-5pm, free) is a fascinating relic of the Old West. Built in 1909, the ground floor was designed as living quarters for the sheriff and his family while the 2nd and 3rd stories housed jail cells, which remain eerily intact. Although never used, a single noose still hangs from an upstairs ceiling with a nearby lever that releases a trapdoor beneath. More than 8,000 prisoners traipsed through the jail before the county opened a new facility in 1974. The museum features a hodgepodge of historical artifacts, such as a saddle that belonged to Larry McMurtry's grandfather, Native American weapons dating back to the 1870s, and replicas of dinosaur bones excavated in Archer County.

★ Booked Up No. 1

Larry McMurtry, the legendary author of the *Lonesome Dove* series, ran four carefully curated bookstores in Archer City until 2012, when he auctioned off about 300,000 of his handpicked titles and shuttered three of his stores. **Booked Up No. 1** (216 S. Center St., 940/574-2511, www.bookedupac.com, Thurs.-Sat. 1pm-5pm) is all that remains, carrying about 150,000-200,000 volumes of rare and scholarly books as well as some first editions of McMurtry's novels. Literature lovers have been making pilgrimages to this iconic bookstore for decades in hopes of soaking up inspiration from McMurtry's personal collection. Allow plenty of time to get lost in the shelves here, since the hours are limited.

RESTAURANTS

The unassuming gas station restaurant **Lucky's Café** (513 S. Center St., 940/574-4431, www.luckyscafeinarchercity.com, Mon.-Fri. 6am-10pm, Sat.-Sun. 7am-10pm; $7-10) serves up one of the best and cheapest breakfasts in town. Sure, that's not saying much in a city of fewer than 2,000 people, but Lucky's home cooking exceeds expectations. You can get a full breakfast for under $7, plus there's a wide selection of burgers, sandwiches, and pizza for lunch and dinner.

Another small-town gem, **Murn's Café** (107 N. Center St., 940/574-2233, Mon.-Thurs. 5am-2pm, Fri. 5am-2pm and 5-9pm, Sat. 6am-2pm; $7-10) is known for the "El Diablo," a chicken-fried steak covered in queso, pico de gallo, and jalapenos. Look for other made-from-scratch daily lunch specials like friend catfish Fridays, and ask about the blackberry cobbler.

Aside from the delicious soups, entrees, and desserts, **Five Forks Tea House** (103 S. Center St., 940/574-4999, www.5forksteahouse.com, Wed. 10:30am-2:30pm, Thurs. 10:30am-2:30pm and 5pm-8pm, Fri.-Sat. 10:30am-2:30pm; $6-8) features a wide selection of loose-leaf tea and gourmet coffee in a cozy atmosphere full of neat knickknacks. Don't skip the artichoke dip, and ask about the day's off-menu specials. From inside the restaurant, you can also access **MillWright Marketplace and Flowers** (105 S. Center St., 940/574-4913, www.millwrightflowers.com, Mon.-Fri. 9am-5:30pm, Sat. 9am-1pm). The gift shop carries Archer City-themed tote bags, mugs, and other souvenirs.

ARTS AND CULTURE

Immortalized in the 1971 Oscar-winning film *The Last Picture Show*, the **Royal Theater** (113 E. Main St., 940/574-2489, www.royaltheater.org) remains the centerpiece of this tiny Texas town. Throughout the 1950s, Archer City's heyday, the Royal functioned as a movie theater and local hangout. In 1965, a fire nearly destroyed the building, and the structure sat in disrepair for decades. In fact, the film crew barely salvaged the façade for the movie (the interior scenes were shot elsewhere). Finally, in 2000, with help from local donors, the city restored the Royal to its former glory, and it now operates as a performing arts venue. Theatrical productions begin in February and continue throughout the year, including a spring drama, a summer musical, and a holiday performance. Tickets cost around $15, and shows usually run for two weekends during the evenings with one Sunday matinee.

HOTELS

For a cozy, middle-of-nowhere retreat, book a room at the historic **Spur Hotel** (101 N. Center St., 940/574-2501, www.thespurhotel.com; $80-100). Built in 1928, the 12-room boutique hotel was restored and reopened in 1990 with a gorgeous western-chic design. There are a few drawbacks, though: the three-story hotel has no elevator, and the rooms have no phones or TVs. Fortunately, there's free Wi-Fi.

PRACTICALITIES

Visitors Center

In keeping with the town's far-flung character, the **Archer City Visitor Center** (103 N. Center St., 940/574-2557, www.visitarchercity.org, Mon.-Wed. 8am-noon, Thurs.-Sat. 8am-2pm) is housed in an old filling station in the center of town. Look for the ironically digital Welcome sign across the front and the classic car mural behind the building. Friendly locals are on hand to clear up any confusion you have upon entering this remote little town.

Media

Pick up a copy of the weekly ***Archer County News*** (www.archercountynews.com) for a glimpse at life in Archer City, which includes Texas's youngest mayor, elected at age 18. You'll also find the ***Times-Record News*** (www.timesrecordnews.com), a larger daily out of Wichita Falls, which is half an hour north.

Getting There and Around

Archer City is almost a straight shot from Fort Worth. From downtown, just hop on I-35W north to U.S.-287. Then, head west on F.M. 174, which turns into Highway 25, leading right into the town's lone traffic light. Getting there from Dallas requires a little more effort and a toll. Take I-35E north from downtown to Highway 183 west. That turns into I-820 and connects to I-35W north.

To get around town, just step out of the visitors center, and look both ways. You'll see all of your destinations within walking distance.

Top: the Royal Theater in Archer City; **Bottom:** Dr Pepper museum at Dublin Bottling Works

Dublin/Hico

While each of these Central Texas towns has a distinct character, their proximity to one another provides the perfect two-in-one day trip just a couple of hours from Dallas-Fort Worth.

As evidenced by its green, shamrock-shaped welcome sign, Dublin is the "Irish Capital of Texas," home to a sizeable Irish American population. The humble town of about 3,700 people celebrates its heritage during the annual St. Patrick's Day parade and pageant. Dublin also claims the original, 120-year-old Dr Pepper factory.

About 20 miles east, the smaller town of Hico has grown from a roadside pit stop into an epicurean getaway. Try not to slip into a sugar coma while splurging on mountainous pies, specialty sodas, and gourmet chocolates. In May, thousands of tourists flock to Hico for the annual **Texas Steak Cook-off and Wine Festival** (www.texassteakcookoff.com), the largest event of its kind in the Southwest. Chefs compete for the title of best 12-ounce rib eye in the state.

Here's the best way to tackle these two towns: Make Hico your home base, because it has more to offer daylong and overnight guests with its excellent restaurants and lodging. Detour to Dublin for the Dr Pepper factory and soda shop, and take a quick peek at the Rodeo Heritage Museum.

SIGHTS

★ Dublin Bottling Works

The first factory to bottle Dr Pepper began operating in 1891, shortly after the drink was invented in a Waco drug store 90 miles east. The facility continued to produce the classic soda in its original form with pure cane sugar, calling it Dublin Dr Pepper. Texans agreed it was far superior to the mass-produced, high-fructose-corn-syrup-laden soft drink sold around the country. That all ended in 2012 when Dr Pepper's parent company sued the Dublin factory, forcing it to sell its rights to the brand. Fortunately, there's a silver lining to what could have been the death of an iconic destination.

While it no longer produces Dr Pepper, **Dublin Bottling Works** (105 E. Elm St., Dublin, 888/398-1024, www.dublinbottlingworks.com, Tues.-Sat. 10am-5pm, Sun. 1pm-5pm) has launched its own line of old-fashioned sodas bottled on-site and served in **Old Doc's Soda Shop,** housed in the same historic building. You can sample Dublin's brand of root beer, vanilla cream soda, black cherry, and other sugary drinks. The history of Dr Pepper remains preserved in the museum, which has troves of vintage artifacts and memorabilia. Tours of the 120-year-old factory run every 45 minutes from 10:15am to 4:15pm and cost $5 for adults and $4 for children and seniors.

Rodeo Heritage Museum

While Fort Worth enjoys much of today's rodeo glory, the sport's beginnings trace back to Dublin. From 1937 to 1959, Dublin was home to the

World's Championship Rodeo, the most famous rodeo company in the country. Owner Everett Colborn and performer Gene Autry toured the United States with professional cowboys and cowgirls trained at the 14,000-acre Lightning C Ranch. The **Rodeo Heritage Museum** (118 W. Blackjack St., Dublin, 254/445-0200, www.rodeoheritagemuseum.org, Wed.-Sat. 1pm-5pm, free) conserves that nearly forgotten legacy through printed records, historical photos, saddles, trophies, and other memorabilia.

RESTAURANTS

For some truly local fare, **Eis** (202 N. Pecan St., Hico, 254/796-2231, www.hicosupstairsinn.com/eis, Tues.-Thurs. 11am-2pm, Fri.-Sat. 11am-4pm) uses ingredients from Texas purveyors to whip up savory sandwiches like smoked chicken salad and jalapeno pimento cheese. The homegrown ingredients include bread from Sulak's Czech Bakery in Clifton just a few towns east and cheddar from the Veldhuizen Cheese farm in Dublin. Eis shares a storefront with Hico Upstairs Inn and the Pecan Street Drink Shoppe.

No day trip is complete without a visit to the local greasy spoon. **Koffee Kup Family Restaurant** (300 W. 2nd St., Hico, 254/796-4839, www.koffeekupfamilyrestaurant.com, daily 6am-9:30pm; $8-12) serves a home-style breakfast, gourmet burgers, and chicken-fried steak. But the real attraction here is homemade pie. Fifteen flavors rotate daily, including favorites like coconut meringue, banana blueberry, and Black Forest.

Set in an adorable pastel-colored cottage, **Wiseman House Chocolates** (406 W. Grubbs St., Hico, 254/796-2565, www.wisemanhousechocolates.com, Mon.-Sat. 10am-6pm, Sun. 1pm-5pm) is filled with fine, handmade chocolates from revered chocolatier Kevin Wenzel. For more than 20 years, he has crafted these confections using only natural ingredients for more complex flavor profiles. The shop even hosts chocolate-making classes in the spring, including a family-friendly beginner course and more intense workshops for serious connoisseurs.

SHOPS

Located in a two-story building in downtown Hico, **Blue Star Trading Co.** (112 Pecan St., 254/796-2828, www.bluestartrading.com, Mon.-Sat. 9:30am-6pm, Sun. 1pm-5pm) specializes in furniture, including both handmade and vintage selections. It's also a prime spot for trendy western apparel and souvenirs.

Named for the restored 1895 theater in which it's housed, **Opera House Antiques** (104 Elm St., 254/796-2210, www.operahouseantiqueshico.com, Mon.-Sat. 10am-5:30pm) features dozens of vendors selling antique furniture, jewelry, clothing, and other finds. The shop also sponsors the annual Hico Spring Antique Fair in downtown.

The family-owned **Sugar Moon Antiques** (101 S. Pecan St., Hico, 254/796-4155, www.sugarmoonantiques.com, Mon.-Sat. 10am-5:30pm, Sun. 1pm-5pm) features a variety of vintage home décor from shabby-chic to classic European. For refab fiends, the shop offers a slew of Annie Sloan chalk paint products. You'll also find one of Texas's largest selections of Flax Designs linen clothing.

HOTELS

Blending a vintage vibe with modern luxuries, **Hico Upstairs Inn** (202 N. Pecan St., Hico, 254/796-2230, www. hicosupstairsinn.com, $140-160) offers three private rooms with cable TV and Wi-Fi. Downstairs, the **Pecan Street Drink Shoppe** (which also houses **Eis** sandwich shop) features specialty soda, tea, and coffee along with Texas wine and craft beer. Swing by for a Saturday afternoon tasting.

PRACTICALITIES

Visitors Center

The **Dublin Chamber of Commerce** (111 S. Patrick St., Dublin, 254/445-3422, www.dublintxchamber.com) doubles as the visitors center, and is stocked with brochures and information on local attractions and events.

Hico greets travelers with its sensationalized connection to Billy the Kid. Rumor has it that he escaped death in 1881 and hid in Hico for rest of his days. The life and disputed demise of the Old West's most notorious outlaw is on display at the **Billy the Kid Museum** (114 N. Pecan St., Hico, 254/796-2523, www.billythekidmuseum.com, Mon.-Sat. 9am-3pm, donations accepted). It's also the visitors center where you can find tourism information and souvenirs.

Getting There

Dublin and Hico lie on the same route from both Dallas and Fort Worth. Take I-30 west, which turns into I-20 west. Head south on US-281 to Stephenville. For Dublin, go south on US-377 straight into town. For Hico, stay on US-281 for about 20 more miles.

Granbury

A historic town square and lakeside views have made Granbury a go-to getaway for Dallasites. Founded in 1887, local legends abound in this town, which claims ties to outlaw Jesse James and assassin John Wilkes Booth. However, the vibrant performing arts scene is perhaps the biggest draw. The Granbury Theatre Company enthralls visitors with professional-grade productions in the town's gorgeous 19th-century opera house.

While located only 35 miles from Fort Worth (a little farther from Dallas), Granbury is best experienced over a two-day trip. Family-friendly outdoor adventure can be found in Glen Rose, 20 minutes south. Spend an afternoon exploring dinosaur tracks or mingling with endangered species before returning to Granbury for dinner and a show.

SIGHTS

Granbury Doll House Museum

Set inside a gorgeous Victorian-style home, this dollhouse within a dollhouse features an enormous collection of the childhood toys, dating back to 1860. The ladies who own the **Granbury Doll House Museum** (421 Bridge

St., 817/894-5194, Fri.-Sat. 10am-4pm, Sun. 1pm-4pm, donations accepted) painstakingly restore each individual doll to its original state. The museum regularly rotates exhibits, and features guest speakers and doll-making demonstrations.

Granbury State Historical Cemetery

Located on a hill above the town square, **Granbury State Historical Cemetery** (801 N. Houston St.) offers a fascinating glimpse into Granbury's past. You'll find graves of veterans dating back to the War of 1812, along with burial sites of descendants of Davy Crockett. One tombstone reads, "Jesse Woodson James Sept. 5, 1847-Aug. 15, 1951. Supposedly killed in 1882." Locals claim this is the final resting place of outlaw Jesse James, who escaped death and retreated to Granbury under an alias. However, the story has never been proven.

★ Granbury Opera House

One of the oldest remaining structures in town, the **Granbury Opera House** (133 E. Pearl St., 817/579-0952, www.granburytheatrecompany.org, Mon.-Thurs. noon-5pm, Fri. noon-7:30pm, Sat. 10am-7:30pm, Sun. noon-2:30pm) has been beautifully restored to reflect its 19th-century origins. Spend some time admiring the ornate chandeliers, limestone walls, and rounded staircases. The intimate space includes floor and balcony seating, all with excellent views of the stage.

Hood County Courthouse

Constructed in 1891 from native limestone, the **Hood County Courthouse** (100 E. Pearl St., 817/579-3200, www.co.hood.tx.us, Mon.-Fri. 8am-5pm) adorns the center of Granbury's historic town square. The three-story structure features a French Second Empire architectural style and original interior woodwork, and still houses government offices.

RESTAURANTS

Whether you're craving classic comfort food or just need a break from it, **Linda's Southern Kitchen** (200 E. Pearl St., 817/573-1952, www.lindassouthernkitchen.com, Thurs.-Sat. 11am-8pm, Sun. 11am-2pm, $8-12) is a good bet. The menu features gravy-smothered chicken-fried steak and homemade pies but also a decent selection of salads, sandwiches, and seafood.

The **Nutshell Eatery & Bakery** (137 E. Pearl St., 817/279-8989, Mon.-Thurs. 7am-3pm, Fri. 7am-5pm, Sat. 7am-7pm, Sun. 7am-6pm) is the go-to breakfast spot before a day of shopping and sightseeing. Housed in a restored building from 1885, the charming café offers a cheap and substantial breakfast. Be sure to try the homemade cinnamon toast.

Located a block from Granbury's town square and housed in a renovated 1930s filling station, **Pearl Street Station** (120 W. Pearl St., 817/579-7233, www.pearlststationgranburytx.com, Mon.-Tues. 11am-6pm, Fri.-Sat. 11am-8pm, Sun. 11am-3pm, $7-12) serves delicious barbecue and Cajun food, including a chopped brisket sandwich, crawfish étouffée, gumbo and other dishes.

ARTS AND CULTURE

Based in the 1950s-era theater in the historic downtown square, the **Big City Music Revue** (114 N. Crockett St., 855/823-5550, www.bigcitymusicrevue.com) performs nostalgic concerts that routinely sell out. Backed by a full band, classically trained vocalists belt out '50s, '60s, and '70s hits along with country and gospel tunes. The themed concerts run every other weekend throughout the year. Tickets are $25 for adults, $22 for seniors and veterans, and $15 for children.

Continuously operating since 1952, the **Brazos Drive-in Theater** (1800 W. Pearl St., 817/573-1311, www.thebrazos.com, $20 per six-person carload) consists of one screen, a wood-frame concession shack, a few rows of covered seating, and plenty of space for kids to roam and play. Family-friendly blockbuster movies premiere every weekend at dusk, and gates open 45 minutes before showtime. The theater accepts cash only.

One of the oldest remaining structures in town, the **Granbury Opera House** (133 E. Pearl St., 817/579-0952, www.granburytheatrecompany.org, Mon.-Thurs. noon-5pm, Fri. noon-7:30pm, Sat. 10am-7:30pm, Sun. noon-2:30pm). Settling in for an outstanding community theater production. The Granbury Theatre Company puts on 8-10 productions a year with a quality that holds its own against professional companies in the big city. Tickets range $20-30 and should be reserved in advance.

Each fall, thousands of visitors flock to the largest outdoor amphitheater in Texas to watch the musical life of Jesus Christ unfold on stage. The **Promise in Glen Rose** (5000 Texas Dr., Glen Rose, 254/897-3926, www.thepromiseglenrose.com) has endured for nearly three decades at the $8.5 million venue surrounded by a 45,000-gallon moat ideal for reenacting biblical stories. Performances run on Friday and Saturday nights throughout September and October, and general admission tickets start at $30.

SPORTS AND ACTIVITIES

Two towering prehistoric beasts greet visitors to **Dinosaur Valley State Park** (1629 Park Rd. 59, Glen Rose, 254/897-4588, www.tpwd.texas.gov/state-parks/dinosaur-valley, adults $7, children free). While the life-sized models may be just for show, real dinosaurs roamed this park a hundred million years ago. The evidence lies in the Paluxy River, where you can walk through the shallow waters and find tyrannosaurus tracks and other fossilized footprints. Pick up a map of all the preserved tracks at the park headquarters and spend the day exploring, or join a guided hike. Due to the unpredictable Texas weather, call the park for a report on river levels before embarking on this 1.5-hour road trip.

Within walking distance of Granbury's town square, **City Beach Park** (623 W. Pearl St., daily 5am-11pm, free) offers a small coastal escape in the middle of Texas. The man-made beach is popular with children and families, so don't expect a peaceful retreat. You'll find sand volleyball, a spray park, kayak rentals, a boardwalk, and covered picnic pavilions.

Come face-to-face with endangered species at **Fossil Rim Wildlife Center** (2299 County Rd. 2008, Glen Rose, 254/897-2960, www.fossilrim.org, Nov. 1-March 11, daily 8:30am-3:29pm, March 12-Oct. 31, daily

8:30am-4:29pm, $25.95 pp). This Glen Rose park researches and conserves threatened animals rarely seen in the wild. On a scenic drive through the park, you can see curious creatures like the wildebeest, rhinoceros, and Arabian oryx along with more familiar friends like giraffes, zebras, and emus who won't hesitate to poke their heads through the car window. Don't waste your money visiting on a hot summer day, when many animals stay hidden in the shade. Start early in the morning to see the most animals, and expect to spend a few hours touring the park, and picnicking. Guided tours are available but must be booked three days in advance.

SHOPS

Granbury's historic downtown square was the first in Texas to earn a spot in the National Register of Historic Places, becoming listed in 1974. Aside from the vibrant arts and dining scenes, the square attracts shoppers from all over the state in search of antiques, knickknacks, and other small-town treasures. You'll want to wander every storefront, but don't skip these spots along the way:

The **Wagon Yard** (213 N. Crockett St., 817/573-5321, www.wagonyard.com, Mon.-Sat. 8:30am-5:30pm) has furniture and home décor, vintage record players, nostalgic advertisement signs, and original weekly issues of *Life* magazine from 1937 to 1972. For culinary connoisseurs, **The Pan Handle** (106 N. Crockett St., 817/579-1518, www.thepanhandle.com, Mon.-Thurs. 10am-6pm, Fri.-Sat. 10am-8pm, Sun. 1pm-6pm) is full of kitchen tools and gifts along with a vast array of gourmet coffee flavors from Mississippi Mud Pie to Swiss chocolate orange. Make your own souvenirs at **Against the Grain Studio** (111 E. Bridge St., 682/936-4443, www.atg-studio.com, Mon.-Tues. 10am-8pm, Wed. 10am-5pm, Thurs. 3pm-8pm, Fri. 10am-11pm, Sat. 10am-10pm, Sun. 2pm-6pm). The arts and crafts store takes walk-ins for mosaics ($7 and up), ceramics ($4.50 and up), and canvas painting ($10 and up). The shop also hosts monthly workshops.

HOTELS

The sprawling lakeside **Hilton Garden Inn** (635 E. Pearl St., 817/579-3800, www.hiltongardeninn3.hilton.com, $130-150) provides direct access to the city beach and boardwalk. The rooms come equipped with all the expected comforts, including flat-screen TVs, cable channels, Wi-Fi, microwaves, and mini-fridges. The hotel is ideal for large groups.

For something a cozier, the **Iron Horse Inn** (616 Thorpe Springs Rd., 817/993-9847, www.ironhorsebb.com, $115-125) is nestled off the beaten path but only two blocks from Granbury's town square. The Craftsman-style mansion features six rooms, plus a separate garden cottage. Guests can indulge in a lavish breakfast served on fine china, or sip some OJ on the front porch.

A historic limestone building located right on the square, the **Nutt House Hotel** (119 E. Bridge St., 817/279-1207, www.nutt-hotelcom, $90-140) is a popular retreat for families who don't want to venture too far from the main attractions. The hotel has gift shopping downstairs, including old-fashioned candy. Ask about the ghost of Mary Lou Watkins, the hotel's former owner who still watches over the building.

PRACTICALITIES

True to Granbury's small-town hospitality, most shop and hotel owners gladly offer up tourism information. To find it all in one place, the **Granbury Visitor's Center** (116 W. Bridge St., 800/950-2212, www.visitgranbury.com, Mon.-Fri. 8am-5pm, Sat. 10am-5pm, Sun. noon-4pm) is stocked with brochures for every local attraction, including adventures in Glen Rose and other neighboring towns.

Getting There and Around

From Dallas, head south on I-35E to I-20 west. Continue past the southern edge of Fort Worth to U.S. 377, and follow that road for another 27 miles until it turns into Pearl Street. You've arrived when you spot the courthouse clock tower. Downtown Granbury and its vicinity are easily walkable. Glen Rose is a 16-mile drive south on Highway 144.

Grapevine

Past the knot of freeways and construction cranes, the heart of this northern suburb presents a very different picture. Grapevine's historic downtown is full of locally owned shops, restaurants, and old-fashioned attractions. It's also a prime spot for tasting Texas wine. With 10 wineries located up and down Grapevine's Main Street, the town serves as a hub for the state's wine industry, the fifth largest in the country.

While adults can indulge in local wine and fancy cuisine, kids come for water parks, vintage train rides, and a magical land of LEGOs. Located just north of DFW Airport, Grapevine is full of hotel options, some equipped with so many attractions that you might not want to venture any farther.

SIGHTS

★ Grapevine Urban Wine Trail

With several different wineries to choose from, winos and connoisseurs alike can sip a wide range of homegrown vino on the **Grapevine Urban Wine Trail** (www.grapevinetexasusa.com). Tasting rooms are scattered along Main Street in historic homes; one noteworthy spot is **Cross Timbers Winery** (805 N. Main St., 817/488-6789, www.crosstimberswinery.com), housed in one of Grapevine's oldest structures. There's also a barn and outdoor seating. South of downtown, **Delaney Vineyards and Winery** (2000 Champagne Blvd., 817/481-5668, www.delaneyvineyards.com) is the largest in North Texas and features a spacious 8,000-square-foot tasting room and 10 acres of Cynthiana grapes. For something a little offbeat, the **Sloan & Williams Winery** (401 S. Main St., 817/527-7867, www.sloanwilliams.com) makes its own wine ice cream in distinct flavors like cherry merlot and peach white zinfandel.

You can tour the wineries at your own pace and price point, or sign up for a guided tour via **Grapevine Wine Tours** (817/259-9463, www.grapevinewinetours.com, departs twice daily, $99.50-109.50), which is limited to three destinations.

Grapevine Vintage Railroad

Known for its enormously popular North Pole Express at Christmastime, the **Grapevine Vintage Railroad** (705 S. Main St., 817/410-3185, www.grapevinetexasusa.com) runs along the historic Cotton Belt route between Grapevine and Fort Worth. The Victorian-era coach is powered by the one of the oldest continuously operating steam engines, from 1896. You can board the train for themed rides like the Jazz Wine Train, featuring live jazz music; the Witches Brew Train with craft beer and Halloween costumes; and the kid-friendly Day Without Thomas, which chronicles the classic tale of Thomas the Tank Engine.

If you still need to squeeze in a trip to the Fort Worth Stockyards, the train offers a 1.5-hour trip to see the cattle drive and spend a couple of hours exploring before returning to Grapevine in the evening. This ride operates every weekend between Memorial Day and Labor Day. Tickets are $18-26 and should be reserved in advance. Prices for other excursions vary.

LEGOLAND Discovery Center

Located inside Grapevine Mills Mall, **LEGOLAND Discovery Center** (3000 Grapevine Mills Pkwy., 877/818-1677, www.dallasfw.legolanddiscoverycenter.com, Mon.-Fri. 10am-6pm, Sat. 10am-8pm, Sun. 11am-6pm, $19.95-31) can get pretty crowded during spring break and summer months, but it's well worth the trip for the little ones. The massive theme park features interactive playgrounds, a mini-land made from millions of LEGO pieces, mechanical rides, and a 4-D movie theater.

It's best to buy tickets at least 24 hours in advance to secure a spot, because the center allows only a certain number of visitors in at a time. Plus, it's cheaper. General admission is $19.95 online and $21 at the door, and free for children under 2.

RESTAURANTS

A.J.'s on Main (651 Main St., 817/488-6112, www.ajsonmaintx.com, Tues.-Sat. 11am-9pm, Sun. noon-4pm, $10-15) is known for its pulled pork sandwiches, beef tamales, and other barbecue staples. The restaurant offers pleasant patio dining alongside a smoker that emits aromas of brisket and sausage. The full bar stocks plenty of local craft beers.

Housed in an old bank building in Grapevine's historic downtown, **Dino's Steak and Claw House** (342 S. Main St., 817/488-3100, www.dinosteakandclaw.net, Mon.-Thurs. 5pm-9:30pm, Fri.-Sat. 5pm-10:30pm, $30-60) features a romantic, upscale vibe. The low-lit, two-story restaurant presents dinner music performed live on a grand piano. The menu of seafood and steak includes popular dishes like horseradish-steamed crab claws and the 20-ounce porterhouse. Ask for a seat upstairs for more secluded dining.

Specializing in European-style handmade breads, **Main Street Bistro & Bakery** (316 S. Main St., 817/424-4333, www.themainbakery.com, Mon. 6:30am-3pm, Tues.-Thurs. 6:30am-9pm, Fri.-Sat. 6:30am-10:30pm, Sun. 6:30am-9pm) serves delicious pastries, especially the almond croissant and the crème brûlée cronut. Stop by first thing in the morning to choose from the case of fresh-from-the-oven treats. The café also serves breakfast, lunch, and dinner. Weekend brunch hours draw huge crowds, so expect to wait for a table.

ARTS AND CULTURE

The art deco-style **Palace Arts Center** (300 S. Main St., 817/410-3100, www.grapevinetexasusa.com) houses the 1940s-era Palace Theatre, which hosts music, drama, and film productions. The First Friday Film Series features family-friendly movies for $6. The smaller Lancaster Theatre, converted from an old 1930s grocery store, accommodates smaller events as well as an art gallery with rotating exhibits.

SPORTS AND ACTIVITIES

Lake Grapevine (www.lake-grapevine.com) covers 8,000 acres of North Texas land, surrounded by several miles of hike-and-bike trails. The North Shore Trail extends 9.5 miles along the northwest end of the lake, offering some of the best sunset views of the landscape. **Murrell Park** (880 Simmons Rd., 817/865-2600) provides easy access to the trail as well as fishing and picnicking spots.

You can also paddle and wake-surf the lake via **DFW Surf** (www.dfw-surf.com, 972/427-4084). Paddleboard and kayak rentals start at $20 an hour. Between May and October, challenge your balance during a stand-up paddleboard yoga session on the lake. The best shoreline access is near **Scott's Landing Marina** (1999 Farris Branch Dr.) on the south side of Oak Grove Park.

SHOPS

Open weekends year-round, the **Farmers Market of Grapevine** (520 S. Main St., Suite 203, 817/527-7446, www.farmersmarketofgrapevine.com) features an indoor and outdoor section of fresh produce and handmade gifts from growers and artisans. Sample fruits and vegetables harvested from farms less than 30 minutes away. Other goodies include gluten-free pastries, fried pies, and gourmet tamales.

Grapevine's historic Main Street is home to dozens of locally owned shops worthy of a peek inside. Some of the best spots include **Vintage Tex** (603 S. Main St., Suite 300, 817/946-6455, www.vintagetex.com, daily 11am-6pm), which carries women's clothing and accessories from the 1920s to the 1970s at fair prices. **Dr. Sue's Chocolate** (417 S. Main St., 817/416-7667, www.drsueschocolate.com, Mon.-Thurs. 11am-6pm, Fri.-Sat. 11am-8pm, Sun. noon-6pm) specializes in all-natural dark chocolate with complex flavor profiles like blueberry ancho chile and ginger fig. For western souvenirs, stop by the **Texas General Store** (406 S. Main St., 817/756-6476, www.texasgeneralgrapevine.com, Mon.-Wed. 10am-6pm,

Thurs.-Sat. 10am-8pm, Sun. 11am-5pm), where you'll find T-shirts, jewelry, homemade snacks, and novelty gifts.

HOTELS

Even though Grapevine is just a 30-minute drive from Dallas, the luxurious theme-park accommodations make it hard to pass up an overnight stay. The massive **Gaylord Texan** (1501 Gaylord Trail, 817/778-1000, www.marriott.com, $270-360) overlooks Lake Grapevine and houses a 4.5-acre atrium of gardens and water features. Its winter ice sculptures and slides make the hotel a popular holiday destination.

For a more natural setting, the **Vineyards Campground and Cabins** (1501 N. Dooley St., 888/329-8993, www.vineyardscampground.com, $93-175) offer furnished cabins and RV sites on Lake Grapevine with access to a kayak and bike rentals, a swim beach, and nature trails.

PRACTICALITIES

Tourist information can be found at the **Grapevine Convention and Visitors Bureau** (636 S. Main St., 817/410-3185, www.grapevinetexasusa.com, Mon.-Fri. 8am-5pm, Sat. 10am-6:30pm, Sun. noon-5pm). Volunteers are on hand with maps and brochures, plus you can buy tickets to many local attractions in one place.

Getting There and Around

Grapevine lies about 25 miles north of downtown Dallas, in the middle of Dallas and Fort Worth amid a web of suburban highways. From downtown Dallas, take I-35E north to Highway 183 west to Highway 114 west. Exit at Main Street. From Fort Worth, take I-35W to Highway 121 north to I-820 north. Follow that to Highway 183 east and then take Highway 121 north to Main Street.

Background

The Setting

With its skyline of luminous steel towers and white arches, and flanked by freeways and interstates, Dallas is a vibrant and fast-paced metropolis, spanning 385 square miles of mostly flat North Texas land. The country's ninth-largest city is home to about 1.2 million people. Despite its distinctly urban landscape, Dallas's defining feature has always been its native blackland prairies and the Trinity River, which flows through the southern and western sections of the city.

What the region lacks in diverse topography it makes up for in the simplistic beauty of its tall woodland grasses that sweep across the landscape, which sits at about 430 feet above sea level. The land rises a few hundred feet south of the Trinity River in Oak Cliff and surrounding areas, offering an elevated view of the city skyline.

Due to the rapid commercial development of Dallas, you have to look pretty hard to see the blackland prairies, which only remain in pockets like White Rock Lake Park, the Great Trinity Forest, and other nature preserves. The Trinity River's more attractive west fork meanders through neighboring Fort Worth, which lies in the Cross Timbers region of Texas, characterized by rolling hills and prairies.

CLIMATE

Dallas-Fort Worth experiences humid and often scorching summers, with temperatures routinely reaching triple digits. While the rest of the year remains warm and mild, locals have come to expect a brief bout of sleet and snow during the winter. The coldest months, January and February, average a low of about 35 degrees while the hottest months, July and August, hover around a high of 96 degrees.

Located in "tornado alley," the region is no stranger to severe and dangerous storms. Although spring brings out the bluebonnets and other gorgeous Texas wildflowers, the weather can be volatile. Heavy rain, flash floods, hail, high winds, and tornados are not uncommon.

ENVIRONMENTAL ISSUES

While it has taken steps to reduce greenhouse gas emissions, the Dallas-Fort Worth area records some of the highest ozone levels in Texas, particularly in the springtime. The air pollution stems mostly from commuter traffic, natural gas wells, and chemicals from coal and cement plants wafting over from nearby counties. Dallas is not kind to travelers with seasonal allergies, either. In the spring, the metro area sees some of the highest ragweed counts in the country.

The native blackland prairie that characterizes the North Texas landscape has shrunk to less than 1 percent of its original size. It's the most endangered large ecosystem in North America.

Previous: Margaret Hunt Hill Bridge; historic Chisholm Trail Mural by Richard Haas in Downtown Fort Worth

History

Like many major cities, Dallas was founded as a transportation hub. John Neely Bryan, an Indian trader from Tennessee, established a trading post on the east bank of the Trinity River in 1841. A natural ford provided ideal passage across the river. The real growth began with the railroad construction in the 1870s, allowing for the regional transport of goods, namely cotton, which boomed through the early 20th century along with the retail industry. In 1907, a high-end store known as Neiman Marcus opened specializing in women's clothing and millinery.

One year later, the natural feature that made Dallas so desirable devastated the burgeoning city. The Great Trinity River Flood of 1908 left five people dead and thousands homeless, and resulted in millions of dollars in damages. The river rose to a record 52.6 feet. It was the worst disaster Dallas had ever seen, thus beginning a new chapter in the city's development. In the years following, Dallas built levees along the Trinity River, diverted rail lines into one depot, and constructed the now century-old Houston Street Viaduct, the first of several bridges connecting downtown to the south side of the river.

Dallasites are less eager to reminisce about the post-World War I era when the city became home to the nation's largest chapter of the Ku Klux Klan. More than 13,000 members strong, the group consisted of lawyers, politicians, judges, police chiefs, and other civic leaders. That period didn't last long, though. The *Dallas Morning News* took an unpopular stand against the organization, helping elect the anti-Klan candidate for Texas governor in 1925. The KKK's membership plummeted over the next four years until the chapter shuttered in 1929.

The Great Depression came with a silver lining for Dallas: the discovery of oil in East Texas. The petroleum industry soared, and so did the economy. The city beat the larger and more historic cities of Houston and San Antonio in a bid to host the Texas Centennial in 1936, the first "world's fair" of the Southwest. After World War II, the Dallas business boom continued into its heyday of the 1950s and '60s.

While the city flourished economically, it was rife with vitriol politically and socially. The sentiments that defined Dallas in the 1920s—racism and socialist paranoia—flared up again amid desegregation efforts of the 1950s and '60s. This time, the *Dallas Morning News* fueled the fire, taking an extreme stance against the Kennedy administration. The assassination of President John F. Kennedy on November 22, 1963, and the events that followed, left Dallas with deep scars and the nickname "City of Hate."

Despite the setbacks, Dallas continued to grow into a major metropolis. The opening of the Dallas-Fort Worth International Airport in 1974 attracted more corporate headquarters, and the facility is now one of the busiest airports in the world. Other commercial and residential development crept north throughout the 1970s and '80s, especially shopping malls.

While Dallas dominated the cotton, oil, and retail businesses, the former army outpost of Fort Worth earned its title of "Cowtown," herding more than four million cattle through town via the Chisholm Trail, a post-Civil War livestock route that stretched from Kansas to Texas. Fort Worth was the last stop before crossing the Red River into Indian territory. After the railroad arrived in 1876, a Boston businessman invested in what is now the Fort Worth Stockyards. By 1900, the city had become more than just a pit stop for cattle drovers. The local livestock industry was born along with the largest meatpacking industry in the Southwest.

In the 1920s, Fort Worth also reaped the benefits of the Texas oil boom, helping the city grow from a livestock exchange station into a small metropolis. Several significant landmarks developed in the years leading up to World War II: the T&P train station, the Will Rogers Memorial Coliseum, and the renowned Casa Mañana theater.

Meanwhile, Texas Christian University was expanding from a small, private college to a sprawling university. By the 1970s, Fort Worth was home to critically acclaimed art museums. Over the next couple of decades, after suburbanization had pulled people north, the historic heart of downtown was revitalized as Sundance Square, attracting residents back to the city center. The same change has occurred in neighborhoods like Southside and West Fort Worth.

Government and Economy

Although historically conservative, Dallas County residents have generally voted blue since the 1990s. For the first time in 75 years, the *Dallas Morning News* endorsed the Democratic presidential candidate, Hillary Clinton, in 2016, sparking fierce protests and a drop in subscriptions. The suburban counties of North Texas remain a conservative stronghold.

The railroad construction of the 1870s sparked Dallas's growth as one of the largest inland cotton markets and the nation's leader in cotton gin manufacturing. By the 1930s, oil reigned supreme thanks to its discovery in East Texas and other parts of the state. Dallas cornered the petroleum market, resulting in a sustained economic boom. Telecommunications became the next industry to take off as major companies like Texas Instruments established headquarters. Today, the so-called Telecom Corridor is home to hundreds of firms including AT&T, MetroPCS, and Cisco Systems.

The Dallas-Fort Worth region also has one of the nation's largest concentrations of publicly traded companies, including Dr Pepper Snapple Group, ExxonMobil, Southwest Airlines, Frito-Lay, JCPenney, and Atmos Energy.

The city has remained a retail giant since Neiman Marcus debuted in the early 20th century. Dallas has two of the state's largest malls, NorthPark Center and Galleria Dallas, along with numerous walkable outdoor developments.

People and Culture

As Dallas and Fort Worth experience business growth and urban redevelopment, the cities have attracted a relatively younger demographic; the median age is 31 years old. The largest trend over the past several decades has been the influx of Mexican immigrants. Their cultural influence is seen everywhere from local cuisine to retail shops to performing arts. The city's largest minority group, Hispanics make up about 42 percent of the population.

African Americans comprise about 25 percent of today's population. Dallas's Black Chamber of Commerce, founded in 1926, is the country's oldest. The city saw a rapid demographic shift between 2006 and 2010, ranking fourth in the nation for the largest number of new African American residents.

Despite its diversity, Dallas still struggles with income and racial segregation. Most poor, nonwhite residents live in blighted areas south of the Trinity River while wealthy white households are concentrated north of downtown.

Although many parts of Dallas and Fort Worth are trending toward pedestrian- and bike-friendly environments, the region as a whole is overwhelmingly car-centric. People are usually in a hurry. Upon a closer look, however, each neighborhood has its own culture—from the wealthy SUV-sporting families of Park Cities to the scrappy thirtysomething artists of Deep Ellum to the *paleteria*-pushing vendors of Oak Cliff.

While English is the primary language spoken in Dallas-Fort Worth, Spanish is also widely spoken in some pockets, especially in southern and western Dallas.

Fort Worth's population of about 800,000 people is growing fast (nearly 4 percent per year) along with the rest of the region. Collectively, the Dallas-Fort Worth metro area encompasses 13 counties and 6 million people.

RELIGION

Dallas and Fort Worth consist largely of Protestant Christians. The roots of Methodists, Baptists, and Presbyterians run deep, with congregations beginning in 1868. The historic First United Methodist Church in Downtown Dallas is more than 170 years old. The nearby Cathedral Santuario de Guadalupe was constructed in the late 19th century, shortly after the region's first Catholic parish was formed. Both churches remain popular stops on downtown sightseeing tours.

The first Reform Jewish synagogue in North Texas, Temple Emanu-El, was chartered in 1875, and is now the largest in the South. The Jewish community played a significant role in the development of Dallas, influencing the city's retail industry and the social conscience.

The more recent decades have seen the growth in evangelical megachurches alongside large Muslim and Buddhist communities concentrated primarily in surrounding suburbs.

ARTS

Beyond the state-of-the-art cultural districts that have formed in recent decades, a number of modern-day artists, writers, and musicians have called Dallas-Fort Worth home.

Ray Wylie Hubbard and Michael Martin Murphy came of age in Oak Cliff, attending the same high school, before becoming country music stars. Two original members of the Dixie Chicks, Emily and Martie Erwin, grew up in North Dallas, performing first as a bluegrass ensemble at local church-run coffee shop. Singer-songwriter Edie Brickell, another Oak Cliff native, helped lead the 1980s resurgence of Deep Ellum, playing regular shows with the New Bohemians. A teenage Stevie Ray Vaughan routinely fell asleep during class at his Oak Cliff high school, after moonlighting as a soon-to-be blues icon. He dropped out to launch his music career in Austin, but he is buried at Laurel Land Cemetery in Dallas.

The cities also bred major music stars of the late 20th century. The Toadies got their start in Fort Worth, joining the droves of alt-rock bands that reshaped Deep Ellum in the 1990s. Dallas native Tim DeLaughter formed the multi-instrumental Polyphonic Spree in 2000, and every year the band performs a wildly popular holiday show in Dallas. After growing up in a prestigious all-girls prep school in North Dallas, '90s darling Lisa Loeb went on to record the hit song, "Stay (I Missed You)."

Although born in Brooklyn, New York, contemporary jazz artist Norah Jones became one of the most notable graduates of Dallas ISD's distinguished Booker T. Washington High School arts magnet downtown. She studied jazz piano at the University of North Texas before moving to New York City and racking up Grammy Awards in 2003.

Soul singer Erykah Badu, another Booker T. grad, is one of the few Dallas-born artists who still lives in her hometown. And she doesn't hide from her local fans. Badu throws her own massive birthday bash in Deep Ellum, and has been known to appear as a surprise DJ at local dance clubs.

More recently, the breakout musician Leon Bridges proudly hails from Fort Worth, having recorded his debut track, "Coming Home," at Shipping and Receiving Bar. He quit his job as a dishwasher at Del Frisco's Grille when Columbia Records signed him.

Before his death in 2013, world-renowned classical pianist Van Cliburn lived out the later years of his life in Fort Worth where the Van Cliburn International Piano Competition was established in 1962. The quadrennial event was created to honor Cliburn's historic win at the first International Tchaikovsky Competition in Moscow.

Essentials

Transportation

AIR

Its location near the center of North America makes Dallas-Fort Worth one of the easiest and quickest metro areas to reach by air. If you choose ground travel, the cheaper alternative, you're in for a long haul. What you lose in hours spent on the road you make up for with extra cash in your pocket.

With more than 1,800 flights a day to over 170 destinations, the **Dallas-Fort Worth International Airport** (DFW, 2400 Aviation Dr., 972/973-3112, www.dfwairport.com) is one of the busiest airports in the world. Located about 20 miles from Downtown Dallas, the airport recently renovated Terminal A as part of a $2.7 billion improvement plan. The plan includes an increase in restaurant and retail space, an expanded baggage claim area, and a new electronic parking guidance system. The airport serves more than 65 million travelers a year on 157 domestic and 56 international non-stop flights on American Airlines, American Eagle, Spirit, JetBlue, and United, along with major international airlines.

The much smaller, city-owned and operated **Dallas Love Field Airport** (DAL, 8008 Herb Kelleher Way, 214/670-5683, www.dallas-lovefield.com) is the headquarters for Southwest Airlines, bringing in about seven million passengers a year. It's also the city's exclusive outpost for Virgin America. The airport is an attractive entrance to the city thanks to its stunning art installations by Dallas artists.

Both airports operate shuttle buses and rental car counters 24 hours a day, and they are served by Uber, Lyft, and Wingz app-based services. These app-based services have a regulated fare of $25-33. There are also taxi stands. The **Dallas Area Rapid Transit** (DART) train's orange line operates stations at DFW Airport and Love Field. The rail line transports travelers to major attractions including downtown and Deep Ellum, running from 1am to 4am seven days a week. For those headed west, the **Trinity Railway Express** (TRE) takes you to Fort Worth, but only out of DFW Airport. Both public transit options cost $2.50 for a two-hour pass.

TRAIN

Amtrak operates out of Dallas's Union Station in downtown (400 S. Houston St., www.amtrak.com). Its Texas Eagle train service runs daily between Chicago and San Antonio, stopping in Dallas. The train also has a station in Downtown Fort Worth (1001 Jones St.). Amtrak excursions take much longer than buses, but you get to see more of the Texas landscape.

BUS

A few blocks from the Amtrak station is the **Greyhound** bus station (205 S. Lamar St.). If you don't mind sacrificing comfort, a cheaper option, **Megabus** (www.us.megabus.com), offers routes to major cities in

Previous: a DART train; the iconic Dallas Pegasus atop the Magnolia Hotel the Southwest, including Austin, Atlanta, Memphis, and Little Rock, as well as a route to Chicago. The double-decker bus service operates out of the DART East Transfer Center (330 N. Olive St.) in Downtown Dallas.

PUBLIC TRANSIT

Over the past decade, Dallas has made considerable progress on public transportation options. In particular, the **Dallas Area Rapid Transit** (DART, www.dart.org) system makes it easy to move between tourist destinations. However, for activities off the beaten path, it's best to travel by car.

All four DART rail lines make stops at the **Pearl/Arts District Station** (2215 Bryan St.) in Downtown Dallas, running about every 20 minutes. From there, you can explore the Dallas Arts District on foot. For the best route across the Trinity River, the free **Dallas Streetcar** runs 5:30am to midnight every day from **Union Station** (400 S. Houston St.) to the **Bishop Arts District** in Oak Cliff. North of the river, the free **McKinney Avenue Trolley,** or "M-Line," (www.mata.org) connects Downtown Dallas to Uptown; its schedules varies daily.

To head west, the **Trinity Railway Express** (TRE, www.trinityrailwayexpress.org) travels from Union Station in Downtown Dallas to the historic **T&P Station** (221 W. Lancaster Ave.) in Downtown Fort Worth.

DRIVING

Driving in Dallas can be stressful for an out-of-towner. Even locals complain about the confusing and ever-changing freeway routes as the roads undergo one construction project after another. Plus, Dallas drivers are not polite to slowpokes.

The main highways in and out of Dallas are I-35E north/south and I-30 east/west. I-45 goes southeast to Houston. U.S. Highway 75 originates in Dallas and goes north all the way to Oklahoma. I-635 makes a loop around Dallas. The Dallas North Tollway begins in downtown and extends to the northern suburbs of Addison, Plano and Frisco.

Rush hour is 4pm-7pm. In downtown Dallas, traffic typically bottlenecks in the east-west stretch that locals call "the canyon," where I-30 crosses I-35 and I-45 and U.S. Highway 75. However, the ongoing "Horseshoe Project" aims to alleviate the problem. Dallas traffic also bottlenecks at I-35 north and Woodall Rodgers Freeway (Spur 366).

The main highways in and out of Fort Worth are I-35W north/south and I-30 east/west. The best route between Dallas and Fort Worth is I-30. The freeway sometimes bottlenecks in Arlington during big events. The suburb is home to several of the region's major stadiums and arenas.

Several major car rental companies operate headquarters in Dallas and Fort Worth, with rentals starting at about $20 a day. Options include **Enterprise Rent-A-Car** (www.enterprise.com), **Budget Car Rental** (www.budget.com), and **Hertz Rent A Car** (www.hertz.com). You can always hitch a ride using apps like **Uber** and **Lyft.**

Travel Tips

WHAT TO PACK

Packing for a trip to Dallas-Fort Worth requires a bit more forethought compared to other big cities. Because the weather changes at will, bring layers and be flexible. A light jacket works well on a cool morning. As the day heats up, you can start shedding down to a breathable shirt or tank top. Comfortable shoes are a must.

The afternoon rays can be brutal, so pack sunscreen, sunglasses, and a hat if you plan on spending a lot of time outside. Dallas may be hundreds of miles from the coastline, but the city is full of fancy hotel pools and party spots, so pack a swimsuit, towel, and flip-flops.

TOURIST INFORMATION

There are several spots that will help you plan your day in Dallas. The main hub for travel information is the **Dallas Convention and Visitors Bureau** (325 N. St. Paul St., 214/571-1000, www.visitdallas.com). You'll find comprehensive tourism brochures, sample itineraries, and ideas for how to tackle the top attractions.

The Fort Worth Convention and Visitors Bureau (www.fortworth.com) operates the **Main Street Visitors Center** (508 Main St., 817/698-3300) in downtown and the **Stockyards Visitor Information Center** (130 E. Exchange Ave., 817/624-4741) in Northside. Both are excellent starting points, whether you're spending a night strolling Sundance Square or watching a rodeo at the Cowtown Coliseum.

Travelers can find event calendars for art, culture, and nightlife in the alt-weeklies, the ***Dallas Observer*** (www.dallasoserver.com) and the ***Fort Worth Weekly*** (www.fwweekly.com) as well as public radio station **KERA**'s Art and Seek program (90.1 FM, www.artandseek.org).

SMOKING

Dallas banned smoking inside restaurants and bars in 2009. As of March 2017, it's illegal to light up in public parks. Violating these ordinances will get you a $200 fine. You'll still find a few people smoking on the patios of bars and clubs, especially in Deep Ellum, even within the 15-foot limit. But the habit has become less and less common over the years.

Fort Worth and Arlington have similar ordinances but still allow smoking inside bars. Many of the music venues in those cities are usually filled with heavy clouds of smoke, so nonsmokers should be prepared for some secondhand inhalation.

E-cigarettes have become more socially acceptable, but rules for vaping indoors vary by establishment.

LIQUOR LAWS

Texas's liquor laws are among the most complicated in the country. The patchy wet-dry restrictions in Dallas County were simplified in 2010 after a referendum made it legal for stores across the county to sell beer and wine (but not liquor). Liquor stores are scattered around the city but essentially do not exist south of the Trinity River. This resulted in the Oak Cliff phrase, "going across," which is code for a booze run.

You can buy beer and wine until midnight Monday-Friday, and liquor until 9pm. Liquor stores are closed on Sundays. Beer and wine cannot be sold at supermarkets between midnight Saturday and noon Sunday.

TRAVELERS WITH DISABILITIES

Travelers with disabilities will be mostly at ease in Dallas and Fort Worth. The main attractions, including the Sixth Floor Museum, Reunion Tower, the Dallas Museum of Art, and the State Fair of Texas, are completely wheelchair accessible without sacrificing any part of the experience. In addition, many bars, restaurants, and clubs have large, private bathrooms. Besides meeting the Americans with Disabilities Act, DART offers reduced fares for travelers with disabilities, along with a free travel training program with quick, one-on-one instruction for how to use the public transportation.

A Fort Worth-based company, Adventures Unbound (www.adventuresunboundtravel.com), provides organized travel led by trained caregivers. Day trips include NASCAR races at Texas Motor Speedway, tours of the Dallas Cowboys and Texas Rangers stadiums, and adventures at the Fort Worth Stockyards.

TRAVELING WITH CHILDREN

Dallas and Fort Worth offer plenty of kid-friendly adventures that also appeal to adults, but not everything is conveniently located. The family could easily spend an entire day in the walkable Dallas Arts District, lounging and romping around Klyde Warren Park's jungle gyms and fountains, or exploring hands-on exhibits at the Perot Museum of Nature and Science. Elsewhere in the region, however, children's activities are more spread out. Build in extra travel time to make it to the Dallas Children's Theater in East Dallas or Casa Mañana in the Fort Worth Cultural District. Both cities have large populations of families out and about, even in downtown areas, so you won't feel out of place pushing a stroller or two.

LGBT TRAVELERS

Home to the largest gay and lesbian population in Texas, Dallas is more than welcoming to LGBT travelers. Oak Lawn, with its strip of bars and dance clubs along Cedar Springs Road, is the most popular gathering place. It's also the site of gay pride parades and events every September. Gayborhoods extend well beyond Oak Lawn and are not limited to entertainment districts.

Many gay and lesbian business owners have set up shop in the Bishop Arts District in Oak Cliff. Several prominent LGBT-affirming houses of worship are peppered throughout the city, including one of the largest in the nation, Cathedral of Hope (5910 Cedar Springs Rd., 214/351-1901, www.cathedralofhope.com). Although it lacks a definitive gay and lesbian entertainment district amid its overt cowboy culture, Fort Worth is on par with Dallas for LGBT friendliness. Dallas-Fort Worth's gay and lesbian atmosphere ranges from loud and proud to relaxed and understated.

There are several organizations and resources in the area: North Texas Gay and Lesbian Alliance, which promotes equality in schools, workplaces and communities in North Texas (www.galanorthtexas.org); Resource Center, which supports LGBTQ communities affected by HIV, and promotes physical, emotional and mental health (www.rcdallas.org); and *Dallas Voice*, a weekly newspaper covering the LGBT community (www.dallasvoice.com)

Health and Safety

While overall crime was down slightly in 2016, violent crime in Dallas increased by about 20 percent, according to statistics from the Dallas Police Department, which attributed many of the incidents to drugs and domestic-violence rather than random acts.

The LGBT community of Oak Lawn saw a spike in assaults in 2016. Not all of the attacks were identified as hate crimes, but they did prompt Dallas police to create a special task force and increase surveillance in the area.

If you're attending an event in Fair Park, don't venture any farther south. The blighted southeast area of Dallas is not where you want to lose your way at night.

Thefts tick up and down, and are likely to happen at random. Travelers should practice the "take, lock, hide" approach when leaving their vehicles, even for a quick stop, and park in well-lit, populated areas.

The safest neighborhoods include Sundance Square in Fort Worth, which has a private security force monitoring the area 24 hours a day, and University Park and Highland Park north of Downtown Dallas, which are actually separate, wealthy municipalities with their own police departments.

Texans tend to take extra precautions against mosquitos amid threats of the West Nile virus and, most recently, the Zika virus, which has been sexually transmitted to several pregnant women in Dallas. The chances of contracting a virus are very low, but it's wise to invest in some high-quality bug repellent.

The region has severe summer heat waves with temperatures regularly soaring above 100 degrees. Stay hydrated, and never leave children or pets in the car for even a few minutes.

For emergencies, contact the police and fire departments by calling **911.** For non-emergent issues, call their business lines: **Dallas Police Department** (Jack Evans Police Headquarters, 1400 S. Lamar St., 214/670-3001, www.dallaspolice.net), **Dallas Fire-Rescue Department** (214/670-5466, www.dallasfirerescue.com), **Fort Worth Police Department** (Thomas R. Windham Building, 350 W. Belknap, 817/392-4000, www.

fortworthpd.com), **Fort Worth Fire Department** (817/392-6800, www.fortworthtexas.gov/fire).

HOSPITALS

The Dallas Medical District, just outside Oak Lawn, is home to the county's public hospital, **Parkland Memorial** (5200 Harry Hines Blvd., 214/590-8000, www.parklandhospital.com), which sees about one million patients a year. It also serves as the primary teaching hospital for the nearby Southwestern Medical Center.

Every Dallas neighborhood has a major hospital, including: **Baylor University Medical Center** (3500 Gaston Ave., 214/820-0111, www.baylorhealth.com) in East Dallas/Deep Ellum area; **Methodist Dallas Medical Center** (1441 N. Beckley Ave., 214/947-8181, www.methodisthealthsystem.org) in Oak Cliff; and **Medical City** (7777 Forest Ln., 972/566-7000, www.medicalcitydallas.com) in North Dallas. Over the past several years, the Dallas area also has seen an influx of emergency care clinics.

In Fort Worth, the hospital district is just outside downtown, where you'll find **Baylor Scott & White All Saints Medical Center** (1400 8th Ave., 817/926-2544, www.baylorhealth.com). There's also **Cook Children's Pediatric Clinic** (1799 8th Ave., 682/885-3301, www.cookchildrens.org), which has a good reputation, but limited hours.

Resources

Suggested Reading

Burrough, Bryan. *The Big Rich: The Rise and Fall of the Greatest Texas Oil Fortunes*. Penguin Books, 2010. This New York Times bestseller reveals the history of the Texas oil boom and its barons, known as the Big Four: Hugh Roy Cullen, Clint Murchison, Sid Richardson, and H. L. Hunt. The latter three were Dallas and Fort Worth legends.

Davis, Steven L., and Minutaglio, Bill. *Dallas 1963*. Grand Central Publishing, 2013. Essential reading on the assassination of President John F. Kennedy, *Dallas 1963* shines new light on the role Dallas played in the historic tragedy. The book examines the volatile political culture of the day that led to the nickname "City of Hate."

Doty, Mark. *Lost Dallas*. Arcadia Publishing, 2012. Of all the Images of America books that chronicle the history of Dallas and Fort Worth, *Lost Dallas* includes the most interesting facts and details you don't often hear about the area. These are the forgotten structures and landmarks that did not survive the city's unstoppable building boom.

Patoski, Joe Nick. *The Dallas Cowboys: The Outrageous History of the Biggest, Loudest, Most Hated, Best Loved Football Team in America*. Back Bay Books, 2013. More than 800 pages of stories fill this ultimate guide to understanding the Dallas Cowboys, one of the most influential teams in NFL history.

Selcer, Richard F. *Hell's Half Acre: The Life and Legacy of a Red-Light District*. Texas Christian University Press, 1991. Chronicling the underbelly of 19th-century Fort Worth, *Hell's Half Acre* examines the entertainment district frequented by the city's prominent residents and drifters, including Butch Cassidy and the Wild Bunch.

Smith, David Hale. *Dallas Noir*. Akashic Books, 2013. Part of the publisher's Noir Series, *Dallas Noir* features 16 creepy crime thrillers inspired by local history. Although the stories are fiction, acclaimed Dallas-born authors capture the city's tone and setting beautifully, with a dark twist.

Tierce, Merritt. *Love Me Back*. Doubleday, 2013. This award-winning breakout novel set at an upscale Dallas steak house is powered by the real-life events of the local author. Employing her raw and raunchy prose, Tierce chronicles the life of a single mom struggling to make ends meet waiting tables and fighting self-destructive urges, while intersecting with the city's high-society patrons.

Internet Resources

INFORMATION

Dallas City Hall
www.dallascityhall.com
The portal to practical information about city services and political memos.

Visit Dallas
www.visitdallas.com
The digital version of the Dallas Convention Center and Visitors Bureau offers just about all the information you could receive in person, including downloads for specialized brochures, neighborhood maps, and more.

Fort Worth CVB
www.fortworth.com
Tourist information for all of Fort Worth's attractions can be found here, along with features on local breweries, the film community, and other scenes of note.

NEWS

Dallas Morning News
www.dallasnews.com
Founded in 1888, this is the major daily newspaper for the entire Dallas-Fort Worth metroplex. After a few visits to the website, however, a paywall blocks the content.

D Magazine
www.dmagazine.com
The city's monthly news and lifestyle magazine presents an accurate picture of life in Dallas. You'll find plenty of "best-of" lists as well as in-depth political reporting and longform narrative.

Dallas Observer
www.dallasobserver.com
The city's alternative weekly is a good resource for finding events and nightlife, as well as snarky commentary on City Hall happenings.

Index

EF

G

H

IJK

L

M

NO

P

QR

S

T

UVWXYZ

Restaurants Index

INDEX

Nightlife Index

Shops Index

Hotels Index

Photo Credits

Title page photo, Longhorn Steers in Pioneer Plaza, sculpture by Robert Summers: © courtesy of VisitDallas

Page 2 (top left) © Joseph Haubert | Fort Worth CVB, (top right) © Andy Rhodes, (bottom) © courtesy of VisitDallas; page 20 (top left) © Andy Rhodes, (top right) © Sean Fitzgerald | Trinity River Audubon Center, (bottom) © Scott McDaniel; page 21 © Emily Toman; page 22 © courtesy of VisitDallas; page 23 © courtesy of VisitDallas; page 24 © Kevin Brown | State Fair of Texas; page 25 © courtesy of VisitDallas; page 26 © Fort Worth CVB; page 28 © Norma's Café; page 29 (top) © courtesy of VisitDallas, (bottom) © courtesy of VisitDallas; page 30 © Ritu Jethani | Dreamstime.com; page 38 (top) © courtesy of VisitDallas, (bottom) © courtesy of VisitDallas; page 42 (top) © Wenling01 | Dreamstime.com, (bottom) © Heinerle | Dreamstime.com; page 47 (top) © Fort Worth CVB, (bottom) © courtesy of VisitDallas; page 51 (top) © Fort Worth CVB, (bottom) © Haynesworth Photography; page 56 (top) © Robert Strickland, (bottom) © Kevin Marple; page 59 © Emily Toman; page 70 (top) © Emporium Pies, (bottom) © Jessica Sepkowitz ; page 84 (top) © Emily Toman, (bottom) © Andy Rhodes; page 94 (top left) © Emily Toman, (top right) © Emily Toman, (bottom) © Billy Bob's; page 100 (top) © courtesy of VisitDallas, (bottom) © Jason Janik | Perot Museum; page 102 © courtesy of VisitDallas; page 110 (top) © Calvin Leake | Dreamstime.com, (bottom) © courtesy of VisitDallas; page 115 (top) © Fort Worth CVB, (bottom) © Calvin Leake | Dreamstime.com; page 121 © Kevin Brown | State Fair of Texas; page 122 (top) © courtesy of VisitDallas, (bottom) © Andy Rhodes; page 127 (top) © Kevin Brown | State Fair of Texas, (bottom) © courtesy of VisitDallas; page 132 (top) © Walter Arce | Dreamstime.com, (bottom) © Trinity River Audubon Center; page 135 (top) © Joseph Haubert, (bottom) © courtesy of VisitDallas; page 136 © Sandi Outland; page 143 (top) © courtesy of VisitDallas, (bottom) © Draper James; page 148 (top) © Darren Braun, (bottom) © courtesy of VisitDallas; page 153 (top) Emily Toman, (bottom) © Andy Rhodes; page 161 (top) © Nicolas Henderson, (bottom) © Joe Thomas | GrapevineTxOnline.com; page 162 © Joe Thomas | GrapevineTxOnline.com; page 166 © courtesy of VisitDallas; page 169 (top) © Nicolas Henderson, (bottom) © Nicolas Henderson; page 180 (top) © courtesy of Visit Dallas, (bottom) © Andy Rhodes; page 186 (top) © courtesy of VisitDallas, (bottom) © Typhoonski | Dreamstime.com.

Also Available